The Shadow of El Centro

The Shadow of El Centro

A History of Migrant Incarceration and Solidarity

Jessica Ordaz

The University of North Carolina Press CHAPEL HILL

This book was published with the assistance of the Thornton H. Brooks Fund of the University of North Carolina Press.

Set in Merope Basic by Westchester Publishing Services
Manufactured in the United States of America

The University of North Carolina Press has been a member of the Green Press Initiative since 2003.

Library of Congress Cataloging-in-Publication Data
Names: Ordaz, Jessica, author.
Title: The shadow of El Centro : a history of migrant incarceration and
    solidarity / Jessica Ordaz.
Other titles: Justice, power, and politics.
Description: Chapel Hill : The University of North Carolina Press, [2021] |
    Series: Justice, power, and politics | Includes bibliographical references
    and index.
Identifiers: LCCN 2020037085 | ISBN 9781469662466 (cloth) |
    ISBN 9781469662473 (paperback) | ISBN 9781469662480 (ebook)
Subjects: LCSH: El Centro Immigration Detention Camp. | El Centro Service
    Processing Center. | Detention of persons—California—El Centro—
    History—20th century. | Illegal aliens—Abuse of—California—El Centro—
    History—20th century.
Classification: LCC JV6926.E43 O73 2021 | DDC 365/.979499—dc23
LC record available at https://lccn.loc.gov/2020037085

Cover illustration: Sleeping barracks at El Centro, 1985. Robert Gumpert Photograph Archive, The Bancroft Library, University of California, Berkeley. Photo by Robert Gumpert, used by permission of the photographer.

Parts of chapter 4 were previously published in a different form as "Migrant Detention Archives: Histories of Pain and Solidarity," *Southern California Quarterly* 102, no. 3 (2020): 250–73.

Chapter 5 was previously published in a different form as "Protesting Conditions inside *El Corralón*: Immigration Detention, State Repression, and Transnational Migrant Politics in El Centro, California," *Journal of American Ethnic History* 38, no. 2 (2019): 65–93.

For Arnulfo and Maria Elena Ordaz.
And for the struggle to abolish all types of prisons.

Contents

Figures

Acknowledgments

My interest in telling this history stemmed from a place of silence. When I was a child, conversations about my father's apprehensions, detentions, and deportations quickly ended. I hope that in highlighting the experiences of detained migrants, the stories of people like my father will be understood within a narrative that affords them dignity, after decades of feeling shame for attempting to maneuver in a system not of their own making.

Despite having been personally impacted by immigration enforcement, I did not come to this research project until having multiple conversations with my mentor and advisor, Dr. Lorena Oropeza. We discussed the possibility of exploring the history of immigration detention centers and the urgent need for such a project. She provided excellent guidance and feedback. Dr. Lisa Materson and Dr. Cecilia Tsu also played a significant role in shaping the early stages of my research. I am extremely thankful for their guidance, mentorship, and support.

While scholars played a central role in developing my research questions, I would not have been able to write this book without the multiple agencies and institutions that generously funded my work. My research travel was made possible with the support of the following agencies: the University of California California Studies Consortium (UCCSC), UC Davis History Department, UC Davis Hemispheric Institute of the Americas (HIA), UC Davis Office of Graduate Studies, UC Davis Institute for Social Sciences, the Society for Historians of American Foreign Relations (SHAFR), University of California Institute for Mexico and the United States (UC MEXUS), Immigration and Ethnic History Society, University of Washington, Duke University's David M. Rubenstein Rare Book and Manuscript Library, Summer Institute on Tenure and Professional Advancement (SITPA), and the University of Colorado, Boulder. This funding was crucial in obtaining the necessary archival sources to write this story.

Countless archivists assisted me as I searched for materials relevant to my study. I am very appreciative of them. From Mexico City, Washington, D.C., San Diego, and New Mexico, the aid of librarians and research specialists was critical in my acquiring INS records and documents from formerly detained migrants. My research assistant at UC Davis, Jasmine Marie Stoltzfus, helped me sort through these primary sources, and she conducted microfilm research for this project. I am also grateful for the various immigration lawyers and community activists who allowed me to interview them. Their experiences and knowledge helped me piece together this narrative. I want to thank Montserrat Haydee Mendivil for providing lodging during various research trips to Los Angeles. Your friendship and support made what could have been isolating occasions fun and enjoyable.

The time I spent at the University of Washington was of particular importance, as the Andrew W. Mellon Sawyer Seminar Postdoctoral Fellowship on Capitalism and Comparative Racialization provided me with the time and space to draft the manuscript. The fellowship also provided me with the opportunity to get extensive feedback from scholars and graduate students, including Megan Ming Francis, Jack Turner, Sophia Jordan Wallace, Moon-Ho Jung, Chandan Reddy, Roneva Keel, and Vanessa Quince. At the University of California, Berkeley scholars Raúl Coronado, Marla Ramírez, Brian DeLay, Christian Paiz, and David Montejano read and commented on the entire manuscript as part of the Bancroft Seminar on Interdisciplinary Latina/o History. They provided invaluable feedback as I prepared to find a press best suited for my project. I also want to recognize the select number of scholars who read and commented on sections of—and in some cases, the entire—manuscript once it was close to completion: Vicki Ruiz, David Hernandez, and Miroslava Chávez-García.

I am extremely grateful to the colleagues and friends I made while working on this research project. Thank you to Melissa J. Gismondi, Marco Antonio Rosales, Anne Pérez, Carrie Alexander, Natalie Collin (deceased), Jessica Blake, Stephen Cox, Pablo Silva-Fajardo, Andrew Higgins, Juan Medel-Toro, Lily Hodges, Patricia Palma, Fiona Viney, Laura Tavolacci, Rajbir Singh Judge, Abby Judge, Diana Johnson, Griselda Jarquín, Melani Peinado, Genesis Lara, and Joel Virgen for sharing writing space, intellectual conversations, and camaraderie in Davis, California. While conducting archival research throughout Mexico and the United States I had the good fortune of meeting Daniel Morales, Amie Campos, Kevan Antonio Aguilar, Raquel Escobar, Jorge Ramírez, Alina Méndez, Rachel Oriol, Araceli Lopez, Hrafnkell Pálsson, and Michael Damien Aguirre. In Colorado, Em Alves, Charlie Beard, Lauren DeCarvalho, Asif Zaman, Diana Aldapa, and Carlos Jiménez have become an incredibly important source of support and friendship.

At the University of Colorado, Boulder, my ethnic studies colleagues have been exceptionally supportive and welcoming. I am particularly appreciative of Arturo Aldama, Seema Sohi, Enrique Sepúlveda, Nicholas Villanueva,

Virginia Kester-Meyer, and Joanne Corson for their mentorship, guidance, and support. During the final stages of the writing process, I had the opportunity to conduct a graduate seminar on Latinx migration and the carceral state. I learned a great deal from my students Lauren Adler, Roberto Monico, Dan Moore, Alejandra Portillos, and José Vásquez Zárate. Our conversations on carceral matters influenced my final conceptualization of the book.

I was fortunate to have several sources of writing support. The junior faculty of color writing group at CU Boulder was a safe space to get the day-to-day writing done. Thank you for sharing this space with me, Natalie Avalos, Kristie Soares, Natasha Shrikant, Maisam Alomar, Nishant Upadhyay, Tiara Na'puti, Joëlle Marie Cruz, Maria A. Windell, Samira Mehta, Jeremy Calder, and Élika Ortega-Guzmán. It was wonderful to have an in-person writing group. I also benefited from online writing support, during which I shared my progress and setbacks with Lily Pearl Balloffet and Stacy Fahrenthold. Thank you for your encouragement! As a Summer Institute on Tenure & Professional Advancement (SITPA) participant I had the good fortune of being paired with a mentor. Thank you to Monika Gosin for all the advice and support. Lastly, it was an absolute joy to work with my editor at UNC, Brandon Proia. I am appreciative for all the guidance and feedback you provided throughout this process.

My family has been an important source of encouragement during my academic journey, especially during the route to complete this book. I am grateful you are such a significant part of my life, Maria Elena Ordaz, Arnulfo Ordaz, Angela Ordaz, Belinda Pereira, and Chase Pereira.

Prologue

Not long after I began to study immigration detention in El Centro, I came to appreciate the inconsistencies of the official record. Some maps included the detention center in El Centro; others did not.

THE FEDERAL GOVERNMENT DESIGNED the El Centro Immigration Detention Center to be temporary. Yet it was open between 1945 and 2014. The center's story is not linear—it was initially operational for five years before immigration officers stopped using the facility on January 12, 1950. However, eighteen months later the Immigration and Naturalization Service (INS) restarted its operations in El Centro.[1]

The history of migrant detention is full of the same absences and discontinuities seen in El Centro. This led me to wonder: What information does the public have on immigration detention centers, considering that many are operational for a specific time and then closed? What records of their existence remain? Where did these sources and memories go? Would the experiences of the people detained in these places simply vanish, leaving the ghosts of those formerly incarcerated to linger in the present? These questions, difficult to answer in aggregate, become more concrete in the consideration of a single center. The shifting history of El Centro presents a way of transcending the temporal nature of migrant detention to provide insight into the incarceration of racialized migrants. The story of the El Centro Immigration Detention Center must also extend beyond the walls of the facility itself, given its larger significance to the Imperial Valley.

Throughout the twentieth century El Centro, situated between San Diego, California, and Yuma, Arizona, became an important place for Mexican migrants attracted to the valley's agricultural economy and proximity to the border.[2] The city of El Centro is located in Southern California's Imperial Valley, a region made up of seven cities surrounded by desert dunes and mountains near the U.S.-Mexico border. It lies approximately fifty miles west of the Colorado River and south of the Salton Sea and the New River, one of the most polluted in the country.[3] Corporate agricultural leaders relied on these natural resources to develop the area. Private irrigation engineer George Chaffey appropriately named the region the County of Imperial in 1907, when the Imperial Land Company advocated that Anglo-Americans settle in the territory. The Imperial Valley developed within the context of settler colonialism as Anglo-Americans moved west and attempted to remove and replace the Kumeyaay and the Cocopah. Local white elites and agribusiness leaders also battled over political power, racialized the region's agricultural workforce, and suppressed labor resistance.[4]

Over time, the policing of migration, racialization of labor, and resistance converged in El Centro. By the 1990s the Imperial Valley had developed from an economy based on corporate agriculture to one dependent on the carceral state, becoming home to Centinela State Prison, Calipatria State Prison, Herbert Hughes Correctional Center, and the El Centro Immigration Detention Center. The federal government currently uses more than two hundred detention facilities and county and local jails to hold migrants throughout the country. El Centro was pivotal to this transformation, and its border facility is critical to exploring how detention has grown and expanded not only in the valley but in the United States as a whole over the past eight decades.[5]

Although the detention of migrants is not a new practice, the number of people held inside detention centers drastically increased during the past seventy-five years. In 1944 the federal government reported detaining a total of 1,504 migrants throughout the country, mostly unauthorized Mexicans.[6] This number jumped to 102,523 in 1949, only a few years after the El Centro Immigration Detention Camp became operational.[7] Throughout the 1950s and 1960s, the number of prisoners fluctuated, but by the end of the 1970s, the number skyrocketed to 340,297, as detention demographics expanded to include people from other parts of Latin America, largely Central American asylum seekers and refugees from the Caribbean.[8] While still fluctuating, since the 1990s, the number of detentions remained above 300,000. This book examines the stories of the people behind these numbers in El Centro, California.[9]

IN APRIL 2014 I toured the El Centro Immigration Detention Center a few months before government officials closed it down to open a private and larger facility seventeen miles southeast from the facility in the city of Calexico. Driving across Interstate 8 east from San Diego, across mountainous terrain, I observed how the very geography that surrounded the detention center framed it as a space of marginalization and invisibility.[10] It was about seventy degrees that day, but I was aware that the heat reached dangerous levels in the summer. At ninety-nine degrees the blood vessels in the human body begin to dilate, making the heart work harder.[11] Under extreme heat the body loses water and salt, resulting in overheating, heat exhaustion, and heatstroke. These are the conditions under which guards held migrants in El Centro.

The drive toward Cuyamaca Rancho State Park, during which I passed Jacumba Hot Springs and then arrived at the heart of the Imperial Valley, was eerie. The rugged terrain made the ride feel longer than its two-hour duration, and I wondered how the landscape and isolation affected incarcerated migrants, particularly when it was rainy, windy, foggy, or snowy on the drive over. Immigration attorney Elizabeth Lopez verified that this landscape made it challenging to reach clients in El Centro. The division between the Imperial Valley and larger cities such as San Diego and Los Angeles meant that the distance discouraged immigration lawyers from working with people in the Imperial Valley. Lopez added, "It's too far for their families to come visit. Most of their families could be from Los Angeles and other places, and it's very time prohibit[ive] to drive all the way out there."[12] One has to cross these geographic barriers to get to the Imperial Valley, a desolate region saturated with the ghosts of the migrants who had been incarcerated inside the El Centro Immigration Detention Center during the past eight decades.

In 2014 the facility held migrant men from various regions of the world, including those convicted of deportable crimes, asylum seekers, and people undergoing deportation proceedings.[13] The center held men only, as INS agents transferred unauthorized migrant women to the county jail.[14] Most detained migrants came from Latin America, but the center also held men from places as far away as China, Iraq, and Somalia. A guard pointed out a total of eight housing units that held 520 men over the age of eighteen, a courtroom, a medical processing center, a dining hall, and a visiting area.

During my visit immigration officials emphasized over and over that the facility functioned as a nonpunitive administrative holding center for people awaiting civil, noncriminal deportation proceedings.[15] Yet this rhetoric has long obscured the realities of detention. The federal government frames immigration detention as an administrative procedure, but immigration guards have treated detained migrants like prisoners for decades. In the words of scholar of immigration enforcement David Hernandez, "Because detention by immigration authorities is a liminal process that occurs, or is supposed to occur, as an administrative procedure pursuant to the execution of deportation or exclusion orders, little is known about it or its history."[16] In spite of the officials' claims, guards surrounded every door and chaperoned the prisoners from place to place inside the facility. As I walked throughout the center, I noticed that the prisoners wore color-coded uniforms. When they first arrived, a processing officer performed a strip search, took their clothes and valuables for safekeeping, and classified them based on their criminal record and security risk. This criminal categorization followed the men everywhere they went, as their colored uniforms and wristbands demarcated their classification level.[17] Blue represented the lowest risk, followed by orange for medium security and red for extreme criminal cases. Guards assigned the prisoners barracks based on their classification. A member of the U.S. Public Health Service conducted a medical screening within fourteen days of the prisoner's arrival.[18] I noticed seventeen individual solitary units used when detained migrants committed infractions such as challenging a guard's authority or protesting, or when they fell ill.

During the tour of the camp, I asked the immigration official to tell me about El Centro in her own words. She shared that residents referred to the camp as "El Corralón" (the corral), known as a place that held Mexican migrants. Although the detention site has held a demographically diverse population since the 1970s, community members remembered the decades when the camp exclusively held Mexican nationals. The U.S. Immigration and Customs Enforcement (ICE) official described the facility as a haunted place where employees followed orders. "This place functions based on secrecy," she said. "We do not know why things are done the way they are, and we do not ask questions."[19]

One reason that local ICE officials and detention staff kept quiet about daily occurrences inside the detention facility was that the center was a key employer of the Imperial Valley's middle class. Today 21 percent of employees working for the Department of Homeland Security are Latina/o, but as scholar David Cortez has shown, few Latinos worked for the INS before 1977. In that year, the INS employed 1,420 Latinos, 1,310 African Americans, 255 Asian Americans, and 36 Native Americans. As depicted in figure 1, the INS transformed from what Cortez describes as "a uniformly white institution to one comprised disproportionately by Latinx—the very people the agency had, for decades prior, worked so diligently to construct as a threat on which to justify its own existence and expansion." Economic stability played a role in why Latinos took so many of these jobs. But, as scholars have shown, working for the federal government was also viewed as a respectable endeavor for working-class communities.[20] In a region with few jobs outside the agricultural sector, locals perceived working for immigra-

FIGURE 1 International border, U.S. Border Patrol, 1977. San Diego Union Tribune Collection, San Diego History Center (UT88_00501-12).

tion services as a step up.[21] This economic dependency generated an atmosphere of silence throughout the Imperial Valley.

I encountered a similar sensation when looking for traces of the El Centro Immigration Detention Center at the Pioneers Museum in the city of Imperial. The feeling might be described as a sense of haunting, defined by Avery Gordon as "that which appears to be not there," a "seething presence, acting on and often meddling with taken-for-granted realties." That ghostly presence is "the sign, or the empirical evidence that tells you a haunting is taking place. . . . The ghost is primarily a symptom of what is missing."[22] Similarly, Ann L. Stoler, who has written about imperialism as a haunted history, describes a haunting as "the space between what we cannot see and what we know."[23]

When I realized that the museum held archival collections of families who had lived in El Centro going about their everyday lives and photos of most of the city, including the fire department and local corner stores, yet no record of the detention center that had operated for sixty-nine years, I experienced an archival haunting. I found no photos of the countless detained men—no trace of their stories, suffering, or resistance. Despite this invisibility, I knew the El Centro Immigration Detention Center had a long history. The silence that surrounded El Centro seemed to hide something shameful. The violent events that occurred in the facility throughout the decades still lingered throughout the Imperial Valley. Yet it was not until I searched outside of California, in places as far away as Washington, D.C., and Mexico City, that I found the sources needed to write this story.

ON SEPTEMBER 30, 2014, U.S. Immigration and Customs Enforcement closed the El Centro Immigration Detention Center, after sixty-nine years in operation.[24] At this time the facility had within its walls 544 prisoners and 428 employees, and it cost $69.31 million per year to run.[25] The facility had been a key place of employment for a county with a 21 percent unemployment rate.[26] Residents argued that closing it would further increase unemployment.[27] The fate of the facility, after decades of human rights violations, boiled down to numbers and local economics, not the people held inside.

Immigration officials moved their operations to a new coed facility in the city of Calexico.[28] The prison contractor Management and Training Corporation (MTC) currently operates the new center, called the Imperial Regional Detention Facility. Before ICE closed the semiprivatized El Centro Immigration Detention Center, it was managed by Asset Protection and Security Services and Ahtna Technical Services and employed 450 guards.[29] Immigration authorities constructed the Imperial Regional Detention Facility with the intent of keeping the number of guards down to 150, to keep the cost of running the facility as low as possible. In Calexico the prisoners are separated into pods, with barracks that hold a maximum of sixty-four people, to allow for greater surveillance. The Fox, or F, unit is designated for women. A local immigration attorney suggested that moving the detention center was not only an economic strategy but a way for the state to wash its hands of dealing with prisoner grievances and protests.[30] As the detention and deportation regime became privatized, the federal government became less accountable. This decreased accountability adds to the erasure and invisibility of migrant detention throughout the Imperial Valley. *The Shadow of El Centro* seeks to fill in the absences that this process has left behind.

A Note about Terminology

I use various terms to describe the central actors of this book: incarcerated migrants. I use the term "migrant" to encompass anyone who moved from one country to another but who did not obtain citizenship in the United States. Influenced by the work of scholars Eithne Luibhéid and Patricia Zavella, I choose this term because of its fluidity. But there are times when I have strategically differentiated between an unauthorized migrant and an asylum seeker, since laws did not always apply to them in the same way. I have tried not to use the terms "undocumented immigrant" or "noncitizen," unless I refer to a source, to highlight that the migrants I write about were citizens of countries outside of the United States. Although there are several terms I could have used to describe the people held inside the El

FIGURE 2 Fenced inside the El Centro Immigration Detention Center, 1985 (photo by Robert Gumpert). Robert Gumpert Photograph Archive, The Bancroft Library, University of California, Berkeley (BANC PIC 2016.033). Used by permission of Robert Gumpert.

Centro Immigration Detention Camp/Center, I have chosen the terms "detained migrant" and "prisoner" to emphasize that guards treated them like prisoners even if their detention was part of an administrative noncriminal procedure. My use of the term "immigration detention camp/center" is intentional. The federal government used designations such as the El Centro INS Facility and the El Centro Service Processing Center, but these words do not encapsulate the process of criminalization and dehumanization that occurred inside the facility. I also made the decision not to use the term "Latinx," which, although a nonbinary alternative, does not capture how the migrants I write about identified. Last, I have included the names of all the migrants I write about unless I was specifically asked not to, in an effort to challenge the invisibility and silence that surrounds their stories.

The Shadow of El Centro

Introduction

Immigration detention has become daily news across the United States, from cases of death inside detention centers, to the separation of migrant children from their families, to hunger strikes protesting deportation. Currently, hundreds of thousands of migrants sit in migrant detention centers as people across the world isolate to avoid the spread of coronavirus disease (COVID-19). Detention conditions are so deplorable that in June 2019 U.S. representative Alexandria Ocasio-Cortez accused Donald Trump of holding migrants in "concentration camps." She wrote, "This administration has established concentration camps on the southern border of the United States for immigrants, where they are being brutalized with dehumanizing conditions and dying."[1] Although these national conversations have been critical in exposing the violent realities faced by migrants, the media has emphasized shock at the expense of presenting a more nuanced and historical context. As philosopher Giorgio Agamben cautioned, "The correct question to pose concerning the horrors committed in the camps is, therefore, not the hypocritical one of how crimes of such atrocity could be committed against human beings." Instead, Agamben asserted that "it would be more honest and, above all, more useful to investigate carefully the juridical procedures and deployments of power by which human beings could be so completely deprived of their rights and prerogatives that no act committed against them could appear any longer a crime."[2] *The Shadow of El Centro* reveals that antimigrant violence is central to the development of immigration detention in the United States.

U.S. Immigration and Customs Enforcement (ICE) currently detains migrants in jails, service processing centers, Bureau of Prisons centers, and facilities managed by private prison companies.[3] Human rights violations have been found in all these sites. In 2000, 10 percent of the women detained inside the Krome Immigration Detention Center in Miami, Florida, declared that guards had raped them. Their claims became news when two of the women became pregnant while still in detention. In the words of immigration lawyer Cheryl Little, "A lot of women at Krome don't feel they can question sexual demands by guards. Basically, they are at the mercy of their offenders."[4]

That same year, on January 12, 2000, a guard by the name of Officer White attacked Luis A. Ogilvie, a Panamanian migrant being held at the Krome facility. Ogilvie, a disabled man with diabetes who had arrived in the United States in 1980, requested an evening snack, a meal he was entitled to because of his condition. White responded by kicking Ogilvie's wheelchair, slamming him against the wall, and calling him a "fuckin cripple." This assault left Ogilvie with severe back pain and bruises. Ogilvie recounted the beating's lasting effects: "My back snapped during the assault and it is causing me a great deal of pain. I have bruises on my shoulder and my neck still hurts from Officer White's assault."[5] Despite the glaring abuse, immigration officials requested that Ogilvie be deported to Panama.

The mistreatment and neglect of detained migrants have also resulted in the loss of life. In 2008 Hiu Lui "Jason" Ng died inside the privately run Wyatt Detention Facility in Central Falls, Rhode Island.[6] Ng had originally arrived in New York as a teen and overstayed his visa. He married a U.S. citizen, had two children, and worked as a computer engineer. ICE agents detained Ng the moment he completed his final interview requesting permanent residency. Although Ng did not have a criminal record and was in the process of adjusting his status, immigration agents sent him to a detention center. While inside the Wyatt facility, Ng complained of excruciating pain. Detention staff dismissed his claims and accused him of faking his ailments. It was not until Ng's family sued ICE four months later that he received medical care, but unfortunately it was too late. Five days later Ng died of liver cancer at the age of thirty-four.

Ng's death was not an isolated incident. In 2009 the *Washington Post* reported that since 2003 there had been eighty-three deaths of people in immigration custody.[7] More than twenty-four migrants have died in the custody of Customs and Border Protection (CBP) during Trump's administration, including seven-year-old Jakelin Caal Maquin, two-year-old Wilmer Josue Ramírez Vásquez, and sixteen-year-old Juan de Léon Gutiérrez. These examples of antimigrant violence not only demonstrate the widespread brutality within the system; they also reflect the geographic spread of migrant detention throughout the entire country. Initially, immigration detention camps like the one in El Centro were largely situated along the U.S.-Mexico border region, but today migrants are held throughout the interior, including in states such as Wyoming, Iowa, and Oklahoma. This growing carceral landscape has resulted in the confinement and punishment of more people.

It is necessary to move beyond shock to explore how violence was deployed inside the El Centro Immigration Detention Center, which, between

1945 to 2014, held migrants awaiting an administrative immigration hearing to determine their deportability.[8] The mistreatment of detained migrants has become more visible, but the incarceration and abuse of migrants are not new. The current immigration enforcement system is not broken but functions exactly as intended. The violence migrant prisoners experience is not unintentional, because this system allows for individuals working in detention and deportation to act violently and with impunity. Within this dense network, known as an immigration industrial complex, which includes the practices of border enforcement, detention, and deportation, this book shows how detention functions at various intersections, including antimigrant violence, the relationship between detention and labor, the racial and gendered punishment of migrant bodies, the production of racial enemies in the context of national security, and migrant resistance.[9]

The history of the El Centro Immigration Detention Center tells several stories. As one of the oldest continuously operating detention centers in the United States (until recently), its history charts the mechanisms of the state's capacity to build detention centers, the larger functions of the detention system, and the changing nature of migrant activism. The local immigration detention center played a prominent role in the history of the Imperial Valley. Its evolution from an INS detention camp in 1945 to an ICE service processing center fundamentally shaped the larger labor regime.[10] Tracing the evolution of this site reveals that the number of people detained has increased throughout the past seven decades. Using migrant prisoners as an exploitable labor force remained constant throughout the decades. The importance of El Centro's labor system today is that detained migrants are still paid only one dollar per day to participate in what ICE calls a "voluntary work program."[11] From the moment the El Centro Immigration Detention Camp became operational in 1945, local INS agents and officials used detained Mexican migrants to labor in their private homes and farms, maintain the immigration detention camp, and construct buildings throughout the Imperial Valley.

The state used dominant constructions about race and gender inside detention centers in relation to discipline, surveillance, and punishment.[12] Framing immigration detention centers as gender-segregated administrative regimes reveals the connections between the carceral state and the control of racialized bodies through labor, isolation, and punishment.[13] Central to this story are the detained migrants themselves. While constrained within the detention and deportation regime, migrants resisted their incarceration from the moment the camp became operational in 1945, such as finding ingenious ways to escape and contesting their confinement. Immigration detention, counter to its administrative aims and bureaucracy, was intended to be punitive and to impose discipline.[14] Yet, in protesting their incarceration, migrant prisoners transformed the detention center into a place of radical possibility and solidarity, engaging in what I call "transnational migrant politics," a set of strategies and solidarities used by migrant prisoners to resist state power.

The roots of today's detention and deportation regime can be traced to major developments in the federal government's restriction of immigration during the turn of the twentieth century.[15] Yet U.S. obsession with confinement, punishment, and exclusion can also be traced back further, to the workhouses, plantations, prison camps, reservations, relocation centers, industrial schools, and penitentiaries that have proliferated since the founding of the republic. This history was tied to the expansion of white supremacy. The federal government gained funding and infrastructure to exclude migrants from the United States, and it focused on restricting people based on race and nationality.[16]

The 1882 Chinese Exclusion Act restricted Chinese migration to the United States and racialized immigrants as unassimilable.[17] Ten years later the Geary Act of 1892 linked immigration control with crime and punishment.[18] This legislation called for the arrest, imprisonment, and deportation of Chinese laborers who did not register with the federal government. It required Chinese immigrants to disclose their name, age, place of residence, and occupation as part of their registration.[19] When Chinese laborers protested, in *Chae Chan Ping v. United States* (1889), the Supreme Court ruled that the federal government had the right to "prohibit immigrants from entering the country" as "an extension of sovereignty and, thereby, a realm of plenary power."[20] As anti-immigrant legislation increased, in 1910 federal authorities opened the Angel Island Immigration Station in San Francisco, which processed and detained arriving migrants in the West.[21]

The federal government formed the United States Border Patrol in 1924. After only five years the Immigration Act of 1929 criminalized unauthorized border crossing to the United States. A first-time offense became a misdemeanor, and subsequent reentries were classified as felonies, punishable by two to five years in prison and a fine of $10,000.[22] As a result of policing unlawful entry and antimigrant legislation, the federal government necessitated the buildup of the detention infrastructure. It used sites such as La Tuna Detention Farm near El Paso, Texas, and the Immigration and Detention Station in Galveston, Texas, to hold unauthorized Mexican migrants.[23] Yet the early history of immigration detention camps remains largely unknown and unwritten.

Deportation scholars have studied and written about immigration law, the scapegoating of migrant communities, and the violence experienced during deportation.[24] Such work has largely focused on the history and practice of the deportation process rather than the workings of the immigration detention center. More recently, scholars such as Tanya Maria Golash-Boza, Patrisia Macías-Rojas, and Kelly Lytle Hernández have taken on this task.[25] *The Shadow of El Centro* is place-based. By mapping geographies of freedom and confinement throughout the Imperial Valley, it shows that migrant detention was intended to function as a violent space. Yet, detained migrants also made it develop as a place to express migrant politics.

Current immigration detention scholarship often puts great emphasis on the link between the privatization of immigration detention and antimigrant violence.[26] El Centro's example demonstrates that this may not capture the full story. As early as 1945 the immigration detention camp functioned as a profit-producing laboratory that regarded migrants as racialized and criminalized security threats. The history of federal immigration camps, as opposed to private facilities, reveals that violence was endemic in detention camps before they were shaped by more recent neoliberal policies.

Thinking about the long history of migrant detention as a ghost that has lingered and haunted the United States also offers a new conceptualization of detention.[27] The metaphor of hauntings permits this book to unearth a history that has troubled the United States but until recently has remained untold. As Joanne Lipson Freed has explained, a haunting "troubles the boundaries between past and present, here and elsewhere, real and unreal, familiar and strange. . . . But for all its immediacy, the traumatic past, like a ghost, remains opaque and inscrutable, and it is the very incomprehensibility of these past events that causes their uncontrollable return."[28]

The Shadow of El Centro is organized chronologically and divided into three parts. The first part narrates the origins of the El Centro Immigration Detention Camp. Chapter 1 examines the opening of the camp within the context of World War II, national security fears, and the creation of a forced labor system. The federal government transported several structures, including the housing barracks and kitchen utensils, from a camp in Fort Stanton, New Mexico, that held Germans and briefly Japanese Americans during World War II, to El Centro, California. Immigration officials then used unauthorized Mexican migrants to assist in erecting the El Centro Immigration Detention Camp in 1945. Under the guise of volunteer labor, detained migrants maintained the very facility that imprisoned them.

Chapter 2 examines the early years of the El Centro Immigration Detention Camp alongside the initial years of the Bracero Program (1942–64). The Imperial Valley contained Mexican workers who came to the United States as current braceros, unauthorized migrants, and braceros who lost their contracted status or skipped out on the program on their own accord. The El Centro Bracero Reception Center and the El Centro Immigration Detention Camp operated only four miles apart from each other, yet the reception center functioned to import Mexican nationals, and the detention camp served to deport them to Mexico. Chapter 3 examines migrant resistance in El Centro and tracks migrant fugitives to reveal how detained Mexican migrant men collaborated to challenge their confinement, negotiate power, and seek freedom.

The second part of the book explores the expansion of immigration detention in the Greater Southwest after 1954, a period when the number of detention centers is believed to have decreased. Yet, as chapter 4 shows, the history of border policing and INS practices in the Greater Southwest—including internal policing and detention at federal immigration camps and border stations—suggests that the detention of Mexican migrants continued to institutionalize violence as border policy. Looking at the Greater Southwest reveals that the detention and deportation regime expanded between the 1950s and the 1970s as immigration agents increased the policing of Mexican migrants along the U.S.-Mexico border. This chapter examines the racialization of Mexican migrants as subversive and criminal, logics that helped to strengthen the detention and deportation regime by increasing border policing and the deportation of migrants. I explore migrant incarceration in places such as the El Centro Immigration Detention Camp and Terminal Island in California, the McAllen Detention Center in Texas, and border patrol stations throughout the Greater Southwest. Chapter 5 chronicles the events surrounding the 1985 El Centro hunger strike to examine how prisoners expressed what I call "transnational migrant politics." Central American men who ended up at El Centro had attempted to escape poverty, dictatorships, and civil war, only to experience similar horrors once apprehended, detained, and deported. This context influenced the migrants' activism as they turned to the hunger strike to protest their detention.

The final part of the book interrogates the continuities of immigration detention after the passage of the Immigration Reform and Control Act (IRCA) of 1986. Chapter 6 centers on migrant punishment and pain inside the El Centro Immigration Detention Center and the Eclectic Communications, Incorporated (ECI) facility for unaccompanied minors. The 1987 INS *Detention Officer Handbook* emphasized that detention was not intended as punishment, yet prisoner testimonies and government sources suggest that punishment served as one of the primary ways to maintain order. Guards used particular places within detention centers in which to punish migrants. The bathrooms inside the El Centro Immigration Detention Center and a punishment room at Eclectic Communications became liminal spaces for immigration authorities to physically abuse prisoners. The final chapter looks to local and national detention transformations between 1994 and 2014, framing the immigration detention center as a place to examine migrant deaths that resulted and could have been avoided if not for immigration enforcement policies. Deaths of unidentified migrants crossing the U.S.-Mexico border became so common in the Imperial Valley that dead migrants started to fill the local cemetery in Holtville, California.

Over the course of sixty-nine years, detained migrants challenged local immigration authorities, while state resources for policing increased. After 2014, the facility ceased operations, but the haunting continues still.

PART I | Hauntings

CHAPTER ONE

The Camp's Skeleton

A Prehistory

> The past is a haunting presence, one that intrudes into
> and dramatically alters . . . lives in the present.
> —JOANNE LIPSON FREED, 2017

Immigration officials opened the El Centro Immigration Detention Camp in 1945 as an administrative holding center for unauthorized Mexican migrants.[1] Local patrol inspectors used this incarcerated population to maintain the detention camp and to assist on work projects throughout the Imperial Valley. For instance, on March 2, 1954, Walter I. Walden, secretary of the Imperial Valley Central Labor Council, discovered that a Border Patrol agent was supervising eight Mexican migrants laying concrete blocks for a building in the Border Patrol and Immigration Service at El Centro.[2] Although agents had been investigated by the FBI for these labor practices in the past, this was not an isolated incident. Just one day later Ernesto Galarza, a Mexican American scholar and activist, wrote a letter to the Mexican consulate in Calexico, informing them that INS authorities were using the labor of eight unpaid detained migrants at the El Centro Immigration Detention Camp to reconstruct the facility.[3] After receiving Galarza's letter the Mexican consulate sent Eugénio V. Pesquería to visit the detention camp in El Centro, where he was told that the INS would stop using the labor of detained Mexicans in reconstructing the camp.[4]

The history of the El Centro Immigration Detention Camp is part of wider scholarship that argues that racialized punishment and carceral spaces existed in the plantation, the boarding school, and the prison.[5] This chapter, however, identifies the wartime roots of migrant detention and the use of Mexican migrants as an exploitable labor force. Disguised as a system of voluntary work by local INS officials, this labor regime proved coercive at best. This story of incarcerated Mexican men is part of the larger history of forced labor in the United States.[6] From indentured servitude, chattel slavery, Native American enslavement, convict leasing, and the chain gang to the coerced labor of Mexican migrants, forced labor has played a central role in institutionalizing white supremacy.[7] Local immigration officials used the El Centro Immigration Detention Camp as a holding pen for an incarcerated labor force.

The federal government opened the El Centro Immigration Detention Camp as World War II was coming to an end. By 1945 the INS had abundant experience in confining people classified as enemy aliens. The El Centro Immigration Detention Camp was created by repurposing the carcass of a former camp. The structures that the federal government used to construct the camp in El Centro were originally part of the Fort Stanton Internment Camp in New Mexico, a place that held Germans and, for a brief period, Japanese Americans. After the Fort Stanton Camp closed, INS authorities hauled its tools, buildings (including the victory huts, prefabricated buildings used during war to house soldiers), and kitchen equipment such as pots, pans, and cutlery to El Centro.[8] This transfer of materials from one carceral space to another speaks to the legacy of confinement in the United States. The prehistory and expansion of the El Centro Immigration Detention Camp was based on a model of war and forced labor.

The SS *Columbus*

On September 1, 1939, the SS *Columbus*, a luxury ship from northern Germany, adorned with the red and black swastika flag, began its voyage home after a cruise along the Caribbean. In addition to a fervidly pro-Nazi crew, about half of whom belonged to the National Socialist Organization, the ship contained 745 passengers.[9] At the very same time, Germany invaded Poland, sparking war throughout Europe and then most of the globe.

The *Columbus*'s route back to Germany suddenly became all but impossible. A British naval blockade prevented the *Columbus* from returning by sea. The Cuban government allowed the ship's passengers to disembark in Havana, allowing the crew to figure out an alternate means of returning to Germany. They attempted an alternate sea route, this time without passengers, by sailing the ship north from Cuba, but on December 19, 1939, the British tracked the ship near New York. Hitler had ordered that the ship should not fall into the hands of the Allies, and so, rather than surrendering to the British, the crew set the *Columbus* ablaze and abandoned ship.[10]

The crew was rescued and transported to the U.S. mainland on the USS *Tuscaloosa* on December 20, 1939. Immigration agents took the men to Ellis Island because they were considered "excluded alien seamen" without valid immigration visas.[11] British and U.S. government authorities allowed German women, children, and men over fifty-two to return to Germany. The remaining crewmen were transported to Angel Island on a train and then a ship because officials believed they could return to Germany on a Japanese steamer from the West Coast.[12] But this did not come to pass. Instead, immigration services were charged with accommodating 512 Germans at the Angel Island Immigration and Quarantine Stations.[13] There were so many people that the guards held several men at the Alameda County Jail owing to lack of space.

In March 1940 Karl Eduard, Duke of Saxe-Coburg-Gotha, and the visiting head of Germany's Red Cross, visited the quarters that held the German crewmen. Eduard concluded that the rooms, while crowded, were neat and contained improvised storage boxes on ropes and pulleys.[14] He was impressed by the fishing wharf, smokehouse, and *biergarten*, although it did not serve alcohol. Since the INS was receiving monthly payments to hold and feed the crew from the German consul, they received various privileges, including salaries and shore leave.[15] The German embassy paid each German crewman $2.50 per week.[16] While confined to Angel Island and unable to return to Germany, the men were not stressed about money. For instance, thirty-one-year-old Kurt Johann Hinsch told INS officials that "by German law" he was "entitled to [his] salary until [he] reached home." German seamen received the same salary whether at port or sailing. Hinsch, having been trained as a merchant marine and having attended a naval academy, had worked as a seaman since the age of sixteen and had served on the *Columbus* for about three years. He was married and counted on his father-in-law, an export and import businessmen, to help support him while he was in the United States.[17]

The crew's relative freedom was challenged once the Germans stepped out of line, however. Joseph X. Strand, inspector in charge of the Detention and Deportation Division, Captain Wilhelm Daehne, and First Officer Ruppert debated if the privilege of shore leave should be discontinued after they discovered that several men failed to return to Angel Island at the designated time. Captain Daehne temporarily suspended shore leave privileges and deducted pay from the violators, but he asked the INS commissioner to reinstate shore leave until more "serious misconduct" had taken place. Daehne and Ruppert asserted that they found the entire crew to be "trustworthy and reliable" and felt that they "could virtually guarantee that there [would] be no desertions."[18] Yet, the crew's stay at Angel Island would soon come to an end.

Fort Stanton

Holding the men in San Francisco grew challenging as anti-German hostility increased. The Justice Department searched for a new and more remote location and selected the Fort Stanton Civilian Conservation Corps (CCC) Camp in New Mexico as the location to hold the German crew.[19] Largely used for cattle raising, this area was chosen because it was in remote mountainous country and few families lived there. Border Patrol agents visited and concluded that it could be well controlled.[20] On January 27, 1941, thirty-nine members of the *Columbus* were transported from San Francisco to New Mexico in a day coach. The media reported that the men were transported in a "prison car with armed guards," but the INS emphasized that this was not the case, "because this crew [was] a well behaved and well-disciplined body of men."[21] Immigration officials were constantly anxious not to present the image that they treated the crew like prisoners. For instance, when officials debated if the new camp should be fenced, Lemuel B. Schofield, special assistant to the attorney general, suggested, that "it might give to some the appearance of a 'prison' or 'concentration' camp, and it seem[ed] to the Central Office very desirable that this be avoided."[22] The remaining crewmen were transported to New Mexico on a Southern Pacific train, making the total number of Germans at the camp 412.

The crew continued to receive preferential treatment at Fort Stanton. William F. Kelly, Assistant Commissioner for Alien Control, and Captain Daehem administered the camp. The U.S. and the German government funded the camp's operations.[23] Because of its prefabricated accommodations, Fort Stanton looked similar to an army camp.[24] As soon as the crewmen settled into their new residence, they painted a Nazi swastika in the camp and put up several photographs of Hitler. They were allowed to re-create life inside the camp as closely as possible to their lives aboard the *Columbus*. This included building a library, constructing a sausage smokehouse and a recreational swimming pool, and organizing two music bands who performed in the camp.[25] The German government continued to compensate the crew regardless of the labor they performed.[26] When the Border Patrol requested help with projects outside of the camp, such as constructing the adobe-walled guardhouse, German laborers earned an additional ten cents an hour.[27]

As war raged throughout Europe, locals expressed frustration with the government's preferential treatment of the German crew held at Fort Stanton. One resident wrote, "They should load the whole damn bunch up and ship them back to Hitler."[28] Another person said, "They should run them out beyond the 12-mile limit and sink them." An ex-serviceman and world war veteran echoed these sentiments when he asserted, "If they [the Border Patrol] would just let a bunch of us legionnaires go up there with our rifles and give them a day off, their problems would be solved." Another resident went as far as to suggest that, if war were declared, they would immediately kill every German crew member who tried to abandon the camp.[29]

The FBI also expressed concern with the liberties the men were granted. In a report to the attorney general, the FBI stated that law enforcement officers informed them that Germans were allowed to roam outside the camp and often visited nearby cities. INS officials responded by informing the FBI that the crewmen were not prisoners of war and should not be "deprived of all liberties."[30] The crewmen were allowed to leave the camp and go on hikes as long as they carried passes granting them permission to do so. Local police officers found this troubling because they believed that if the United States entered the war, the Germans would certainly try to escape.

From the perspective of Captain Daehne, granting the men certain privileges kept them content. He was in favor of making small compromises, such as serving beer in the camp's canteen, "to prevent dissatisfaction or to keep the crewmen's time occupied."[31] These privileges might have kept the crew more relaxed, but they outraged locals. When bids were received for supplying the Fort Stanton Camp with lamb, L. A. McDonald, the local manager of Armour and Company, included his opinion about how the camp was operated. He said, "The German crewmen of the former SS 'Columbus' . . . lived like kings and queens," and that "it might help to put some arsenic in their food."[32] Soon, conditions inside the Fort Stanton Camp would become stricter.

The United States entered World War II after the Japanese navy attacked Pearl Harbor on December 7, 1941. The federal government called for the opening and construction of additional detention facilities to hold enemy aliens.[33] Presidential proclamations 2525, 2526, and 2527 granted the federal government full authority to detain enemy aliens and confiscate their property.[34] The Justice Department apprehended, detained, and interned hundreds of thousands of "natives, citizens, denizens or subjects of Japan, Germany and Italy" who the FBI classified as dangerous or suspicious.[35] When the United States declared war on Germany, the German crewmen held at the Fort Stanton Internment Camp became enemy aliens. Many of the freedoms the internees had been granted ended. Guards began patrolling the new watchtowers and the barbed-wire structure with trained dogs, weapons, floodlights, vehicles, and horses. Increased funds allowed for the hiring of twenty-six new employees, including tower guards, relief guards, and foot, car, horse, and dog patrols.[36] When the men broke the rules, they were promptly punished. For example, in February 1942 nine German crewmen escaped from the camp.[37] They were quickly caught and placed inside the El Paso County Jail. Patrol Inspector George W. McCombs allowed them to return to Fort Stanton after the fence was secured around the camp and after the men wrote a letter promising not to attempt future escapes. The camp's food and gasoline became rationed, and Border Patrol agents played a larger role in the facility's operations.[38] Yet, even with these stricter measures, the men received treatment that would not be seen in future detention camps. For instance, the German crewmen continued to receive payments from the U.S. and German governments, and they could accept funds from family and friends.[39]

As the war unfolded, divisions grew between detained Nazi sympathizers and anti-Nazi advocates. Ammon M. Tenney, the Border Patrol agent in charge of the camp, requested that internees who did not support Nazism be kept away from Fort Stanton to prevent potential violence.[40] Fort Stanton was transformed into a concentrated place of detained Nazis. Then, in 1943, the INS established "disciplinary camps" within the Fort Stanton Internment Camp to hold enemy aliens classified as agitators. The first subcamp held Germans, and the second unit, called Japanese Segregation Camp No. 1, held Japanese Americans.[41] The segregation camps were constructed to minimally meet the requirements of the Geneva Convention, to avoid making these spaces seem appealing to potential dissidents.[42] The German subcamp included six prefabricated buildings, four barracks, a dining room, a recreation hall, and a washroom.[43] Immigration officials claimed that "for psychological and disciplinary reasons," they would not disclose the location of the subcamp.[44]

The men transferred to Japanese Segregation Camp No. 1 were accused of being pro-Japan agitators. They were originally part of a group of 366 Japanese American men sent to the Santa Fe Internment Camp from Tule Lake.[45] At Fort Stanton, they lived in two-man portable wooden huts, and their camp included a latrine, laundry room, recreational room, kitchen, and small walking area.[46] The Japanese Americans transferred to the segregation camp were considered segregants rather than internees and were to remain separate from the rest of the men at Fort Stanton. Their living location was much smaller and self-contained. It was located near the main camp, but they did not have the same privileges or accommodations as the German crewmen. When the camp held Japanese Americans, Germans continued to receive money from the U.S. and German governments every month. Also, if the Germans worked in the kitchen, cleaned the camp, cared for the stock, or plowed or harvested on the farm, they were compensated with eighty cents per day. If they were injured and unable to work, they qualified to receive forty cents per day. They could use the football and volleyball fields, tennis courts, boxing ring, athletic field, and swimming pool or read one of more than six hundred books in German, Spanish, English, French, or Italian.[47] If they became bored, the German internees might join the camp's orchestra, listen to the radio, or watch a film. The men in the segregation camps, however, were not entitled to any of these benefits, as they were treated as troublemakers.

German racial privilege led to treatments and wages, even after the start of World War II, that differed for Japanese Americans and later Mexican migrants. The U.S. marshal even went out of his way to pay formerly detained Germans if there was a discrepancy. For example, after Walter Eiler and Heinrich-Friedrich Jahn were repatriated, the U.S. marshal tracked them down and ensured that they received their wages.[48] The U.S. marshal also ensured that professional craftsmen were hired when repairs needed to be made inside the Fort Stanton Internment Camp.[49] For this work assistant engineers earned a dollar an hour, and truck drivers received seventy-five cents per hour.[50]

When Germany surrendered on May 7, 1945, the U.S. government requested that the Fort Stanton Internment Camp close and that the portable, prefabricated CCC-type barracks be sent to various INS facilities.[51] By August 12, 1945, 347 German internees had been sent to Germany. A month later, on September 14, twenty Japanese American men were temporarily transferred from the Santa Fe Internment Camp to assist in tearing down the Fort Stanton Camp. The officer in charge of Fort Stanton and the supervising engineer, Mr. Wahls, requested that the men assist with the "crating, packing, and removal of property from the camp."[52] Confined nonwhite labor was used to expand the carceral state. The camp officially closed in October 1945, and its disassembled parts were transported to El Centro, California, to be repurposed as the newest immigration detention camp for unauthorized Mexican migrant men.[53] The Japanese Americans held inside Segregation Camp No. 1 were transferred to Terminal Island in San Pedro, California.[54]

Life at Fort Stanton shows that the mechanisms of war merged with the practices of the INS. Although the different experiences of German, Japanese American, and Mexican migrants reveal that immigration officials treated prisoners in different ways based on racialized ideas about labor productivity and value, World War II shaped the growth of migrant detention.

The Imperial Valley

El Centro was formed by a history of racism and labor exploitation long before the 1940s. The city of El Centro developed within the context of corporate agribusiness during the early twentieth century. In 1900 the valley was an unproductive desert, but beginning in 1908 a multiracial set of migrants played a pivotal role in developing the Imperial Valley. Local white elites reaped the benefits as the Colorado Desert transformed into an "agricultural empire."[55] White farmers turned to the indigenous Cocopas people to help with the construction of irrigation canals and ranch labor. Local growers recruited Japanese migrants to harvest cantaloupes, and African American and Southeast Asian migrants to pick cotton. Filipino and Korean migrants harvested crops on a seasonal basis as early as 1914. Yet Mexican migrants would come to occupy a more permanent role in the Imperial Valley's labor force. As early as 1908, Mexican migrants were recruited to work on local railroads and ranches. The presence of Mexican workers, which increased due to the migration of Mexican residents fleeing violence sparked by the Mexican Revolution of 1910, became so prevalent that one of the neighborhoods in El Centro was called "Little Mexico."[56]

The railroads kept the city segregated from east to west. Nonwhites lived on the east side, and the west was reserved for white residents.[57] By World War I Mexican workers harvested cantaloupes, melons, lettuce, and cotton throughout the Imperial Valley. In 1927 the Mexican population rose to twenty thousand, in a region that had fifty-four thousand residents, yet the power of the local elite continued to grow.[58]

The policing of Mexican migration was rampant throughout the Imperial Valley before the El Centro Immigration Detention Camp was constructed in 1945. On May 6, 1940, the International Longshoremen's and Warehousemen's Union wrote a declaration condemning the "intimidation and terror" of laborers in the Imperial Valley.[59] The union claimed that INS agents used records from clinics funded by the state of California and the federal government to identify and deport Mexican workers on the basis that they would become public charges. The federal government established two venereal clinics in the Imperial Valley, one in Brawley and one in El Centro, to contain the spread of communicable diseases and provide basic care to locals. The Hollywood League of Women Shoppers also denounced this practice, and, as a result, the Los Angeles district director agreed to investigate the matter.[60] Regina Raglia, executive secretary of the Hollywood League, wrote, "Several Mexican workers are now being held for deportation [based on the assumption that they would become public charges], most of whom have been residents of Imperial Valley for a quarter of a century, some of them having lived in Imperial County before the Americans."[61]

The Los Angeles district director discovered that on March 15, 1940, Miguel Gutiérrez stopped by the Calexico Immigration Office to renew his U.S. resident border-crossing card. When Inspector William E. Addis asked Gutiérrez to provide evidence of residence in the United States, he presented a treatment card he received after visiting one of the clinics in Brawley, during which he was treated for syphilis. Addis took away Gutiérrez's crossing card and threatened to arrest him if he left the country and attempted to re-enter. He based this on the notion that Gutiérrez suffered from a "loath-some and dangerous contagious disease."[62] Patrol Inspector Richard L. Williams of El Centro was assigned to obtain a warrant of arrest to apprehend Gutiérrez. During his investigation, Inspector Williams came up with the idea of tracking down deportable Mexicans by obtaining information from the local clinics, even if most of the patients had lived in the United States for ten or more years. In 1940 the clinics treated about 234 patients, 84 of whom were Mexican citizens. Along with Patrol Inspector Bryon A. Maxson, Williams visited the venereal clinic in Brawley and asked Dr. Paul V. Yingling, who was in charge of the clinic, to provide him with relevant information. But Dr. Yingling asserted that he could not do so without the approval of his superior officer. Williams and Maxson stood in front of the clinic and proceeded to question the Mexican men as they attempted to enter. Based on these conversations, they were able to secure warrants for the arrest of the men.[63]

Although the INS investigation concluded that there was no evidence to suggest that the patrol inspectors sought to deport workers with a history of unionization, they confirmed that Williams and Maxson attempted to use clinic records to find deportable Mexicans in the valley. This practice reveals one of the ways INS agents identified people for deportation. In 1940 most patrol inspectors working in the Imperial Valley apprehended between ten and thirty people each month.[64] They received tips from informants and then submitted a report to the inspector in charge to obtain a warrant. In other instances, patrol inspectors visited places such as agricultural fields and local jails to interview people they suspected were unauthorized. They subsequently submitted a written report to the inspector in charge to be used as a basis for obtaining a warrant.

Then, in 1942, the regional and national labor regime changed with the introduction of the Bracero Program, a guest-worker initiative that temporarily brought Mexican nationals to work in the United States. As a direct result of this program, in January 1943, 1,800 braceros arrived in the Imperial Valley.[65] Growers paid them a mere fifty cents an hour, a wage set by government and industry, sparking the beginning of an exploitative labor practice that lasted until 1964. As unauthorized Mexican migration increased because of the Bracero Program, in 1945 immigration officials zeroed in on El Centro as the location of a new immigration detention camp for migrants awaiting deportation.

The Origins of El Centro Immigration Detention Camp

The racialization of Mexican men as forced labor impacted the imaginations of immigration authorities. In 1945 patrol inspectors suggested that "the cost of setting up the buildings from Fort Stanton [at El Centro] would be very nominal because of the fact that all common labor could be performed by detainees."[66] From the start Mexican migrants were used in constructing and maintaining the El Centro Immigration Detention Camp.

INS officials opened the camp in January 1945 with the intent to close it within three months.[67] The government constructed the facility as an emergency measure when Mexican authorities refused to accept Mexican nationals from the Imperial Valley unless they had lived in Baja, California, for at least six months.[68] Patrol inspectors kept the camp filled from the moment it opened. In 1944 the INS had arrested 31,174 unauthorized entrants, and, as policing increased along the Imperial Valley, the Arizona Yuma Valley, and the Lower Rio Grande Valley of Texas, the INS hoped the El Centro Immigration Detention Camp would provide temporary space to hold the increasing number of unauthorized migrants generated by the Bracero Program.[69] The INS commissioner defined the function of the camp as "an assembly point for Mexican nationals apprehended in the immediate vicinity of the border."[70] Although most unauthorized migrants were allowed voluntary deportation to avoid legal proceedings, the INS held as many migrants as the immigration camp and local jails allowed.

Small and makeshift, the El Centro Immigration Detention Camp could hold up to a hundred men. Sixteen guards, two cooks, two general laborers, one clerk stenographer, and a physician staffed the facility managed by

Patrol Inspector Donald B. Anderson. According to INS records, "The camp was constructed to meet an emergency brought about by the refusal of the Mexican authorities to accept for deportation through ports in this District."[71] The purpose of the camp was to process, hold, and transport detained Mexican men within three days. Los Angeles district director Albert Del Guercio wrote that migrants "[were] to be held for transportation to either Nogales, Arizona, or El Paso, Texas depending upon the outcome of negotiations with the Mexican Government."[72] In practice local patrol inspectors kept migrants at El Centro for up to thirty days.[73] The Los Angeles district director wrote to officers stationed in El Centro and inquired why detained migrants were being held longer than thirty days if the purpose of the camp was to expedite their removal. According to Chief Detention Officer Bern Berard, the INS detained "aliens that had been recently apprehended and their status needed to be determined, aliens that had been processed and [awaited] deportation, aliens that were awaiting further information from the U.S. Marshal, and aliens held as witnesses."[74] The length of stay for each man varied. Detained migrants with a criminal background were turned over to the court for prosecution and then placed back inside the detention camp after serving their sentence.[75] Deportable migrants who were not excludable based on crimes, immoral or subversive grounds, or defects might be allowed voluntary departure without formal procedures because this practice was less expensive for the INS.[76]

But local patrol inspectors also had individual motives in encouraging detention over deportation, including profiting from migrants' labor. Holding them in immigration-specific camps made border policing more cost-effective because INS officials could count on detained migrants to aid with construction and maintenance.[77] For instance, in 1947 Officer J. E. Riley admitted that "aliens in the process of being deported, or given voluntary departure," had been used as laborers without being asked.[78] Acting Commissioner T. B. Shoemaker added, "Some of the officers in your district . . . overstepped the bounds of propriety in the employment of illegally resident aliens to assist in construction and other types of work on government buildings and grounds, and in at least two instances on their own private ventures."[79] In El Centro immigration authorities used the detention center as a holding site for an unpaid labor force.

Despite the government's initial intent to close the El Centro Immigration Detention Camp, local INS agents and officials quickly realized the benefits of keeping the facility open. They argued that they needed the camp, given its strategic border location.[80] By 1946 the Border Patrol had apprehended a total of 99,591 unauthorized migrants across the United States and deported 14,375 people.[81] As a result, in 1948 local INS officials requested the enlargement of the El Centro Immigration Detention Camp, not its dissolution. The INS expanded the holding capacity of the camp from 100 to 300 detained migrants by installing additional barracks, enlarging the dining area, and requesting additional guards and kitchen personnel.[82] The camp was transformed from being temporary and makeshift to a more permanent building within the Imperial Valley.

A System of Forced Labor

Life inside the El Centro Immigration Detention Camp was structured around work. Immigration officials expected detained Mexican men to labor outdoors in up to 115 degree weather. Yet, as W. A. Carmichael reveals, local INS employees were not content living under such weather conditions. He wrote, "Each summer several officers from the El Centro sector experience heat strokes or due to failing health, which is aggravated by the extreme heat in Imperial Valley, petition the Service for permission to transfer, at least temporarily, to the coast or some other locality with a more favorable climate."[83] Carmichael proposed transporting old victory huts from El Centro to Jacumba, California, to construct summer living quarters for the Border Patrol. He claimed that detention staff were unsatisfied working in El Centro because they felt ill due to the extreme temperatures.[84] Jacumba, a tiny town in the mountains off Interstate 80 and about forty-five minutes from El Centro, had a cooler climate. Moving INS personnel to Jacumba would help reduce the number of people who requested transfers during the summer months. Yet these same immigration officers believed Mexican migrants were perfectly suited to work in these conditions.

In 1947 immigration officer M. H. Scott asserted that migrant labor proved critical in helping to maintain immigration facilities. He wrote, "One of the big problems with regard to the operation of our detention facilities that I have encountered is general repair and maintenance of the facilities. For the past 20 years it has been our practice to utilize the service of detained aliens to assist us in meeting this problem." Many INS employees blamed this practice on the lack of government resources, but Officer Scott presented an alternative reason for using the labor of detained migrants. He argued that by working, "detainees might improve their time" by "learning the value of maintenance and repair."[85] But they were not paid for this "learning experience." Instead, local officials asked the men to volunteer with repairs, irrigation, and landscaping. Detained migrants worked in the mess halls, cleaned the barracks, and monitored the yard.[86] They maintained the very facility that imprisoned them and subsequently supported their loss of liberty.

Patrol inspectors justified treating migrants in this way by claiming that the men agreed to serve as volunteers and that they compensated them with food. Yet guards penalized migrants who did not fit the model of an ideal inmate, using punishments that included volunteering for work assignments. Officer Scott wrote:

> If [a detainee] refuses to be orderly or to comply with camp regulations . . . that is, being loud, boisterous, overbearing, and otherwise making himself a nuisance — he is instructed as to his conduct by the barrack orderly in the presence of an officer. If he . . . is subject to punishment for improper conduct in the mess-hall, or taking his fellow prisoner's clothes, etc. and/or refusing to do the necessary work about the camp . . . he is separated from the others, placed in a room apart from the others, and not permitted to associate with the men of the camp or enjoy the privileges of the camp for as long as 24 hours.[87]

An in-depth INS investigation revealed that local authorities also used detained migrants in what they called "work parties" to help with construction projects throughout the Imperial Valley. The investigation began when INS Patrol Inspector Charles E. Wilson, who was stationed at Calexico, informed a personal friend and FBI agent in San Diego about his coworker's questionable practices. Wilson learned of these labor practices when he arrested a Mexican migrant working on a construction project in El Centro. Patrol inspectors James E. Parker and Alva L. Pillied threatened Wilson for bothering the worker because, unbeknownst to Wilson, he was helping them with a project.[88] Wilson claimed that Chief Patrol Inspector Richard H. Wells used unethical practices to construct the Border Patrol Office in Brawley. Contractor Rafael Ortis provided the Border Patrol with carpenters, bricklayers, and plasterers in exchange for the labor of unauthorized Mexican men who could dig ditches for the sewer and water lines and clean up his yard.[89] When Deputy Commissioner T. B. Shoemaker asked Wilson why he contacted the FBI, he stated that he did not come forward with this information out of self-interest. He affirmed that "he did not make the complaint to win any particular reward in the Immigration and Naturalization Service as he ha[d] applied for a position as a California State Police Officer and believe[d] he w[ould] be accepted."[90] According to Wilson, he was motivated to make a report because he believed these practices were ultimately detrimental to the INS and the government more broadly.

During the investigation Patrol Inspector Joseph W. Alexander, head of the Brawley Substation, confirmed Wilson's allegations. When asked if the men volunteered for this work, Alexander responded, "Well, let me say that in the beginning the aliens were asked whether they preferred to spend the time intervening their arrests and their voluntary return, in the jail quarters or if they would rather be outside and assist us in our work. After a period of time the choice was unanimously in favor of being outside and helping us than spending the day in the local jail quarters awaiting their turn to be written up and later transported to the border." Patrol Inspector Alexander further disclosed the frequency of this type of practice. He wrote, "I am fully aware of the fact that the El Centro Office and the Detention Facility down there were built with the assistance of this labor. . . . Frankly, it never occurred to me that either specific permission would be required or that there was any reason why we should not use this type of labor."[91] Alexander's statement suggests that this custom was widespread and accepted. These labor practices seemed like common sense, given the historical link between labor and detention in the United States. It had not been that long since people classified as convicts were forced to labor outdoors in brutal conditions along highways and county roads as a form of punishment.[92]

The officers had tremendous power over the migrants they asked to work, including providing food and potentially influencing their deportation, making this labor system coercive at best. Patrol Inspector Wilson reported that INS officers used "unethical and unbecoming" labor practices in building, repairing, and maintaining INS facilities. He said, "Mexican nationals under deportation proceedings, or in the process of being allowed voluntary departure in lieu of deportation, were asked to volunteer to assist in this work."[93] With the promise of extra food rations, Mexican migrants participated.

The INS investigation sparked by Wilson's allegations also revealed the discretionary nature of border policing during the 1940s. Local INS agents determined when to enforce immigration laws based on their economic agendas. For example, Patrol Inspector Gruwell, stationed in Brawley, used migrant workers in construction projects such as repairing the Border Patrol building by handing out "get out of jail free" cards with his name to protect the workers from apprehension and deportation while he used them as unpaid labor.[94] On July 30, 1947, Fernando Alvarez, employed as an irrigator on a farm owned by Patrol Inspector Albert J. Smith, was arrested in Brawley and granted voluntary departure to Mexico. As soon as Inspector

Smith found out, he used the immigration inspector in Calexico to have Alvarez brought back to the United States. Smith claimed that Alvarez was valuable because he had provided him with information on the whereabouts of other unauthorized migrants. Yet Alvarez also worked on his farm, which suggests that INS agents bent the rules if it benefited them.[95]

The INS investigation revealed that local officials, agents, and guards used detained Mexican migrants as forced labor. Officer J. E. Riley stated, "There is no question but that aliens in the process of being deported, or given voluntary departure, have at times been directed to work on Border Patrol construction projects without being asked to volunteer."[96] But Riley blamed this practice on lack of funding. He asserted, "It is a matter of regret that the money this Service has been able to spend for the erection of suitable quarters to handle its work has been so small that it has been found necessary to ask Border Patrolmen to offer their time and services and to use Mexican laborers to work for nothing to erect them."[97] Officer Riley blamed this exploitative labor practice on the lack of funding and economic resources. Although immigration officials found these accusations unethical and embarrassing, they did not fire any agent for engaging in such inappropriate practices, according to the investigation.

Patrol inspectors throughout the Imperial Valley treated Mexican migrant men as disposable and turned the El Centro Immigration Detention Camp into a holding pen from which they could select men to participate in a regime of involuntary labor disguised as a volunteer work system. Local immigration officials claimed that they needed the labor of Mexican migrants to make up for a lack of funds, to give them something to do, and to train them.

THE LABOR PRACTICES that developed inside the El Centro Immigration Detention Camp, especially when examined alongside the confinement of the German crewmen held at Fort Stanton suggest that immigration camps did not simply function as administrative centers but rather holding pens for exploitable laborers. The detention conditions at Fort Stanton changed once the United States entered World War II, and this context shows that Mexican migrants continued, after the war, to be treated as national security threats.

The men held inside the El Centro Immigration Detention Camp might not have been prisoners of war, but the skeleton of the camp was constructed in a context of war and militarization. The carcass that was converted into an immigration detention camp held the spirits of warfare. The following chapter builds on the detention of Mexican migrants within the context of the Bracero Program.

CHAPTER TWO

The Spectral Door

Migrant Fluidity

> And this being-with specters would also be, not only but also,
> a politics of memory, of inheritance, and of generations.
>
> A spectral moment, a moment that no longer belongs to time.
>
> —JACQUES DERRIDA, 1993

In 1951, at the age of fourteen, Ramiro Cortez Martínez, a migrant from Pu-répero, Michoacán, crossed the U.S.-Mexico border from Tijuana, Mexico. Although young, he was able to secure a job in Palo Verdes, California. After gaining some experience he became a gardener for a wealthy family, whom he later found out included the head of the Los Angeles INS. Ramiro asked the INS official if it was a problem that he was *sin papeles* (without papers), and the officer responded by saying, "Don't worry, if you are working for me, the INS won't do anything. No one will bother you."[1] Ramiro recalls that the family treated him well because of a near-tragic incident. While watering some plants, he witnessed the young daughter of his boss nearly drown in a swimming pool. He jumped in and pulled her out just in time to save her life. Despite the family's gratitude and promises that the INS would leave him alone, three years later INS agents showed up at Ramiro's home. Agents apprehended him and sent him to Tijuana on a bus.

Within a few months, Ramiro was able to reenter the United States. This time he made his way to northern California. He was hired to work in the beet fields of Tracy, but INS agents apprehended Ramiro and sent him to an immigration station in Stockton, where he was held along with two hundred other migrants. The room was so crowded that he felt nauseous and witnessed several people pass out from the tight space and lack of water and food. Agents placed the migrants on top of trucks used to transport cattle and drove until they reached Nogales, Mexico. The drivers stopped a few times to eat but refused to give the migrants any food or water.

Ramiro stayed in Mexico after his second deportation, until 1957, when he was older and could apply for a Bracero contract.[2] He obtained work in Stockton, California, along with his brother and father. But when the grower selected him to pick cherries, he was separated from them. There were people from every state in Mexico at the labor camp. After a few months, he asked the cook to help him track down his father. They discovered that he was working at a farm down the street. Ramiro visited his dad and found out that he had recently fallen off a ladder. Although his father was injured and had bruises all over his body, Ramiro was grateful that he had survived the fall, because several braceros had lost their lives after falling from similar fifty-foot ladders. After only a few years, Ramiro skipped out on the Bracero Program because he felt it was very exploitative. He worked as an unauthorized migrant for a few more years before becoming a permanent resident and then eventually a U.S. citizen.

The various stages of illegality and legality that Ramiro experienced exemplify the fluidity of this moment. Scholar James D. Cockcroft referred to the practice of dual migrant importation and deportation as the "revolving door" of immigration. He claimed that this practice allowed "employers [to] keep the border doors revolving at a rhythm that suit[ed] their needs."[3] Ramiro's experience as an unauthorized worker, bracero, and someone who ultimately skipped out on the Bracero Program to have greater agency over his movement was a common migration experience. The migrant men who inhabited the Imperial Valley had similar labor stories of precarity, uncertainty, and nonlinear paths. These seemingly juxtaposed identities, of working as a bracero and an unauthorized migrant worker, came together and coalesced in El Centro.

The El Centro Immigration Detention Camp was opened shortly after the start of the Bracero Program. This labor regime was based on creating a reserve of surplus labor intended to benefit corporate farmers. Prior to the establishment of the Border Patrol, agricultural growers throughout the United States had relied on vigilantism to smash dissent, and the Bracero Program was crucial so that farmers could hire braceros to replace disgruntled workers who sought to unionize.[4] Yet, in documenting workers who had been traditionally unauthorized, the state made them visible in new ways, as they became trackable and at risk for deportation if they lost their work contract and stayed in the United States. In the 22 years that the program was in operation, about 4.8 million contracts were allocated.[5] The work contract, an agreement among the individual Mexican national, the grower or growers' association, a Mexican government official, and a U.S. Department of Labor representative, guaranteed braceros a minimum wage, transportation, and housing. Payroll deductions were to include food and health services.[6] Yet, despite these guarantees, there was disillusionment. A recipient said, "I have read my contract, but it is not worth the pain to insist on the clauses. . . . [It] has no value."[7] One day his work crew of about fifty men stopped working in the middle of the field. They were not necessarily on strike, but they demanded that they not be charged for room and board unless they were allowed to work and earn eight hours' worth of pay. The next day the manager took one of the men into the fields and told him that there were plenty more workers where he came from. The threat of being replaced, denied future contracts, or having their contract terminated with subsequent deportation made it difficult for braceros to protest their exploitation.

Although a Bracero Reception Center and an immigration detention camp served opposite purposes, reception and removal, migrants called both of these places *el corralón* (the corral), to link their experience of confinement with that of animals.[8] Since the Imperial Valley workforce was heavily dependent on Mexican migrants, including braceros, unauthorized migrants, and former braceros whose contracts had expired or who had chosen to skip out on their own accord, many of the men who passed through the El Centro Immigration Detention Camp had at one point or another worked as a bracero.[9]

Mexican officials recruited potential braceros in Mexico, but after 1947 growers also hired "specials," or formerly unauthorized Mexican workers legalized as braceros. Migrants were recruited at farms, transported to the border, issued documents, and returned to the United States in a process called "drying out."[10] As Ernesto Galarza, Mexican American scholar and activist, said about this time period, "Many Nationals have come back to occupy [bracero] camps in which they were housed as illegal migrants only one or two years ago."[11] Thus, migrants moved through various stages of legality and illegality. Their status was fluid and could be changed depending on labor needs. Grower exploitation also led many braceros to skip out on their work contracts, becoming unauthorized yet again. Although braceros were subject to U.S. laws, they were not U.S. citizens, and this limited their abilities to advocate for themselves.

The Bracero Program encouraged unauthorized migration by limiting contracts to men and engendering the idea that jobs were abundant in the United States. Scholars argue that this was not an unintentional side effect but was planned by policy makers "to strengthe[n] the pool of migrants that growers could employ at meager wages, while also avoiding bureaucracy."[12] The number of unauthorized Mexican migrants increased along the Imperial Valley, the Yuma Valley, and the Lower Rio Grande Valley of Texas because agribusiness leaders continued to hire unauthorized migrants, who were ultimately more profitable than braceros, despite the stability of contract labor. Ranchers hired unauthorized migrants with zero labor protections, for less money, and with less bureaucracy. A bracero was paid about $4.80 per week, while an unauthorized migrant earned about $3.00.[13]

The Bracero Program spurred growing rates of migration through the Imperial Valley, and this shift influenced the government's opening of the El Centro Immigration Detention Camp in 1945. You cannot tell one story without the other because they are co-constitutive histories. It was at this time that white Americans associated Mexicans as "iconic illegal aliens." As Mae M. Ngai has written, "Illegal status became constitutive of a racialized Mexican identity and of Mexicans' exclusion from the national community and polity."[14] The importation of braceros worked with the detention and deportation operations occurring inside the detention camp. Placing the history of the Bracero Program alongside that of immigration detention in El Centro elucidates the intersecting experiences of Mexican migrants and their fluid status in the Imperial Valley. Because Mexicans were racialized as "illegal" regardless of their actual status, it is impossible to untangle both of these developments.

Policing Race and Labor in the Imperial Valley

When I was researching in El Centro, California, I drove around asking locals if they would be open to sharing their experiences of living near the El Centro Immigration Detention Camp. Rather than discuss migrant detention, people encouraged me to visit the former Bracero Reception Center. Although the Bracero Program was also difficult to examine, locals seemed to find it more manageable to discuss because it ended fifty years ago. The fact that I needed to consider immigration detention by contemplating a distinct yet related labor regime reveals a discomfort on the part of locals that made this matter further invisible.

After doing some digging, I found the site of the Bracero Reception Center, located at the intersection of West McCabe Road and South La Brucherie Road, which had been repurposed in the 1960s from a major administrative site for braceros in California to a six-acre private residence. The Bracero Reception Center for all arriving Mexican migrants to California was located in El Centro, only four miles from the immigration detention camp. I knocked on the door and was greeted by the homeowners, a lovely couple who welcomed me in and helped me to think about the links between corporate agriculture and the carceral state in the Imperial Valley. The current property owner, Gretchen Laue, summarized the importance of the government receiving center by saying, "I think in many ways, the story of this house is the story of the Imperial Valley. . . . It was both a place of despair and a place of hope."[15]

The Imperial Valley's white elite benefited from the precarious nature of Mexican migrant lives. The noncitizenship status of both braceros and unauthorized migrants made them vulnerable to exploitation by agricultural growers.[16] Local farmers and INS authorities viewed Mexican migrant workers, regardless of their legal status, as docile and fit for backbreaking and cheap labor. Mexican men had been racialized as ideal agricultural workers throughout the twentieth century, and this racialization continued during the Bracero Program. The federal contract lent the appearance of a more equitable labor system, but this was not the case.[17] In fact, despite the bracero contract, Mexican migrants were racialized as nonhuman, criminal, and disposable laborers.

The exploitation of Mexican workers started before they came to the United States. The US government paid for the transportation of Mexican nationals seeking to participate in the Bracero Program from recruitment centers in northern Mexico to Bracero Reception Centers throughout the United States. Hopeful braceros, such as Isidoro Ramírez, remembered one of the recruitment centers being like a concentration camp. He said, "The concentration camp was in Empalme, Sonora, Mexico."[18] A representative with the American Friends Service Committee documented the case of a Mexican man who hoped to become a bracero at a Mexican contracting station in Empalme. The man died while he waited for a temporary contract, not to last more than six months, and when authorities investigated the cause of death, doctors discovered that the man's stomach and intestines contained nothing but paper.[19] He had eaten paper to stay alive long enough to secure a work contract.

It was common for hopeful men who waited in Empalme to accrue debt or experience homelessness while waiting, making them vulnerable to people with promises of securing them a contract for a fee.[20] The men who survived these conditions were transported in boxcar trains to Bracero Reception Centers along the border. They faced "backbreaking labor, low-quality food, a lack of water and rest, and segregated, substandard housing," which often resulted in "respiratory illnesses, permanent spinal injuries, malnourishment, the mental effects of isolation," and in some cases death.[21] Loss of life was a fairly common occurrence, as evidenced by the death certificates of braceros who died while working in the United States located in the Secretariat of Foreign Affairs in Mexico City.

References to a Mexican migrant's ability to work in deplorable conditions were widespread. For instance, grim conditions plagued the El Centro Bracero Reception Center, which braceros should have left within hours but sometimes stayed at longer owing to delays in getting them to a farm.[22] In 1958 Labor historian Hank Anderson inspected the facility and labor camps throughout the Imperial Valley. He claimed that there was no source of heat in colder months at these locations. He spoke with the local compliance man, who asserted, "The heat from [the detainees'] bodies [should be] enough to keep it warm all night, even on the coldest nights of the year."[23] The Bracero Reception Centers in the United States set the standard for the local labor camps, which suggests that conditions were not any better once Mexican nationals received a job assignment and that their welfare was controlled by growers. The U.S. Department of Labor specified that workers receive one blanket regardless of weather conditions, which was an essential item in winter.[24] A field representative with the Department of Labor argued that Mexicans were best suited to labor in the summer heat of the Imperial Valley. He said, "The combination of the heat and the humidity is just about more than a human being can take. . . . I'm not going to ask an American . . . to do it. I don't know of anybody except the [braceros] who can take it."[25] Government officials and agricultural growers used this type of biological justification, common since the 1920s, to rationalize the conditions migrants faced. But these conditions also encouraged braceros to skip out on their work contracts.

Local INS agents played a pivotal role in enforcing and manipulating the perceived and real threat of deportation, allowing for harsher migrant treatment. As Cristina Salinas has shown, "agents patrolled both a border and a labor system."[26] Testimony from the 1950 President's Commission on Migratory Labor showed that the INS and agricultural growers worked together. An immigrant rights group, the Los Angeles Committee for the Protection of the Foreign Born, argued that "the INS used its authority to convenience the big growers; condoning and expediting the entry of 'wet-backs' during harvest; shutting their eyes to un-American wages and living conditions; conducting mass deportations at 'timely' intervals, often before Mexican workers could collect back wages due."[27] Mexican migrant workers, whether braceros, legal permanent residents, or unauthorized migrants, were racialized as ideal workers in the Imperial Valley, and policing was a central component of regulating labor in the region. But this was not a new tactic. As historian David Montejano has pointed out about Texas, the Border Patrol was used as a form of labor control, discipline, and repression since its inception in 1924.[28] It was common for Anglo farmers to leak the names of unauthorized Mexican farmworkers to INS agents to avoid payment of wages.

Local INS officials used detained migrants held inside the El Centro Immigration Detention Camp as unpaid labor, and they often sought out braceros to work in similar conditions. In 1958 an INS employee needed a sewer line dug up at his residence in Calexico, so he asked the head of transportation services at the El Centro Bracero Reception Center to let him borrow two men. The braceros were driven between Calexico and El Centro every day for about a week. When they finished digging the sewer line for the INS officer, they received a new work contract, but no compensation for their labor.[29] This practice suggests that despite the status of Mexican migrants, local immigration officials and agents exploited them.

Mexican Migrants and Public Health

Public health officials regulated migration through racist ideas about science and disease along the U.S.-Mexico border for decades. John Mckiernan-González has written that, during the turn of the twentieth century, "using germ control as their lens, public health officers saw and separated *Mexicans*—people who had been considered part of the general landscape of West Texas—from the suddenly American landscape in which they lived and worked. Rather than treating 'Mexican' afflictions as an important part of life on the border, this newer 'dangerous bodies' approach treated domestic laborers in El Paso as the medical threat that needed regulation, symbolically cleaning the people cleaning El Paso."[30] As the U.S. Department of Labor processed Mexican nationals at five Bracero Reception Centers in California, Arizona, and Texas, this form of policing dominated.

The El Centro Bracero Reception Center was no exception. Walter Francis managed the El Centro Bracero Reception Center, where up to four thousand Mexican nationals waited between three to four weeks.[31] When the men arrived, medical staff deloused and inspected their bodies. Former bracero Isidoro Ramírez recounted how there was no privacy during medical examinations. He was forced to undress, and for that he felt shame and embarrassment. Ramírez waited at the El Centro Bracero Reception Center until a rancher selected him for work.[32] He was treated like an animal during these procedures, he lamented. Health officials also dusted the braceros with dichlorodiphenyltrichloroethane (DDT), a chemical used as an insecticide and believed to prevent germs from spreading.[33]

DDT was introduced in 1940, and it quickly became a widespread method of controlling insects and insect-borne diseases during World War II. Diseases such as louse-borne typhus killed over 2.5 million soldiers and civilians during World War I.[34] To combat these death counts, the War Department worked with researchers to develop the insecticide, which was widely distributed to the army by 1943. The use of DDT on Mexican migrants further shows the connections between migrant detention and the technologies of war. Since the early twentieth century, health officials associated Mexicans with disease, poverty, and crime. As Alexandra Minna Stern has shown, the United States Public Health Service (USPHS) and the Bureau of Immigration worried about disinfecting arriving migrants from Mexico as early as 1916.[35] Immigration officials and staff continued to treat detained men inside the El Centro Immigration Detention Camp in a similar fashion.

During the 1940s Americans largely believed that DDT was harmless to humans, although tests suggested otherwise. For instance, the *New York Times* revealed that experimental trials demonstrated that DDT not only controlled mosquitos but killed nearby animals in the process.[36] Despite ecologists' efforts to show the dangers of using DDT, this remained a widespread practice until the late 1960s, when the Department of Health, Education, and Welfare linked DDT with carcinomas. When the camp was sprayed with DDT, detained migrants were left surrounded by toxic, persistent, and migratory poisonous chemicals.

When INS agents first brought Mexican migrants into the El Centro Immigration Detention Camp, staff dusted them with DDT to eliminate fleas and lice, fingerprinted them, and dressed them in white coveralls for easy identification in the case of an attempted escape.[37] In the May 10, 1948, issue of *El Imparcial*, Mexican newspaper editor Manuel Acosta Meza published an article titled "Our Cousins Kick Us," criticizing INS practices inside the El Centro Immigration Detention Camp. Meza stated that the hair cropping of Mexican laborers' was a "discriminatory act" committed by American authorities "who then later deport[ed] them."[38] The INS practice that Meza refers to was the hair cropping of detained men to kill lice and avoid scalp diseases, a practice many slave masters had used to punish enslaved women.[39] Immigration officials used this procedure at the El Centro Immigration Detention Camp starting in February 1946. Before this date, they dusted the heads of prisoners with DDT powder to stop vermin from spreading.[40] INS officials turned to hair cutting because it was seen as a safer method, although DDT was still used on other parts of the migrants' bodies. The Los Angeles INS district director mentioned that it was common practice for the INS to cut the hair of detained migrants as soon as they arrived in the camp as part of their processing, which included a hot bath and the spraying of their clothing with DDT.[41]

In response to Meza's article, INS officials claimed that the only men who objected to hair cutting were "those of the 'zoot suit' class with long hair, many of whom [had] body lice, and interpret[ed] the act as a personal affront to their dignity."[42] Despite acknowledging that some prisoners challenged the practice, INS officials claimed that hair cutting was done for health and sanitation and that it was limited to a few. This practice was on display on the streets of Mexicali, as it was common to see recently deported migrants with shaved heads, a look reminiscent of military haircuts.[43] On July 15, 1948, INS officials received a letter from the consulate in Tijuana, Mexico, that expressed concern over this approach. The INS responded by assuring the consulate that this practice was a safer alternative to spraying chemicals that could cause skin irritation and injuries to the face.[44] The stereotyping of Mexican migrants as diseased and potential carriers of lice had a longer historical trajectory that racialized Mexicans as dirty and diseased. This form of dehumanization and negative rendering of the bodies of Mexican men helped to justify the harsh treatment inside the camp.[45]

On March 8, 1957, body lice emerged as an issue in immigration detention centers throughout the United States. Immigration facilities, including the El Centro Immigration Detention Camp, became infested with body lice. Immigration officials claimed that they could not get rid of the lice, which had become immune to DDT. David H. Carnahan, the regional Southwest commissioner, wrote that lice could not be eradicated even though "all mattresses and blankets in the camps [were] periodically fumigated [and the] barracks and buildings [had] been systematically sprayed with DDT solution." INS officials requested advice from the Public Health Service. Officials determined that the only means of combating lice would be to strip prisoners upon entering the facility, sterilize their clothes for fifteen minutes at 115 degrees, have them deeply scrubbed with disinfectant soap, and then shave their heads. INS officials expressed hesitation at completely shaving the heads of all the detained migrants, as the Mexican government had made objections to this in the past.[46]

Immigration officials received advice from Dr. C. B. Spencer of the Surgeon General's Office in Washington, D.C. He suggested that the INS use DDT more aggressively. They would have to "process the clothing of new detainees in a fumigation chamber (or building) or in a sterilization chamber; to issue coveralls to the detainees while their clothing [was] processed; to continue the use of DDT and other compositions with other measures, and to fumigate the camp buildings twice (at 8-day intervals) in order to control the breeding cycle of the lice population."[47]

In addition to exposing Mexican migrants to dangerous chemicals, the INS often prohibited braceros from receiving the medical care they were eligible for. When they got sick, INS agents often deported them and claimed that their ability to work was restricted as a cost-saving measure. Imperial Valley doctor and Brawley city council member Ben Yellen was horrified by this practice. He published newsletters informing residents about this issue. He wrote, "This trick of sending the sick workers back to Mexico and thereby avoiding the payment of medical expenses and avoiding payment of disability payments is really sick. The laborer often does not know that he should have been sent to the hospital. Many do not know that they are entitled to weekly disability payments."[48] In addition to poor health, if a bracero was injured he was in danger of being sent back to Mexico so that he would have to pay for his medical expenses.[49] For example, in 1958 Henry Anderson interviewed braceros held inside the El Centro Bracero Reception Center. One man confided, "Last October, I began to feel a pain in my stomach. . . . I went to a doctor [who] said I should be put in the hospital. Instead, the association ended my contract. Now that I am trying to get another contract, they tell me it isn't my stomach that is causing the pain, but tuberculosis in my lungs."[50] Despite the protections the bracero contract claimed to guarantee braceros, they faced medical conditions similar to migrants held inside immigration detention camps, experiencing precarity regardless of their status.

Bracero Labor Camps

Food is political. It can reveal social hierarchies. In El Centro, food became a method of extracting labor and money. As Bryan Finoki has emphasized, "power is contested and transmitted" through sources such as food in prison, "as a weapon in the disciplinary tactics of the jailer."[51] Food became a form of making a profit and controlling Mexican migrants at bracero labor camps throughout the Imperial Valley. For the Bracero Program to benefit private growers, braceros were provided with the bare minimum. Bracero labor camps received one dollar per day, deducted from braceros' paychecks, to feed them food such as oatmeal and sandwiches. If braceros refused to eat meals at the camp, employers threatened to fire them from a particular job or send them back to Mexico.[52] If managers received $500 they were to feed five hundred braceros for a day.[53] But the food served to braceros was not worth nearly the amount of money received, leaving local camp managers with a healthy profit.[54] The tactic of restricting food as discipline and to save on costs had been practiced in carceral places since the 1700s.[55] The Bracero camps followed this long tradition. Ernesto Galarza, a labor activist who was very familiar with the conditions of labor exploitation throughout the Imperial Valley, wrote that the "feeding of hundreds of thousands of Mexican Nationals bec[a]me a profitable business, a lucrative sideline that impinge[d] on the rights and privileges granted workers by law."[56]

Although braceros worked under a legal contract, their rights were violated daily. Their living arrangements were another source of profit for employers. Labor camps included stores with goods such as clothing, shoes, soap, and cigarettes. Store owners overpriced the items in exchange for making them available to workers. They encouraged braceros to exchange store products for credit, which often left them in debt when they worked fewer hours than expected. The El Centro Immigration Detention Camp also included a commissary. If prisoners wanted razor blades, toothbrushes, matches, and cigarettes, including Lucky Strikes and Camels they had to purchase such items at the commissary.[57] One of the reasons that Mexican braceros made significantly less money than they anticipated was that growers set up a system that disadvantaged braceros. Mexican workers were not always given the number of work hours promised, and growers limited the amount of money they could make. Besides, although a pay rate was listed in the work contract, growers did not always abide by this. Agricultural growers hired a large number of workers yet assigned them work for only 30 to 40 percent of the time.[58] This tactic allowed growers to get their crops harvested but did not permit braceros to make a lot of money. One bracero recounted that, after completing two weeks of work, he still owed the camp two dollars for room and board because he had so much debt.[59]

Braceros living in the El Centro Associated Farmers Camp claimed that it was so cold that they often had to ask for additional blankets. They slept in their work clothes, and their bunks were overcrowded and physically constructed in a space intended for cows. Yet lodging was not free. Braceros paid for housing, which added up to about $12.50 per week, regardless of the climate, how many hours they worked, or if they were laid off and waiting to be transported.[60] Mexican nationals complained about the "lack of facilities for washing, poor ventilation in summer, lack of recreation facilities, isolation, frozen pipes in winter, lack of good drinking water and nearness of passing trains."[61] Agricultural employers throughout the Imperial Valley treated Mexican men similarly whether they worked with or without a contract.

Agricultural growers and INS employees viewed Mexican migrant workers, regardless of their legal status, as a source of labor and profit. The distinction between legality and illegality was blurred throughout the Imperial Valley, as was made clear by the proximity of the El Centro Immigration Detention Camp and the Bracero Reception Center. Contracted Mexican nationals had legal protections on paper, but their noncitizen status and their deportability made their lived realities similar to each other. Local immigration officers and growers had tremendous power throughout the valley, and they marked braceros and unauthorized Mexican laborers as a disposable, detainable, and deportable source of labor.

CHAPTER THREE

Migrant Fugitivity

On Disappearance as Survival

> A fugitive, and fugitivity, references stolen life. Fugitivity marks
> a kind of outlawish indiscreet disavowal of and disengagement
> from the project of hegemony.
>
> —MARQUIS BEY, 2019

> To suppose that one can identify fugitive movements in the hollow
> of fungibility's embrace is to focus on modes of escape, of wander,
> of flight that exist within violent conditions of exchange.
>
> —C. RILEY SNORTON, 2017

Mexican migrants throughout the Imperial Valley challenged their labor exploitation and incarceration. On January 22, 1945, Border Patrol inspector
trainees Leo L. Lewis and Findlay J. Postles, who were relatively new to the
INS, placed four Mexican migrants waiting for their immigration proceedings inside an INS truck. They transported them from the El Centro Immigration Detention Camp to a gravel pit located about ten miles from the camp
and a quarter-mile from the international line, near the unincorporated community of Mount Signal.[1] The chief patrol inspector had ordered the volunteer work crew to bring back gravel, to be used in surfacing the INS
headquarters and the camps' walkways and driveways. While the final load
of gravel was being placed in the truck, David Calderón-Cisneros dashed
toward the bushes. Initially, Postles was not alarmed because he assumed
the detained migrant needed to relieve himself. When Calderón-Cisneros
continued running past the nearby bushes, Postles panicked and demanded
that he halt. It was then that Calderón-Cisneros dropped his shovel and
darted as fast as he could toward the border.[2] He managed to outrun the inspector and successfully escape to Mexico, because, according to Postles,
"the terrain around th[e] gravel pit was rough desert country sparsely covered with low brush," making it difficult to catch up to Calderón-Cisneros.
Lewis agreed that "it was impossible to overtake him" because "the International Boundary line was too close." INS officials considered allowing a prisoner to escape a severe misstep, but since Lewis and Postles had worked for

the INS for fewer than seven months and had little experience taking detained migrants to the gravel pit, they concluded that reprimanding the trainees was sufficient. Mexican migrants were not willing participants in this system of "volunteer" labor. Calderón-Cisneros took advantage of the proximity to Mexico to escape his incarceration and labor exploitation.

On June 27, 1940, Congress passed the Second Deficiency Appropriations Act, allocating $2 million to the Border Patrol for additional equipment and employees. These funds were sufficient to hire 769 new employees and purchase 191 patrol cars, twenty-five horses, watercraft, airplanes, firearms, and radio equipment.[3] Despite these resources, the El Centro Immigration Detention Camp was a place where local patrol inspectors and detained migrants contested power. Mexican migrants frequently fled and attempted to escape their mistreatment and dehumanization. Between 1945 and 1949 INS officials recorded that twenty-one prisoners fled from the El Centro Immigration Detention Camp.[4] Local patrol inspectors were still figuring out how to enforce immigration policies in the Imperial Valley as prisoners challenged their power and control. Although the detention of migrants was not intended as legal punishment for crossing the border without proper authorization, the lived realities of these men indicate that their confinement was punitive. Immigration authorities went beyond the law to ensure that Mexican migrants remained incarcerated and they subsequently used them as forced labor.

This chapter shows that Mexican migrants were not passive victims. They frequently fled from the El Centro Immigration Detention Camp and attempted to escape their mistreatment and dehumanization. I view the following stories of migrant flight as examples of freedom and survival. The exact reasons why each detained migrant chose to escape are unknown, but this chapter suggests that they took every opportunity at their disposal to flee from conditions of labor exploitation and dehumanization.

Double Fugitivity

The detention practices employed by the larger INS apparatus provide insight into the agency's larger bureaucratic view on prisoner escape. Taking a look back at the Fort Stanton Internment Camp in New Mexico provides a larger view of escape. To prevent German flight at the Fort Stanton Camp, guards made two check-ins every day. They reported this information to the headquarters in El Paso and Alpine, Texas. If a German crewman attempted to escape, patrol officers reported the incident; conducted a search; worked with local police and sheriffs to patrol the highways, trains, and buses; and contacted "keepers of roadside restaurants and inns, peace officers, rangers, ranchers, and railroad employees."[5] Local agents were encouraged to contact the FBI and use army airplanes if necessary. For instance, in the fall of 1942, German crewmen Bruno Dathe, Johann Grantz, Willy Michel, and Hermann Runne fled from the Fort Stanton Camp. Agents used all available resources to track them down. They searched for the men in cars and on horses, blocked the highways and roads, and meticulously followed their footprints. However, it was local ranchers who spotted the men. One of the escapees was shot in the leg when the rancher apprehended him.[6] At their hearing, it was discovered that they had escaped by constructing a tunnel at the camp. For this transgression, the officer in charge sentenced them to thirty days' confinement.

Although escape was a serious matter, and while there was an elaborate emergency protocol if an escape was attempted, this act was not a criminal offense.[7] In 1945 Congress passed legislation that made assisting in the escape of a prisoner of war or enemy alien punishable with a fine of up to $10,000 or incarceration for ten years. Such assistance could include providing intelligence or advising, aiding, transporting, harboring, concealing, sheltering, protecting, or corresponding with prisoners of war or enemy aliens. This measure targeted potential assistants and not escapees themselves. Focusing on curtailing resources available to fugitives helped ensure that they would be caught and reincarcerated. INS officials later rejoiced about having apprehended all the German escapees during wartime. They wrote in the INS *Annual Report* of 1945, "Since the war started, no internee has succeeded in making good his escape from the custody of this Service, except in the single case of a German internee who departed from a railroad work project in connection with which only minimum surveillance was maintained. He was apprehended some months later by agents of the Federal Bureau of Investigation."[8] This tactic was further reinforced when on June 24, 1948, attempting to assist an escapee "arrested with a warrant or other process issued under any law of the US, or committed to the custody of the Attorney General" became further criminalized with fines or imprisonment.[9]

Prisoner escapes became a growing problem for immigration authorities during the 1940s. As Kelly Lytle Hernández has shown, immigration agents had little training in border regions such as El Centro. Border agents charged with great responsibility often had less than two years of experience. She has written, "It was an unenviable job, particularly since undocumented workers had increasingly taken to running to escape apprehension and the task of chasing them across cotton fields, plowed ground, canals and resacas, and brush and sand in the blazing 100 degree plus temperature and choking dust has become a grueling and exhausting task."[10] Boundary making and policing were still being developed in the Imperial Valley, leaving room for migrant flight. The first escape in the region occurred before the El Centro Immigration Detention Camp was operational. In 1944 local INS agents transferred sixteen prisoners held at the Imperial County Jail to the El Centro Immigration Detention Camp as it was still being constructed. The jail was under quarantine because of an outbreak of spinal meningitis, and the agents used the camp as a temporary space while it was under construction. Holding the inmates at the camp was beneficial for the jail and local patrol inspectors, who sought assistance in finishing the construction of the camp. The prisoners were asked to help in the erection of the victory huts and the perimeter fence. During the night guards placed the prisoners inside one of the huts and watched over them. Yet, on the morning of January 1, 1945, when the guards counted the inmates, Patrol Inspector Leland Wasson discovered that Mexican prisoner Aristeo Castañeda-Agredano was missing.[11] The patrol inspectors could not figure out how he had escaped, but they concluded that he might have slipped out unnoticed while the officers changed work shifts. The fence that would be placed along the camp's perimeter had not yet been put up, and Castañeda-Agredano could have easily fled. These challenges to the authority of local patrol officers continued when the camp opened.

By the end of the first month, detained Mexican migrants felt they were ready to attempt group escapes. On the night of January 25, a guard stationed at the camp's southeast watchtower observed Luis Ramírez-Ruiz, Geronimo Ríos-Rubio, Trinidad Díaz-Ramos, José Beltrán-Chávez, Miguel Lopez-Zazueta, and Francisco Molina-Flores crawl under the east fence and flee from the facility.[12] The guard looked toward the northwest tower, where his coworker should have been stationed. What he did not know was that the escapee had taken advantage of the fact that the guard on the northwest tower had left his post. He came down to open the west gate for a couple of men arriving to complete a paint job at the camp. The guard in the southeast tower immediately came down from his post and ran after the men, but he was unsuccessful in his pursuit. Only after trying to catch the prisoners himself did the guard notify the patrol inspectors of the incident. They reprimanded the guard, but INS officials were aware that the real problem was the lack of communication technologies available to them and the number of guards present in the camp. At the time of the group escape, nine men guarded the El Centro Immigration Detention Camp. Immigration officials had the funds to hire a total of sixteen guards, but it was difficult to recruit men for a temporary job in the middle of the Imperial Valley. Los Angeles district director Albert Del Guerico wrote, "To recruit even this number we have had to content ourselves with accepting for employment as guards persons of more or less substandard qualifications, who would not be considered in normal times."[13] Concerned with the number of escapes, Del Guercio visited the camp a few months later. He requested that phones be installed inside each watchtower to allow the guards to immediately connect with patrol inspectors.

The detained migrants collaborated and thoroughly planned their escapes. They picked a time when the guards were distracted. For instance, the detained men waited until the dirt around the fence was softened by the rain, making it easier for them to crawl under and escape.[14] On another occasion, a prisoner lay flat on the ground against the fence and then used a plank to lift the barbed wire and climb under it. Escapes were anything but spontaneous.[15] Cedric J. Robinson's concept of "fugitivity" helps to contextualize the multiple meanings of these escapes.[16] Referring to enslavement, Robinson contended that the term "runaway" did not fully capture the enslaved act of escape. "Children run away, but what these people were doing was achieving fugitive status," he wrote.[17] Conceptualizing this act as a fugitive action more fully encapsulates the agency of confined Mexican migrants. They were fugitives because they fled the detention camp, but they were also already rendered fugitive because of their unauthorized legal status. Mexican migrants attempted to escape a system that rendered them outlaws.

Surveillance at the Migrant Detention Camp

During the camp's early operations, local INS authorities had trouble exerting control over Mexican migrants, who frequently fled. Despite using all available resources to recover escapees, such as contacting law enforcement, welfare organizations, and hospitals, patrol inspectors had trouble keeping migrants confined.[18] On the night of April 22, 1945, Leland J. Shanks, who had been employed as a guard for three months, was stationed at the observation tower at the southeast corner of the camp. From there he could see several prisoners walk about the compound. It was cloudy because it had rained earlier in the day, but he was still able to see Oscar Bermúdez-Fimbres walk from the central area of the camp near the huts to the east fence, where he proceeded to jump over the nearly nine-foot barricade. The fencing was composed of a nearly eight-foot fence with barbed-wire arms that extended fourteen inches. Shanks called Patrol Inspector Armand J. Molleur in the radio room, as instructed, and asked him to sound the escape signal, three beeps followed by one long blast to represent the east fence. Patrol Inspector Leland R. Crawford responded to the alarm and went looking for Bermúdez-Fimbres, while Molleur contacted Chief Patrol Inspector Richard H. Wells, who arrived within twenty minutes and assisted in searching for the escapee. Bermúdez-Fimbres managed to escape into the darkness, despite the efforts of the inspectors.[19] They followed his tracks for about two hundred yards, but his footprints eventually disappeared in the grass. Immigration officials wrote: "Any hopes of reapprehending an alien were remote. With a short start they are lost in the dark. They can travel much faster than you track them."[20] Although detained men had escaped from the El Centro Immigration Detention Camp in the past, this was the first time someone fled by jumping over rather than climbing under the exterior barricade, which left District Director Guercio with the urgent desire to make the camp more secure.[21]

Immigration officials were shocked that Bermúdez-Fibres was able to jump the fence with ease. They claimed that "it was constructed with the best means available under the supervision of Mr. Wells," while adding that it could be improved by anchoring it to the ground between posts, making it taller, and using materials other than wire mesh.[22] Del Guercio was dissatisfied with the wire-mesh barbed-wire fence. Despite his desire to fortify the barrier, there was a scarcity of chain-link fencing. Instead, he prioritized increasing the number of guards. Del Guercio increased the number of night guards to four, two of whom were stationed near the fence. Only four months after the camp opened, the district director provided the guards with rifles and blanks, to send a message to the confined men and to alert officers if a prisoner attempted to escape.[23] A curfew was implemented so that the detained men did not roam around at night, and guards locked them inside the huts with bolted locks.

As a result of the successful escape of Bermúdez-Fimbres, the district director gave patrol inspectors new policies that stipulated how to manage the camp. One guideline stated, "Physical force may be used against an alien detainee only in self defense or to prevent an escape or to overpower an escapee, or to preserve order among detainees."[24] This rule authorized the use of violence to maintain control and order. The guards assigned to the observation towers were encouraged to keep a closer watch over the prisoners. INS officials hoped that this type of panopticism would function as a deterrent and would make detained migrants think twice about escaping.[25] Immigration authorities viewed state surveillance and the technologies of militarization as among the best methods of regulating the actions of prisoners. As Rachel E. Dubrofsky and Soshana Amielle Magnet have outlined, "State surveillance practices . . . are processes that are simultaneously about seeing and not-seeing—that is, some bodies are made invisible, while others are made hypervisible."[26] Local INS officials and agents viewed the bodies of Mexican migrant men as both disposable and deportable yet capable of performing backbreaking labor throughout the Imperial Valley. They turned toward the tactic of surveillance, a method as old as settler colonialism, when Spanish colonizers employed sexual surveillance of native peoples in the mission system, to manage their workforce.[27] By watching over the prisoners' every move, INS officials made Mexican migrants' movements hypervisible and their exploitation invisible.

Continued Escapes

Despite increasing surveillance at El Centro Immigration Detention Camp, in May 1945, guard Glover C. Smith, who had been employed with the INS for four months, witnessed Salvador Aguilar-Montañes and Alfonso Hurtado-Velásquez escape from the camp.[28] Stationed at the north observation tower at night, he observed a man run toward the north fence. Smith immediately made a call to the main office, during which he realized that a second man had scaled the fence on the east side. He tried to shine a light on the men, but it was too late. Officer Shanks, who was stationed outside the fence, noticed the two detained men. He ran after them but was unable to catch up. During the chase, he saw the men run toward the irrigation canal, where he then lost track of them. INS inspectors continued the search in vehicles, but they were unsuccessful in locating Aguilar-Montañes and Hurtado-Velásquez.

INS authorities were once again on alert on May 21, 1945, when three out of seven detained migrants escaped while in transit to a job site near New River. They were on their way to gather cane for the construction of shade in the camp's yard.[29] Patrol Inspectors John J. Moore and William D. Keirsey, both relatively new to the INS, drove the government truck and made the mistake of letting the men ride in the back of the vehicle without supervision. While en route to the job site, the three Mexican men jumped off the truck and ran away, for which the patrol inspectors were suspended from duty without pay for three days.[30] This story shows that, contrary to INS claims, prisoner work parties were not always composed of voluntary and willing participants. Detained migrants escaped at the first opportunity presented to them and perhaps even volunteered for jobs that took them outside of the confines of the camp to plan an escape. Writing about convict labor and the longer lineage of resistance, Talitha L. LeFlouria has emphasized the importance of recognizing the defiance of incarcerated people. She has written, "The prisoners were always watching for a chance to get away."[31] This was also true of the men in El Centro. Mexican migrants took any opportunity to liberate themselves from the confines of the camp.

The following story illustrates the meticulous planning prisoners used in challenging the INS, including working together if necessary. On the morning of August 21, 1949, eighteen-year-old Andres Silva-Sánchez and twenty-three-year-old Ramon Ochoa-Durán escaped from what was called the "bull-pen." The bull-pen was a room, near the main entrance of the camp, used to temporarily hold migrants before they were processed and assigned barracks inside the camp.[32] Silva-Sánchez was held at the El Centro Immigration Detention Camp because he had attempted the enter the United States via Calexico by falsely claiming U.S. citizenship a few days before his detention. Had he not escaped, Silva-Sánchez would have faced the local commissioner the next morning, who would have initiated criminal proceedings for making false allegations. Ochoa-Durán had also been arrested earlier that week, for entering the United States without legal authorization and for having a prior deportation on his record. Along with Silva-Sánchez, Ochoa-Durán was scheduled to meet with the local commissioner to undergo criminal proceedings the following day.

Silva-Sánchez and Ochoa-Durán escaped from the bull-pen, where guards held them along with thirteen other Mexican men, by making a narrow hole in the wire-mesh ceiling.[33] They started making the small hole the day before they escaped by standing on top of a trash bin while the detained men sang and played cards. Sometime between two and four in the morning they got out by enlarging the hole and climbing into the facility barbershop's open window. Once inside the barbershop, the two men opened the door and escaped. The flight of these two men reveals the importance of collaboration among prisoners. For the men to have crawled out of the bull-pen, they would have needed the assistance of "two men to hold them and push them through the opening they had made."[34] Yet this solidarity could never be assumed, because sometimes migrants turned on one another. For instance, guards first heard that the two men had escaped about five in the morning, when detained migrant Jesús Alcala-Camarillo told Security Officer George S. Chapman of the event.[35] Alcala-Camarillo was a Mexican citizen who had entered the United States without authorization fifteen days before the escape. According to him, another prisoner by the name of Chato suggested that he tell the guard about the missing men. The two prisoners noticed that Silva-Sánchez and Ochoa-Durán were missing when they were awoken by crickets. When INS officials investigated the escape, they found that Silva-Sánchez and Ochoa-Durán had not only run away, most likely to avoid criminal prosecution, but had taken two pairs of hair clippers with them.[36] Perhaps they sold them or took them as weapons.

New Federal Detention Policies

In 1955, as detained migrants continued to escape from the El Centro Immigration Detention Camp and other facilities throughout the United States, the Department of Justice published the *Manual of Instructions for Detention Officers* to provide federal guidelines on matters such as escapes. For instance, on March 1, 1953, a total of thirty-two prisoners fled from the Indio Border Patrol Station.[37] Immigration officials worried about these continued challenges to their authority and wrote about it in the INS *Annual Report*: "The report on Border Patrol reflected an increasing belligerence on the part of Mexican aliens apprehended. This same attitude has made the job of security officers increasingly difficult. The number of aliens who escaped from custody increased during the past year, particularly along the Mexican Border."[38] The officers who expressed these frustrations were not aware that migrant escape had a long history in the United States. They complained that "in the past, Mexicans have been a fairly docile group of individuals, requiring only minimum safeguards and limited detention personnel. . . . He now frequently resents apprehension, detention, and efforts to deport him, is abusive and displays little respect for authority."[39] Mexican migrants were not "docile," and many organized elaborate techniques to escape their incarceration.

The manual stressed the importance of preventing escape and placed this responsibility as high as averting emergencies such as fires and loss of life. If employees permitted such an escape, they could be subject to charges. As a precaution, detained men identified as potential escapees were not allowed to participate in work projects that made it easier to flee. Also, guards were to keep track of each prisoner by counting them three times a day, not leaving their posts, recording suspicious behavior, watching for trouble-making, and inspecting the facilities' doors, screens, gates, and fences throughout the day. To keep the detention camp secure, guards were further charged with checking for ways to get away. This included routinely inspecting ladders and other means of escape. If a prisoner had been convicted of a crime and successfully fled, an official had to make a report to the FBI within an hour. The *Manual of Instructions* also framed detained migrants as highly devious: "Detention Officers, while on duty at any time or any place, should never be so distracted by other duties as to forget the possibility of escape. Prospective escapees often attempt to gain confidence in order to take advantage of the situation and to escape at an opportune moment. They will feign sickness, hunger, thirst and other ruses to distract detention officers."[40]

PRISONER ESCAPES are as old as prisons themselves, but the migrants held in El Centro were not legally defined as prisoners. The frequency of escape attempts and the lengths to which Mexican migrants went to be freed from the camp suggest that this practice needs to be further contextualized as an example of migrant politics.[41] Detained Mexicans did much more than simply escape. They challenged a system completely designed to police their movement and mobility. In choosing to escape from the El Centro Immigration Detention Camp, detained Mexican men strategically removed themselves from their circumstances. Mexican migrant men, whether directly or indirectly, challenged local INS employees from continuing to use their confined bodies as sources of profit. Prisoners could have confronted their confinement in various ways, such as protesting their conditions, but in this case, they elected to become fugitives.

Local immigration authorities had a lot of power, particularly because they were in a geographically remote area, but detained Mexican men challenged this authority through their fugitivity and proximity to Mexico. Despite the efforts of the immigration officials to make the El Centro Immigration Detention Camp more secure by increasing surveillance, detained Mexican men still found ways to escape their confinement. Prisoners escaped to avoid removal, potential criminal prosecution, impending deportation, and their previous fugitive status and to remove themselves from participating in the Imperial Valley's local labor regime. The detention camps' proximity to Mexico provided them with greater access to flee and avoid apprehension. Yet prisoners sometimes used this same system to get outside the confines of the camp and then escape from the INS. Escape has historically occurred when people have been forced to flee cruel and inhumane conditions.[42] For example, in the past exploitative conditions resulted in the escape of thousands of convicts throughout the United States, suggesting that escape was a testament to bad conditions. The fact that prisoners escaped should have been an indication that something was wrong. But immigration officials turned to increasing policing rather than contemplating why so many detained migrants risked their lives to become fugitives.

PART II | Ghosts

CHAPTER FOUR

The Shadow of Migrant Detention
in the Greater Southwest

> By engaging immigration enforcement with the carceral state, we
> learn that in the shadow of practically unchecked state power over
> prisoners is a flexible, biased, productive, and deeply advantageous
> state power over immigrants.
>
> —DAVID MANUEL HERNANDEZ, 2019

Within just a few years of its opening in 1945, the El Centro Immigration Detention Camp was rife with mismanagement, escapes, and labor controversy. In 1949 INS officials briefly closed the camp because it had become too expensive to operate, was difficult to manage, and seemed less necessary. Officer W. A. Carmichael argued that the INS should expect a reduction in the number of migrants needed to be held at El Centro, making the detention camp less necessary.[1] Owing to new detention procedures, only seventy-eight Mexican nationals sat inside the El Centro Immigration Detention Camp in October 1949. It cost the federal government $101,342 per year to pay for salaries, food, supplies, and materials, which the assistant commissioner did not think was worth paying to keep the camp operative. Carmichael instructed Border Patrol agents to transport the men held in El Centro to Camp Elliott in San Diego.[2] Camp Elliott was a temporary detention camp patrolled by sixteen guards. The navy lent the INS the facility in 1946.[3] By January 3, 1950, the El Centro Immigration Detention Camp operated on a reduced scale, as INS agents transported twenty-eight detained migrants to Camp Elliott and several others to the Imperial County Jail.[4] INS officials formally closed the camp twelve days later.

While at Camp Elliott, detained Mexican nationals experienced the same mistreatment and labor exploitation as they had at El Centro. Officer M. H. Scott disclosed that prisoners were required to assist with feeding, housing, and policing.[5] But the El Centro closure did not last long, because anxieties about criminal and subversive migrants triggered the massive apprehension of unauthorized migrants along the border once again. Imperial Valley locals racialized Mexican migrants as transient, criminal, alcoholic, violent, promiscuous, and deportable laborers. The *Imperial Valley Press* and the *Brawley News* described temporary migrant workers as dangerous criminals whom locals should be cautious of.[6] Besides, on January 15, 1951, the navy reactivated its activities at Camp Elliott, forcing INS officials to reopen the El Centro Immigration Detention Camp on June 1, 1951, just in time to commence a deportation airlift of Mexican nationals. Despite scholarly claims that migrant detention was reduced during this period, the Imperial Valley became a central location to hold unauthorized migrants.[7]

The year 1954 is considered a time when a pivotal shift occurred in the history of immigration detention in the United States. Scholars emphasize the pre- and post-1954 detention experience, when U.S. Attorney General Herbert Brownell Jr. declared a monumental change in detention practices.[8] He proclaimed: "In all but a few cases, those aliens whose admissibility or deportation is under study will no longer be detained. Only those deemed likely to abscond or those whose freedom of movement could be averse to the national security or the public safety will be detained. All others will be released on conditional parole or bond or supervision."[9] INS practices in the Greater Southwest, including internal policing and detention at federal immigration camps and border stations, reveal that the detention of Mexican migrants was very active. The Department of Justice discontinued activity at INS detention centers in New York, Boston, Seattle, San Francisco, and Honolulu, but new facilities became operational at the same time. The detention and deportation regime did not shrink during the 1950s, however, because immigration agents continued to police Mexican migrants along the U.S.-Mexico border.

The Mexican as "Subversive and Criminal"

In 1947 John McDowell, a Republican member of the U.S. House of Representatives and the House Un-American Activities Committee, warned the nation that a massive flood of communists was coming across the Mexican border. He urged the Border Patrol to increase surveillance and use planes if necessary to reduce the growing rates of unauthorized migrants.[10] Before this, INS agents deported people on foot, buses, and trains.[11]

Americans increasingly equated unauthorized migration with subversion. Journalists proclaimed that communist agents were entering the United States from the Mexican border. On February 19, 1951, the *Los Angeles Daily News* declared that alien communists were crossing into the United States disguised as farmworkers. Mexican migrants who harvested crops through-out the Imperial Valley were now rendered not only cheap labor, dirty, and diseased, but also highly suspicious, subversive, and dangerous. Journalists claimed that Border Patrol agents found communist propaganda in the possession of Mexican migrants, playing into U.S. wartime anxieties.[12]

On June 1, 1951, the INS began a "wetback" airlift. INS agents flew unauthorized migrants a thousand miles into the interior of Mexico with the hopes of reducing migration and reentry throughout San Diego and the Imperial Valley.[13] They used the Flying Tigers cargo airline, also used as a military charter operator, to deport about 1,200 Mexican migrants per week from the El Centro Auxiliary Air Station to Guadalajara, San Luis Potosì, and Durango, Mexico.

The Internal Security Act of 1950, or the Subversive Activities Control Act, made national security a top priority. Communist organizations were required to register with the attorney general, and the newly created Subversive Activities Control Board investigated people they deemed subversive. The president of the United States was also authorized with the power to detain anyone believed to be conspiring in espionage or sabotage. In 1951 the federal government investigated 2,363 migrants based on suspicions of subversive behavior. Migrants were apprehended, detained, and deported based on presumptions about their subversion and criminality. Immigration Commissioner Argyle R. Mackey published government documents that stressed that the nation was permeated with communists and aliens who threatened the security of the United States. He underscored the importance of internal security. Mackey wrote, "[Aliens] are susceptible to communist influence because of their exploited and depressed economic situation in their own countries, and in many instances, in the United States after their arrival. From any point of view, those who seek admission in this manner are highly undesirable." He further noted, "The crescendo of communism with its devious schemes of infiltration, has made enforcement for internal security of primary importance. . . . The second major enforcement problem is the perennial one of the Mexican migrant laborers who enter illegally."[14]

Before 1952 the vast majority of Mexican migrants were apprehended and then released on voluntary departure. The INS reserved formal deportation mainly for migrants who had a record of reentry or immorality. Voluntary departure was the government's preferred method of enforcing immigration because it was the most cost-effective. But this practice changed in 1952 when INS officials concluded that formal deportation was a better deterrent than voluntary departure.[15] Border Patrol agents began detaining a greater number of Mexican migrants inside the El Centro Immigration Detention Camp to await formal deportation.

Congress approved the McCarran-Walter Act, or the Immigration and Nationality Act, in 1952. It "prohibited suspected communists and other subversives from immigrating" and provided the legal justification for deporting migrant workers who attempted to organize or demand rights.[16] Under this law, the importation of unauthorized workers became a felony, although employers were not penalized for hiring such workers.[17] The McCarran-Walter Act confronted policy makers' fears about insurrection throughout the United States. It granted the INS additional power by increasing their weapons of enforcement, encouraging the denaturalization of subversives, and, for the first time, excluding narcotic addicts and narcotics traffickers.[18] INS Commissioner Mackey proclaimed that preventing illegal aliens from entering the United States could stamp out subversion.[19] Consequently, immigration agents deported 19,845 people during the 1953 fiscal year, based on grounds of crime, subversion, and drug enforcement.[20] The McCarran-Walter Act strengthened the detention and deportation regime and emphasized that subversion could be quelled through immigration enforcement.

Although immigration officials, politicians, and journalists warned the U.S. public that unauthorized migrants were dangerous, local businessmen, agricultural growers, and Border Patrol officers continued to use Mexican men as a profitable workforce. In 1953 General Joseph M. Swing, a future INS commissioner, proclaimed that migrants throughout Southern California and Texas committed 75 to 95 percent of all crimes, including theft, vagrancy, and murder.[21] Then, in 1954, Willard F. Kelly, assistant commissioner of detention and deportation, decried that "during the past ten years a mere trickle of 'wetbacks' into the United States has turned into a flood."[22] He asserted that reports were submitted to the attorney general that expressed a "worsening situation," including "the misery, disease, crime, and many other evils attendant upon this illegal influx."[23] Kelly spoke about an unauthorized migrant from Calexico who stepped behind an X-ray machine, only to discover that he had active tuberculosis. Kelly shared this story as evidence that Mexicans spread disease. Furthermore, he cautioned against prostitutes and other "violators of law," because, according to him, those who committed a crime were more likely to continue. This was dangerous, he said, because "there gr[e]w a deterioration in moral character among those who violate[d] the law, and the growth of that social fungus infect[ed] many who c[a]me in contact with it."[24] Kelly named Imperial County as the "focal point of the 'wetback' tide in California." He stressed that it was a place filled with migrant criminals, where the felony rate was 31 percent compared to a statewide average of 15 percent. A full "55% of those violations are committed by aliens illegally in the US," he declared, without providing a single source.[25]

It was no surprise that in 1954 the INS initiated a campaign that racialized Mexican migrants as criminals. In May 1954 U.S. Attorney General Herbert J. Brownell announced a new militarized campaign against Mexican migrants called Operation Wetback. INS officials used the Immigration Act of 1952 as the legal mechanism to justify the apprehension and deportation of, according to the INS, 1.3 million Mexicans.[26] In February 1954 the *Imperial Valley Press* reported that "the illegal alien traffic has greatly increased the traffic of narcotics" and that the "El Centro police estimate[d] that 75 per cent of all violations [were] attributable to 'wetbacks.'"[27] A full 50 percent of the total apprehensions during Operation Wetback occurred in the Imperial Valley.[28] INS agents used the El Centro Immigration Detention Camp as a focal point for apprehensions, and personnel from the El Centro INS station screened migrants deported to Nogales and Mexicali.[29] During 1954, 508,566 migrants were held in service and nonservice detention facilities, "the highest in the history of the Service," emphasized the INS.[30] Mexican migrants were stereotyped as criminals because they entered the United States without legal authorization but also because politicians and journalists racialized them as inherently culpable.

Although immigration officials framed Operation Wetback as a short and successful campaign, immigration enforcement was a priority long before and after 1954.[31] Migrant policing in the Imperial Valley had a lasting significance, as Mexican migrants were further linked to crime. Although INS agents were often negligent and physically abusive in policing migration, the government disavowed these acts and focused instead on migrant criminality. Minor offenses, as illustrated in the following case, became a bigger deal in the context of the 1950s. For instance, on May 11, 1954, Judge James E. Marable sentenced Mexican migrants Vincent L. Olivia, Francisco M. Ferrosca, and Roberto H. Rodríguez to ninety days in the El Centro County Jail when property managers for George M. Buffum caught them robbing grapefruit from a ranch.[32] Residents believed imprisonment was justice. Journalists claimed that deporting Mexicans would reduce the crime rate, and on June 15, 1954, the *Imperial Valley Press* reported that the "crime rate in th[e] community," including petty thefts, car thefts, and burglaries, "ha[d] been reduced nearly to the vanishing point by the stepped-up border patrol program," or Operation Wetback.[33]

The Greater Southwest

In addition to El Centro, McAllen, Texas, was a key site during Operation Wetback. In 1952 the McAllen Detention Camp was an "open-air-wire stockade" located south of McAllen. On June 17, 1952, Carlos Villenave, a journalist for the Mexico City newspaper *Novedades*, asserted that "Texas kept migrant Mexican farm workers in a concentration camp."[34] Fletcher Rawla, chief inspector of the McAllen Border Patrol District, denied the claim. Laughing, he said, "I've heard everything else but that!"[35] According to Villenave, he visited the McAllen Detention Camp, where he observed men "packed in like cattle, [lying] on the ground in the open air, exposed to the burning rays of the sun by day and torrential rains by night. Whippings, clubbings and other punishments [were] the rule for those who protest[ed]."[36]

On March 6, 1953, the stockade was converted into a formal detention camp. It sat on eleven acres and could hold up to 640 detained migrants overnight and process between 1,000 and 1,200 migrants daily.[37] In the beginning, prisoners remained in the camp for about a day. When they were held for longer durations, guards at McAllen complained to the Central Office about migrant disturbances. On one occasion a Mexican national woke up at three in the morning and screamed that breakfast was ready. As a response, patrol inspectors requested that a separate building be built for "agitators" and "trouble-makers."[38] Sometimes INS agents made deportation decisions that simply served to harm deportees. In April 1953 the Border Patrol began deporting migrants by transporting them from McAllen to Zapata, Texas.[39] At this time Zapata did not have public transportation, and migrants released without money were forced to walk forty-five miles in 110 degree weather across the rattlesnake-infested desert just to reach the Monterrey highway. The heat was also an issue during apprehension.

The death certificates of Mexican nationals who labored and died in the United States are held at the Secretariat of Foreign Affairs in Mexico City, including that of Cesareo Resendez. His family requested that the Mexican consulate assist them in obtaining compensation from the INS for the death of their relative, who passed away on July 27, 1954, near San Benito, Texas.[40] Resendez was an unauthorized migrant who worked in the cotton fields. On the day of his death, he was caught by INS agents in a raid and apprehended with several coworkers. It had been up to 109 degrees all week. Agents had the men sit on the sidewalk, where they waited for four hours, before transporting them to the McAllen Detention Camp. That evening Resendez started to feel sick, and at 8:20 p.m. he was pronounced dead.

A doctor declared sunstroke to be the cause of death. Although Resendez was forced to endure the heat for hours, the INS refused to take responsibility for his death or to compensate his family in any way. The secretary of the state wrote to the Mexican ambassador that "since Mr. Resendez entered this country illegally and was working in the cotton field of his own volition and no one informed the officers of the United States Immigration and Naturalization Service that he was ill until he arrived at McAllen, the circumstances are not such as to impose any responsibility upon the Immigration authorities or upon the Government of the United States to pay compensation to the widow and family of the deceased."[41]

The McAllen Detention Camp, like the El Centro Immigration Detention Camp, became even more significant in the context of Operation Wetback. Between July 14, 1954, and January 3, 1955, INS agents transported 52,885 migrants, to be held for as little as a few hours and as long as several months, to the McAllen Detention Camp. From there the INS deported migrants via boat, train, or bus. The number of detained migrants far surpassed detention space, and INS officials temporarily held people awaiting camp space aboard the SS Emancipation.[42] On November 1955, the chief regional enforcement officer conducted an inspection of the camp, during which he discovered a situation that he could not overlook. He pointed out that "certain discriminatory practices existed" at the camp, including the lockup of deportable migrants in an overcrowded space for up to thirty-five days.[43] During the inspection, he also noticed that the men were separated from the women's and children's quarters by only a loosely woven wire fence. Overcrowding resulted in increased frustration at the camp, triggering escapes and demonstrations. For example, on December 10, 1955, six prisoners escaped from the camp. As a response, the chief Border Patrol officer suggested increasing surveillance and vigilance by improving illumination near the fence, moving the watchtowers to more central locations, and adding fencing around the camp. The use of McAllen, Texas, as an additional site to hold Mexican migrants shows that detention was expanding during the 1950s in the Greater Southwest.

The federal government opened the Federal Correctional Institution, Terminal Island (FCI Terminal Island) in San Pedro, California, in 1936. The facility could hold 280 prisoners.[44] It is located opposite the San Pedro Navy Supply Depot and next to the U.S. Coast Guard Station. It was surrounded with barbed-wire towers with armed guards. During the 1950s many of the people held at Terminal Island were noncitizens accused of subversion, including the infamous Terminal Island Four. Miriam Stevenson, David Hyun,

Frank Carlson, and Harry Carlisle were arrested on October 22, 1950, and detained without bail for their political activism based on the 1952 McCarran-Walter Act. They were openly critical of the Truman administration's position on the Korean War, wages, taxes, and profits for big industrialists and bankers. Stevenson was English-born and had lived in the United States for more than thirty years. He was a trade unionist. Hyun was a Korean architect and a member of the Distributive Processing and Office Workers Union. Carlson was from Poland and an active labor organizer. He worked as a shipyard worker and had attempted to apply for U.S. citizenship, but his application was denied. Carlisle was born in England and had lived in the United States for thirty years. He was a novelist and a labor journalist.[45] In addition to holding people based on ideological beliefs, guards held Mexican nationals the INS hoped to deport within five days. Detention operations at Terminal Island increased with Operation Wetback. James V. Bennett went before the U.S. House of Representatives and requested $918,000 of additional funds to hold an additional thousand prisoners and to expand operations at Terminal Island. He said, "We are in a serious situation with respect to the number of prisoners who have flooded in upon us during the last year. Our institutions are quite seriously overcrowded."[46] Bennett added that detention rates had increased due to a 37 percent rise in immigration law violators.

Border policing also increased at Border Patrol stations, where INS agents often mistreated migrants. In 1956 Juana Galván of Harlingen, Texas, contacted an attorney to dispute how INS employees were negligent in her apprehension. This case resulted in an INS investigation after Attorney Lerma continued to push the INS to examine the case. The assistant commissioner of enforcement was left wondering if the training INS agents received was sufficient. He admitted that while at the Border Patrol Academy, officers received information on immigration laws, work standards, inspections, apprehensions, and duties but not necessarily how to treat migrants.[47] In May 1956, Patrol Inspectors James E. Seabourn and Joseph G. Maskornick knocked on the door of Juana Galván's home in Santa Monica, Texas. They inquired about the citizenship status of her two sons, Ricardo and Panfilo.[48] Galván proceeded to show the officers the birth certificates and baptismal records of her children. The agents claimed that they could not verify the information and proceeded to apprehend her and the two boys, who were transported to the Border Patrol Unit Headquarters, where they were held for nine and a half hours before being released. During this time Juana, Ricardo and Panfilo did not receive any food or access to the restroom. The service admitted that it was wrong for the "officers that participated in the action . . . in detaining the women and her children for such a long period and for not having accorded them humane and considerate treatment, including the furnishing of daily necessities." Yet they denied other charges, such as "striking the female alien with a pencil, shining a flashlight into her eyes, using abusive or harsh language, and entering her home without permission," because Juana did not have evidence to prove her claim.[49] In the end, Senior Patrol Inspector Alton L. McDonald was held accountable for the incident because he was responsible for the conduct of all Harlington officers. Regional Commissioner David H. Carnahan proposed that McDonald be charged with neglect of duty and that Maskornick and Seabourn be reprimanded with a written notice.

The 1950s climate of fear and suspicion shaped immigration enforcement practices in the Greater Southwest, as Mexican migrants became increasingly linked to crime, communism, and subversion. These logics strengthened the detention and deportation regime by increasing border policing and the deportation of migrants. Mexican migrants were marked as culpable regardless of their actions. These attitudes helped transform the El Centro Immigration Detention Camp and the larger detention and deportation regime. Additional transformations occurred during the 1970s, as depicted in figure 3, when the federal government transformed the El Centro Immigration Detention Camp of the 1950s into a service processing center in 1974. The government defined this as a facility for "those who entered the United States illegally or violated their immigration status" and for those awaiting "completion of their deportation case, release on their own recognizance, or pending release."[50]

From a Camp to a Service Processing Center

By the end of the 1970s, the number of people detained in immigration facilities totaled 340,297 across the United States.[51] The groundbreaking Immigration Act of 1965 shaped migration rates by ending the immigration nationality quota system in the United States. The legislation was significant for civil rights, yet it numerically limited legal migration from the Western Hemisphere for the first time.[52] After 1965 the rate of migrant apprehensions increased, as curtailing legal entry to the United States simply made the flow of Latin American migration illegal. The U.S. government's involvement in Central America shaped the revolutionary movements that emerged as a response to Cold War politics. U.S. officials funded, trained, and armed counterrevolutionaries under the auspices of protecting Latin

FIGURE 3 A Central American migrant leaves his mark, Federal Detention Facility, El Centro, 1974. San Diego Union Tribune Collection, San Diego History Center (UT88_L7395-24).

American countries from communism. Consequently, Latin American emigration increased because of violence in part orchestrated by the United States.[53] It was at this time that the demographics of migration from Latin America to the United States changed for decades to come.

Immigration officials viewed these growing rates of migration as "a problem of very serious proportions," and detention and deportation were seen as the solution. During this time Central American migration to the United States increased, and the demographics of the prisoners held inside the facility changed from predominantly Mexican to other Latin Americans. In 1975 INS Commissioner Leonard F. Chapman wrote that when the public visualized a migrant worker, they thought of a "Mexican agricultural worker toiling in the hot sun in Texas or California hoeing lettuce for one to two dollars a day." But, he explained, "that is not the situation any longer. Last year in the industrial states of the Northeastern seaboard, where many illegal aliens hold jobs in manufacturing and industry, 97 percent of those we apprehended were non-Mexican."[54] By the 1970s detention centers that once exclusively held Mexican nationals now included people from countries including Greece, Afghanistan, Nigeria, Brazil, Yugoslavia, Japan, and Costa Rica. Latin American migration increased during the 1960s and 1970s, at the

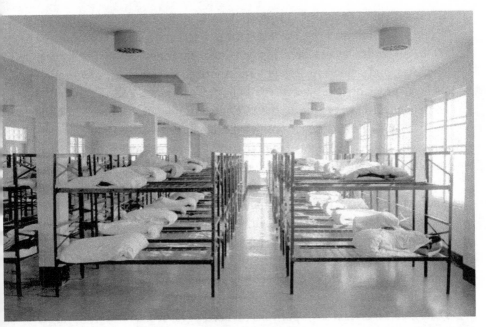

FIGURE 4 The sleeping barracks, Federal Detention Facility, El Centro, 1974. San Diego Union Tribune Collection, San Diego History Center (UT88_L7395-32A).

same time as the global turn toward neoliberalism, which granted more power to economic elites. This economic model encouraged limited state intervention and supported free trade. Advocates encouraged property rights, deregulation, privatization, and a limited welfare state.[55] U.S. policy makers and transnational corporations meddled in the politics, economies, and militaries of Latin American countries, which resulted in political repression and economic strain throughout the region.[56] These factors led to migration from instability.

As the apprehensions of migrants increased, the federal government expanded the infrastructure for detention and deportation. The INS enlarged the El Centro Immigration Detention Center between 1971 and 1973, and when the facility was complete it could hold 632 migrants throughout four dormitories.[57] It included a staff of forty-eight and an immigration judge who presided over deportation and exclusion hearings. The federal government added new technological advancements to the detention center, including automatic location services and all-weather remote-control surveillance.[58]

Regardless of the name change and new construction, poor conditions continued to plague El Centro. On December 28, 1973, Albert R. García, president of the Mexican American Association, wrote a letter to INS

Commissioner Leonard F. Chapman. García requested that Chapman respond to several concerns, including the physical and sexual abuse inflicted by INS guards; agents breaking into and entering private residences, churches, and schools to seek out unauthorized migrants; the deportation of legal permanent residents; the killing of migrants; and the inhuman treatment of migrants inside the El Centro Immigration Detention Center.[59] Chapman responded a month later. He agreed that there "were problems with the management of the El Centro Detention Facility" but asserted that those complications had been rectified. Chapman disagreed with the claim that INS employees treated migrants inhumanely. He wrote: "The El Centro facility is our newest and most modern facility. The toilet, lavatory, bathing, and drinking water facilities meet the national plumbing codes and have proven to be ample. The capacity of the ventilation system exceeds the recommended capacity for the size and occupancy." Chapman maintained that the feeding of prisoners was excellent. According to him, qualified cooks prepared the meals and provided menus to the office for review.[60] Daily meals included large portions of meat, eggs, vegetables, fruit, salad, bread, and a beverage.

This account contradicted descriptions from only a few years prior. In 1972 Mexican journalist Jesus Saldana went undercover as a prisoner to witness what went on inside the El Centro Immigration Detention Center for himself. He called the site "El Infierno," or hell. While detained he was served dinner at six in the evening. "Detainees have to walk in a straight line and cannot talk. We ate a small portion of beans and mashed potatoes, while the guards watched us," he said.[61] He described the facility as so overcrowded that some men had to sleep on the floor. Guards woke them up at five in the morning to eat breakfast, which included coffee and toast with jam.

In addition to inadequate meals, the press pointed out the lack of medical treatment. INS Commissioner Chapman maintained that detained migrants could be seen by a local doctor if needed. He affirmed, "All requests for medical attention are honored by a prompt referral to a physician."[62] Immigration rights activists were not convinced that prisoners received this treatment. Chicano activists frequently referred to the El Centro Immigration Detention Center as a concentration camp where "prisoners were kept for months with no regard for their legal rights."[63] One of their main concerns was the inadequate medical care. On occasion staff from the facility also spoke out against these conditions. In December 1973 the facility's new supervisor, Omer G. Sewell, admitted that "some difficulties" existed at

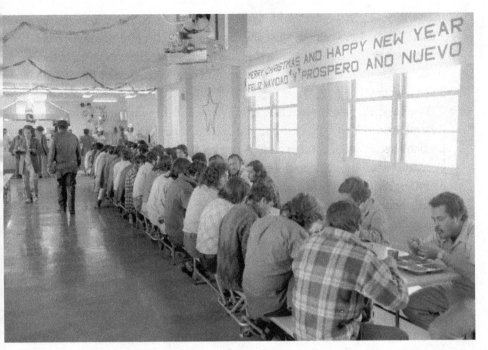

FIGURE 5 The dining commons during the holidays, Federal Detention Facility, El Centro, 1974. San Diego Union Tribune Collection, San Diego History Center (UT88_L7395-18A).

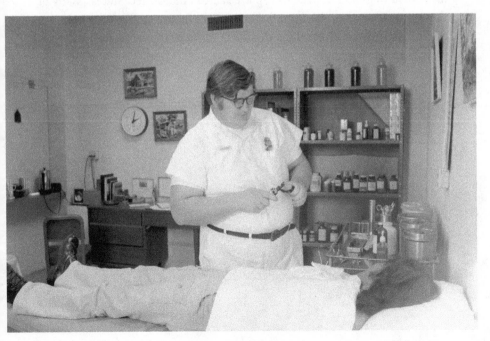

FIGURE 6 The infirmary, Federal Detention Facility, El Centro, 1974. San Diego Union Tribune Collection, San Diego History Center (UT88_L7395-32).

the facility. An INS officer said, "You know what we've got to care for the aliens? Band-Aids. That's it—just one first-aid kit."[64] Despite assurance from authorities that prisoners received proper medical treatment, a guard told reporters that the local doctor came around only when he felt like it or in an emergency.

The Mexican government also expressed concerns with conditions and treatments inside of U.S. immigration detention centers. On June 19, 1974, Mexico's secretary of foreign affairs, Emilio O. Rabasa, sent a letter to the U.S. ambassador to Mexico, Joseph John Jova, where he demanded the end of immigration detention centers.[65] Stories highlighting the conditions guards held Mexican nationals under continued to be published in the Mexican press. A few weeks later journalist Miguel Lopez Saucedo published a piece that called out shortcomings inside detention centers at Port Isabel, Texas, and El Centro, California. He wrote that detained migrants "are held in prisons. Migrants are not fed enough and the sleeping quarters are ovens."[66] These criticisms persisted years later. In 1976 the newspaper *Sol de Mexico* ran an article that called detention centers "nothing more than concentration camps."[67] In the United States, California representative Edward Roybal described detention centers "as fit only to house dog food."[68]

Although harsh conditions persisted at the El Centro Immigration Detention Center, detention facilities expanded, and by 1978 the federal government held migrants in over sixty places across the United States. Many of the issues faced when the detention camp in El Centro first opened went unaddressed. Just as in previous decades, antimigrant repression was met with migrant resistance.

CHAPTER FIVE

The Conjuring

Transforming Traumas into Transnational Migrant Politics

> The performative and political effects of the hunger strike expose
> the modern relations between bare life, revolt, human rights,
> and the violence of sovereignty.
>
> —EWA PLONOWSKA ZIAREK, 2012

In 1985 the U.S. attorney general presented immigration officials at the El Centro Immigration Detention Center with a plaque commemorating the squelching of a hunger strike. Employees placed the plaque inside the detention center's lobby to celebrate the quick put-down of the demonstration, the largest in the facility's history.[1] The tribute suggested that the response was regarded as a model for how to manage detention centers—striking, given the brutality with which the strike had been handled.

The hunger strike had begun on May 27, 1985. Fifteen detained men from countries around the world led the protest. They stormed the mess hall, prompting between 175 and 300 additional prisoners to join their strike.[2] More than 50 percent of the demonstrators were Salvadoran asylum seekers, who made up 33 percent of all detained migrants at El Centro at that time.[3] The group refused to work, go inside the barracks, or eat until government authorities found solutions to the grievances eighty-five prisoners had previously agreed on. The protesters asserted that the detention facility was overcrowded and unsanitary and that guards inflicted flagrant physical and psychological abuse.[4] Within a week between fifty and sixty guards in full riot gear marched into the facility and forcibly moved the hunger strikers indoors.[5]

The migrants held inside the El Centro Immigration Detention Center protested the state's use of verbal and physical abuse, isolation, and neglect. They illuminated the violence that had permeated the facility for decades. They also showed that the legal proceedings within the facility were arguably unconstitutional. The due process clause of the Fifth Amendment requires that immigration officials explain to apprehended migrants what they are legally entitled to. These rights include representation by an attorney at the migrants expense; a deportation hearing to determine a migrant's deportability and potential access to bail; the ability to apply for political asylum if they believed they were being persecuted; and the freedom to request voluntary departure in exchange for giving up the right to a hearing and eligibility for asylum.[6] Although detained migrants were legally entitled to these processes, their activism emphasized the frequency that the INS violated such protections.

Yet the protests were not just the product of El Centro's abuses—they were also conceived and executed by a group of migrants whose actions were shaped by a common set of experiences. Latin American men who ended up at El Centro had attempted to escape poverty, dictatorships, and civil war, only to experience similar horrors once apprehended, detained, and deported. Confined in this liminal space, where the immigrant detention center was not legally defined as a prison, yet in practice operated as a space that housed so-called criminals, the detained men made claims on the state by expressing what I call "transnational migrant politics."[7] I view transnational migrant politics as the emergence of a set of strategies and solidarities used by migrants and immigration advocates to resist and protest state power within the detention and deportation regime. The development of this form of politics arose from the migration experiences of the detained men along circuits of violence. This context influenced the prisoners' activism at El Centro, as they turned to politics they had forged before being placed in detention, where they subsequently experienced punitive and exploitative conditions.

The Expansion of Detention during the Reagan Era

Cold War politics and U.S.–Latin American relations shaped the immigration policies of the 1980s, which in turn affected the detention experience of the El Centro detained migrants and the hunger strike of 1985. President Jimmy Carter signed the Refugee Act of 1980, which expanded the definition of a refugee and set the minimum number of annual refugee admissions to the United States at fifty thousand.[8] Before 1980 refugee policy backed U.S. foreign policy goals and prioritized applicants who escaped communist countries such as Cuba, Cambodia, Vietnam, and the Soviet Union.[9] In the wake of the Vietnam War, the Refugee Act of 1980 was designed to "replace the Cold War-influenced, anticommunist-centered definition of 'refugee' with one much less grounded in early Cold War political ideology."[10] Yet the act provided a false sense of hope for Latin American asylum seekers. When Ronald Reagan came to power, his administration used executive actions to reduce the number of people being granted asylum and to give refugees who fled communism preferential treatment, thereby excluding people escaping right-wing regimes in Latin America.[11] As Julio Capó Jr. has shown, "The Reagan administration found ways to continue its anti-Communist foreign policy, which privileged refugees from Communism within the limitations of the Refugee Act of 1980."[12] Another reason Central American migrants had a difficult time gaining political asylum was because of the United States' continued military involvement in the region.

By 1982 Reagan was certain that the Latin American "refugee problem" needed to be addressed head-on. This same year Congress passed the Immigration Emergency Act, which legalized the president's right to declare an immigration emergency and require the detention of any migrant during such an emergency. The INS also received additional funding to expand the immigration detention system.[13] Congress allocated $1,821,000 to be used in the maintenance and construction of permanent detention centers.[14] The 1982 Immigration Emergency Act made detention mandatory for all "arriving aliens without valid travel documents," including asylum seekers, as a strategy for making political asylum gains more difficult. This resulted in detention wait times of up to two years.[15]

These policy changes transformed the operations of the El Centro Immigration Detention Center and the experiences of the men detained inside. As Tom Riebe, a staff member for Democratic representative Howard Berman, explained, "The El Centro Camp was intended to be [a] short term [place] for Mexicans, but the INS changed this policy when Reagan became president."[16] This shift was reflected in the rates of detention at El Centro. In 1981 the INS held a total of 3,900 men, but by 1984 the number had risen to 9,800.[17] It was common for guards to hold prisoners in El Centro for up to three weeks before they were told what would come next. When a detained migrant was finally able to speak with a judge in immigration court, he was encouraged to accept deportation. If he agreed, INS agents quickly transported the migrant back to his home country. Most prisoners were not informed that they could contest their deportation or apply for political asylum. Some of the men without criminal backgrounds were released from the detention center on bonds averaging about $500 while they awaited future immigration proceedings, but many lingered for months, if not years, if they were unable to pay, did not qualify for a bond, or had filed for political asylum.[18] Ironically, as depicted in figures 7-10, increasing the time that a migrant spent inside a detention center also provided him with greater opportunities to foster solidarity.[19]

The Reagan administration played a critical role in expanding the carceral state and transforming federal detention centers into semiprivate and private facilities to increase detention space across the United States. By mandating that all unauthorized immigrants be detained, the law effectively required an increase in detention centers. For decades the Department of Justice paid state and local jails to temporarily hold migrants for whom there was insufficient space in immigration-specific detention facilities.[20] By the 1980s this had become unfeasible, as carceral sites reached capacity and were unable to guarantee bed spaces. As a result, the government created the Co-operative Agreement Program (CAP) in 1982, which guaranteed bed space for the INS and allocated federal resources to construct new jails. The U.S. Marshals Service requested the construction of additional federal detention centers, and the Bureau of Prisons received funds to increase the number of detention beds at existing Federal Bureau of Prisons facilities. Government officials claimed that providing these resources was essential because "if adequate bedspace to detain thousands of potentially dangerous prisoners [was] not acquired, public safety and the Federal Criminal Justice System itself could be threatened."[21]

But constructing new facilities was expensive. To hold down costs the Reagan administration sought to privatize or at least create semiprivate detention centers by encouraging the INS to hire employees managed by corporations, including guards, transportation workers, and medical personnel.[22] In 1982 President Reagan established the President's Private Sector Survey on Cost Control, or the Grace Commission, named after head commission member and business mogul J. Peter Grace. The goal of the commission was to "root out waste in the federal government" and determine which government services could become more efficient if privatized.[23] Committee members suggested that over $143 million could be saved on costs related to prisons if the government "accelerat[ed] privatization/contracting out of construction activities."[24]

Private groups found ways to hold detained migrants for less money. They advocated that costs be cut on food, medical care, and transportation. In addition to privatizing key components of the detention industry, the federal government moved to hire corporate providers to detain migrants. One of the corporations that was the most aggressive in responding to this new demand was Corrections Corporation of America (CCA), an organization based in Nashville, Tennessee. Newly committed to privatization, the INS signed contracts with four new facilities in San Diego, Los Angeles, Houston, and Denver, and in 1985 a new detention facility opened in Boston, Massachusetts.[25]

Despite the opening of new privatized facilities, the rates of migrants held in privately owned and federally run detention centers far surpassed the number of detention spaces throughout the United States. Instead of reducing the number of migrants held in detention, INS officials continued to fill detention facilities beyond their capability. For instance, on May 31, 1984, detention rates at El Centro were 6 percent over capacity.[26] Overcrowding magnified everyday issues inside detention, including poor sanitation, labor exploitation, and physical violence. It would not be long before detained migrants would fight back.

Activist Lineages

When detained migrants commenced the hunger strike inside the El Centro Immigration Detention Center in 1985, they employed transnational solidarity tactics that had been used decades prior. On February 5, 1977, the Black Panther Party for Self-Defense (BPP) ran a story about José Jacques Medina, a Mexican activist who fled to the United States to escape political persecution in the newspaper *Black Panther*. Titled "José Medina Fight Highlights Struggle of Undocumented Workers," the story featured the activism sparked by the policing of Medina, who was targeted by military and paramilitary forces in Mexico and by the FBI and the INS in the United States.[27] Medina's detention inside the El Centro Immigration Detention Center and his struggle to gain political asylum highlight the migrant activism of the 1970s, when detained migrants and migrant activists spoke out against imperialism, the detention and deportation regime, and capitalism. This activism was often reported by Mexican newspapers, which frequently referred to U.S. immigration detention centers as concentration camps.[28]

José Jacques Medina was an influential social justice activist in Mexico and the United States. Medina attended law school at the National Autonomous University of Mexico (UNAM) in 1966. He quickly became known for his defense of people's rights.[29] In 1968 students elected him to the National Strike Committee, composed of organizers leading Mexico City's student movement. Medina's involvement placed him at the Plaza of Three Cultures on October 2, 1968. The gathering started as one of many demonstrations against the state, but the protest culminated in the massacre of Tlatelolco. The demonstration occurred just days before the Summer Olympics would take place in Mexico City, and the Mexican government used army troops and police to murder between four hundred and six hundred people.[30] Elena Poniatowska described the massacre: "There were shots from all directions,

FIGURE 7 Detained migrants, Federal Detention Facility, El Centro, 1974. San Diego Union Tribune Collection, San Diego History Center (UT88_L7395-14).

from the top of a building in the housing unit and from the street, where the military forces fired round after round from the machine guns mounted on their light tanks and armored transports."[31] Medina was one of the thousands of people arrested during the massacre.[32]

In 1968 students mobilized against the repressive Partido Revolucionario Institucional (PRI), the reigning political party since 1929. The party "was adept in organizing, co-opting, buying off, and if necessary suppressing oppositional movements among the workers, peasants, and middles classes," because it viewed challenges to its authority as grounds for repression.[33] After the massacre, the military rounded up thousands of protesters and placed them in police custody. Many political prisoners were held at jails in downtown Mexico City and in the notorious Black Palace of Lecumberri, which functioned as a prison between 1900 and 1976 until it was converted into the National Archives in 1980.[34] Between 1971 and 1973 the Mexican state used security forces called *halcones*, or hawks, to repress the student movement. They did not wear uniforms and kept a close eye on activists to inform the government about their actions. Their goal was to sabotage political activity with death, if necessary. *Halcones* conducted the dirty work of the state by using intimidation and violence against students, peasants, and labor organizers.[35]

Medina sought refuge in the United States in 1972.[36] He entered the United States on a temporary student visa and continued to organize around migrant rights. He conducted training sessions on labor and immigration law and participated in strikes throughout the country.[37] Medina became an instructor at People's College of Law in Los Angeles and a member of Centro de Acción Social Autónomo (CASA).[38] Then the FBI learned of Medina. They followed him very closely, and on March 29, 1976, FBI agent Benavides arrested and transported him to the Federal Building in downtown Los Angeles. FBI agents accused Medina and members of CASA of trafficking drugs and weapons to be used in overthrowing the federal government.[39] Charging political activists with drug infractions was common during the 1960s and 1970s. One member told reporters, "The FBI is clearly using immigration laws as a political tool."[40] After the interrogation the FBI released Medina to the INS, charging him as an "undocumented revolutionary."[41]

The FBI handed Medina over to the INS in Los Angeles, who then transported him to the immigration facility in El Centro. The detention experience was instructive for Medina. He was moved to what he called the "largest concentration camp in California," along with a hundred other men. Detention staff examined and registered the prisoners as part of the processing phase. The prisoners removed all of their clothing and waited for half an hour during the procedure. INS employees called each man and asked how much money he had to pay for bail as a way of making fun of them. They took their money except for twenty dollars and stored it in an office. But Medina asserted that proof of the amount of money confiscated was not provided. Migrants lost items all the time during this process. Some of the men Medina traveled with had lost their shoes en route to El Centro, and many were stripped of their valuables in Los Angeles during the apprehension and processing procedure. INS personnel told prisoners that their belongings would be sent to El Centro, but this rarely happened, as it often took longer for the items to arrive than for the men to be deported.[42]

Once processed, Medina and his companions received a bed in the barracks. Guards woke prisoners up at six in the morning by yelling that it was time to have breakfast. While the men were in line at the kitchen, guards shouted insults to assert their authority. Once the detained migrants ate, guards sent them outdoors into the corral. The men waited outside until they could come in at five in the afternoon. They experienced this same monotony until the INS released or deported them. Some of the men waited up to three months. During this time guards constantly violated the rights of detained migrants. During Medina's short time at El Centro, he learned that undocumented workers lived in constant fear of being captured and sent to such places.[43] The sheer thought of ending up in El Centro instilled terror and distress.

On June 16, 1976, Medina submitted a political asylum application.[44] He decided to apply "to force the U.S. government to publicly recognize that persecution in Mexico exist[ed]."[45] Medina was released from detention on $5,000 bail.[46] He hoped that his case would gain rights for undocumented people, such as the right to free counsel. In 1975 only 5 percent of deportees were represented by legal counsel, because the INS was not required to pay for legal representation in civil proceedings.[47] As an attorney and advocate of migrants, Medina believed migrants should be given the necessary resources and time to collect the evidence necessary to defend themselves at hearings.[48]

The incarceration and surveillance of Medina led to the creation of a solidarity movement called the Committee for the Defense of José Jacques Medina. Committee members demanded that Medina be granted political asylum and advocated for the general amnesty of all undocumented workers in the United States.[49] CASA was one of the leading organizations involved in the campaign to defend Medina. They stressed that if Medina were deported to Mexico, he would face prosecution, if not death. The committee argued that INS agents should not deport Medina from the Southwest because the region had historically belonged to Mexicans. They highlighted the imperialist legacy of the United States by writing, "We are not just fighting for Medina. We are also fighting for thousands of Haitians, Africans and other third world people fleeing fascist, US supported regimes, who have the courage to seek asylum here in the heart of imperialism."[50] Organizers conducted press conferences, protests, and rallies in major cities throughout the country, including Los Angeles, New York, Chicago, Detroit, Houston, San Francisco, and Seattle. They chanted, "Jail the INS, not José Medina!"[51] The committee gained national support from leftist groups and individuals, including the Workers of the World Party, Youth against War and Fascism, the National Lawyers Guild, the Chicano Federation, and Olga Talamante, Chicana activist and a former Argentine political prisoner.[52]

The first time INS officials reviewed Medina's political asylum application, in February 1977, they concluded that they did not believe he would be persecuted if deported.[53] But Medina had ample evidence indicating that persecution continued in Mexico and that he would be imprisoned if deported. Part of Medina's evidence consisted of historical analysis from key Chicano scholars. Affidavits from professors described the political context that Medina would face if deported. Dr. Timothy F. Harding, a history professor at California State University, Los Angeles, provided background on the use of *halcones*, arguing that this paramilitary group was trained by the Mexican army and had been used to repress dissent.[54] Dr. Rodolfo Acuña, a Chicano studies professor at California State University, Northridge, also spoke up on behalf of Medina, stressing the repressiveness of the Mexican political system against dissidents. Acuña wrote: "I am concerned for the safety of Mr. José Jacques Medina who was an activist in the Mexican scene for many years. . . . During these years, he became very unpopular with government authorities since they were very sensitive about this issue. His activities unmasked the government's false image as a democratic nation."[55] The U.S. government never granted Medina political asylum. However, nationwide protests made it difficult for INS agents to deport him, and they dropped his case.

Medina's case highlights the challenges that people faced inside detention. He studied law and had many activist connections, which helped his case. Yet, as Medina pointed out, this was not the experience of most people caught inside the immigration system. The activism sparked by Medina's detention is an early example of transnational migrant politics as people throughout the United States and Mexico came to his support. It was also a harbinger of activism to come.

Central American Solidarity

People fleeing El Salvador confronted a system that disproportionately refused to grant them political asylum. Robert Kahn has demonstrated that, despite the Refugee Act of 1980, the INS denied Salvadorans "the right to legal counsel—by threats, lies, beatings, sexual abuse, drugs, and occasionally torture—anything to get a refugee to sign INS form 1-274, which waive[d] the right to seek asylum and request[ed] 'voluntary repatriation' to Central America."[56] During the 1980s only 2 percent of Salvadorans who requested it were granted political asylum in the United States, and the first

Salvadoran to gain this status from inside the El Centro Immigration Detention Center did not do so until 1984.[57] During asylum hearings, applicants had to provide substantial evidence and convince an immigration judge that they had a well-founded fear of persecution. Their evidence had to be document-based, and the deaths of family members frequently were not interpreted as sufficient proof.[58] INS officials did not consider the testimonies of migrants without sources credible.

In addition to systematically denying Salvadorans asylum, guards targeted them inside detention centers. By this time many of the guards identified as Latino. The shift from a largely white INS force to one that employed almost 30 percent people of color occurred with the passage of the Equal Employment Opportunity Act of 1972.[59] A Salvadoran held at the El Centro Immigration Detention Center testified that he "fled El Salvador because it [was] not safe for young men to walk the streets unless they [were] members of the government's security forces." He stated, "I was arrested by INS agents on September 14, 1981 . . . There they put us into a corral and an officer separated the Salvadorans from the Mexicans. [Then] they took us (the Salvadorans) out of the corral and officials insulted us by saying, 'You who are so brave, why don't you stay in your country and get fucked over, why don't you stay and die in your country rather than coming here, Latinos sons of whores?'"[60] The experience of this individual was all too common. René Ernesto Torres García, a migrant held at El Centro, testified that he believed guards treated Salvadorans "in a different manner than the other detainees due to [their] acts of protest."[61]

One of these Salvadorans, José René Flores, acted on a developing sense of transnational migrant politics following a trajectory similar to that of many migrants in El Centro. Fleeing an attack by the National Guard of El Salvador at the age of eighteen, Flores migrated from San Salvador to Los Angeles in 1980. "There was terrible repression in El Salvador. I was criminalized for having long hair and black glasses. Just looking different and being young meant you were a criminal, *marijuanero*, *guerillero*, and drug addict," he said.[62] Like many, he wanted to get far away from El Salvador to escape the violence of the civil war. Flores was involved in Frente de Acción Popular Unificada (FAPU), or the Unified Popular Action Front, a revolutionary organization composed of students, union members, peasants, and teachers. He also worked in a factory involved with a trade union called Federación Nacional Sindical de Trabajadores Salvadoreños (FENASTRAS). Four of his coworkers had been murdered for their involvement in the union, and Flores would have been the fifth had he not survived an attempt on his life. Flores was shot five times, but he was able to escape and eventually recover from the attack. Yet the assault left him traumatized, injured, and convinced that he needed to flee the country.

In the summer of 1981, INS agents apprehended Flores while he was looking for work in Santa Monica, California. Immigration agents took Flores to the El Centro Immigration Detention Center, where he applied for political asylum. "I didn't want to go back to El Salvador," he recalled, "because I was scared." Represented by Concilio Manzo, an immigrant aid group based in Tucson, Arizona, Flores was released on bond on December 3, 1981. The brutality Flores encountered during six months inside the detention center sparked him to participate in a protest at the facility. Flores claimed that prisoners were encouraged to volunteer for jobs throughout the center. Migrants were not paid for their labor but worked in the hopes of getting larger food portions, which consisted mostly of eggs and potatoes. The lack of adequate nutrition resulted in severe weight loss among many of the detained men. Conditions inside detention quickly took a toll. Flores observed that several migrants stopped shaving their faces. They also refrained from speaking with anyone at the facility.[63] He got sick once and had a fever of 105 degrees. When he attempted to get medical attention, guards sent him to solitary confinement, where he sweated out the fever. If prisoners attempted to complain about these conditions, their requests were often met with violence.

Although the El Centro Immigration Detention Center held men from all over the world, Flores claimed that the Salvadorans were the most united, because in 1981 they made up the largest group at the facility. Cuban asylum seekers were also pretty closely knit, and they saw Flores as one of their own. The men participated in a fifteen-day hunger strike to draw attention to their confinement and political asylum cases. They wanted out of El Centro. Flores participated because he did not like injustice. "I always speak up. . . . I always defend myself. . . . I don't like to be humiliated," he said. This frustration developed into a shared sense of oppression and solidarity. "We all felt the same. Offended. Mistreated. We wanted to tell each other not to be sad. That we were all in this together," Flores said.[64] Despite the causes of the Salvadoran Civil War, men from the Salvadoran military and left-wing groups joined together in the detention center's hunger strike. Many of the strikers were university students, but some had been law enforcement agents. Flores argued that their differences were temporarily reconciled inside the detention center because the guards treated everyone terribly.

Through the efforts of the Sanctuary Movement, a religious and political undertaking that sought to provide a safer environment for Central American refugees, the discrimination faced by asylum seekers attempting to escape violence perpetrated by United States–backed regimes gained national attention.[65] For instance, in 1982 plaintiffs brought a central district suit against the INS in *Orantes-Hernandez v. William French Smith*.[66] The plaintiffs included Crosby Wilfredo Orantes-Hernandez, a Salvadoran violently apprehended and harassed by the INS, and eighteen other Salvadoran migrants.[67] Supporting organizations included Casa El Salvador–Farabundo Martí, Concilio Manzo, the Central American Refugee Program, and El Rescate. They claimed that thousands of Salvadorans "fled political persecution, torture and death in El Salvador in the hope of finding refuge in the United States," only to face "a removal process, usually carried out by the INS with little or no regard for the procedural or substantive rights of aliens under United States immigration law." This included the right to counsel, the right to apply for political asylum, and the right to a hearing before deportation. The suit called for the INS to stop using intimidation as a strategy to get migrants to accept voluntary departure. It also alleged that INS employees failed to provide prisoners with information about counsel and political asylum, placed them in solitary confinement, and commenced deportation hearings when migrants requested political asylum.[68]

The evidence presented in *Orantes-Hernandez v. William French Smith* highlighted the poor conditions experienced by prisoners held in jails in Pasadena, Los Angeles, and Chula Vista and at the federally run facility in El Centro. INS officials did not allow detained migrants to possess written materials, except for the New Testament of the Bible, claiming that they might start a fire or clog the toilets. Detention guidelines established by the INS also stipulated that guards could place prisoners in solitary confinement without having to provide justification. For instance, José Sanchez-Flores, a migrant held at El Centro, testified: "I have been placed in 'La Loba' [solitary confinement], on three different occasions. . . . I was punished in this way for not staying in my place in the line that forms at meal time, for throwing a piece of soap on the roof, and for playing with a friend. I was never given a hearing regarding whether I should be punished for such acts."[69] Guards used solitary confinement to isolate and punish prisoners who challenged their authority. For instance, they placed Carlos Gilberto Bance Pivaral, a Guatemalan migrant, in La Loba for five days and accused him of instigating a strike in 1983.[70]

Central American asylum seekers faced threats to their lives if deported. For instance, a Salvadoran migrant and politically active union member held inside the El Centro Immigration Detention Center told reporters, "There are Salvadorans at the detention camp here who say they will not survive long if sent back."[71] In 1981 the case of twenty-four-year-old Santana Chirino Amaya made headlines when he was denied asylum, deported to El Salvador, and killed within two months. Amaya's decapitated body was found in San Vicente, El Salvador, where officials often found the victims of military death squads.[72] The murder of Amaya was upsetting but not surprising, given the climate asylum seekers attempted to escape. In 1982 at least thirty thousand civilians were killed in El Salvador.[73] In 1984 the Human Rights Commission of the Catholic Archdiocese of San Salvador reported the murder of "30 percent of returning deportees."[74] Groups such as the U.S. Committee in Solidarity with the People of El Salvador (CISPES) initiated a campaign to call out the atrocities that resulted from deporting asylum seekers. The fear of being sent to El Salvador during the war was so great that Salvadoran migrants often lied about their nationality, hoping to be sent to Mexico if deported. In preparation, they memorized the Mexican national anthem and tried to learn Mexican slang.[75] Francisco Rivera, one of the founding members of the Santana Chirino Amaya Committee, described the "circuits of violence" endured by Central American migrants as prevalent even when prisoners were released on bail. He said: "The problems of Salvadorans here are enormous. People come, get arrested and sent to El Centro. If they're bailed out and come to Los Angeles, the whole city feels like a detention center. . . . People without work, traumatized by repression, in fear of the INS."[76]

Solidarity groups helped to document and disseminate information about detained migrants to the public. For example, Sister Jo'Ann De Quattro, the Los Angeles director of the Interfaith Task Force on Central America, recorded that during a trip to investigate conditions at El Centro in 1983, twelve delegation members witnessed some of the asylum seekers engaged in a hunger strike. The strike was initiated to protest the discrimination and brutality, as well as the facility's food and prisoners' lack of access to phones and attorneys. Prisoners also protested being exposed to temperatures above 100 degrees. Standing on a levee, delegates from the Interfaith Task Force on Central America could see the detention center. As the group prepared to leave, the protesters managed to toss a sheet toward their car. Sister Jo'Ann would recall, "Its message, written with a combination of fruit punch and blood which has faded through the years, became a source of inspiration for

FIGURE 8 In the sleeping barracks, 1985 (photo by Robert Gumpert). Robert Gumpert Photograph Archive, The Bancroft Library, University of California, Berkeley (BANC PIC 2016.033). Used by permission of Robert Gumpert.

us as we participated in the ministry of Public Sanctuary. [The sheet said], *En el nombre de Dios*. HELP us!"[77] By 1983, by her recounting, conditions inside the El Centro Immigration Detention Center were already boiling over.

Although many prisoners expressed solidarity with one another, there were also divisions inside the center. During the 1983 hunger strike, some migrants did not join in the demonstration. José Santos Lemus, a Salvadoran national seeking political asylum, described how during the time he was held inside the El Centro Immigration Detention Center in 1983, Saleshi Juni, a migrant from Tonga, ran the center's laundromat along with a few other prisoners from Iran and Tonga.[78] He took over the laundry operation, monopolized all the soap at the facility, and forced the men to pay him if they wanted their clothes washed. Those who could not afford to pay for this service washed their clothes in the shower. Then, on June 2, 1983, a confrontation arose. Jesus Estrada, a Salvadoran migrant, went to collect his clothes. He claimed that his clothes had not been washed even though he had paid two dollars. Juni hit the man in the face. The guards intervened, but not to stop the altercation. Instead, they dragged the Salvadoran prisoner to solitary.

Twenty detained migrants, mostly Salvadorans who had already planned to go on strike to protest the discrimination against Central American asylum seekers, yelled for the prisoners to strike.[79] When one of the demonstrators attempted to take a shower later in the day, he was met by a guard and placed inside La Loba. Lemus claimed that when guards released the Salvadoran from solitary, "he had bruises on his chest and face." A Mexican national who spoke up against this abuse experienced a similar fate.[80]

The Hunger Strike as Transnational Migrant Politics

At the end of May 1985, fifteen detained men from various nationalities came together to discuss organizing a hunger strike inside the El Centro Immigration Detention Center. They concluded that the strike should be peaceful and agreed to notify their attorneys in case they needed legal assistance during the protest.[81] A total of eighty-four prisoners signed a letter sent to Graciela Zavala, an attorney for Centro de Asuntos Migratorios (CAM). They wrote to notify her that they had attempted to report their mistreatment to the INS, but after months of inaction had decided to strike. The men had spoken with Robert C. Rolls, who held the title of acting supervisor at El Centro, but claimed that he and other immigration authorities ignored their reports.[82] The letter they sent Zavala detailed the strikers' grievances, which included physical abuse, psychological intimidation, solitary confinement, threats, misrepresentation, and other forms of coercion. Between 175 and 300 prisoners would participate in the strike.

The strikers' demands contradicted the INS officials accounts of how the detention center operated. According to William A. Thompson, assistant regional deportation officer in San Pedro, California, the detention center was intended to be a place where migrants awaited their deportation hearings, and not a place of punishment. INS officials asserted that their role was to secure a safe place and to provide migrants with care and custody, including access to food, housing, emergency medical and dental care, clothing, and recreational facilities. Thompson wrote, "The well-trained staff of Detention Officers at El Centro are zealous in maintaining high standards of conduct in providing humane and considerate treatment of detainees."[83] INS employees framed the quality of life inside the detention center in idealized terms. Yet the actions of the detained men revealed that they saw their detention as inherently and unfairly punitive. Strikers' stated refusal to eat or work until INS officials met their demands and challenged the definition of the detention center as simply an administrative space.[84] The INS claimed to

FIGURE 9 Exercising at the El Centro Immigration Detention Center, 1985 (photo by Robert Gumpert). Robert Gumpert Photograph Archive, The Bancroft Library, University of California, Berkeley (BANC PIC 2016.033). Used by permission of Robert Gumpert.

pay prisoners one dollar per day to do custodial and kitchen work, and protesters hoped the demonstration would interrupt functions at the detention center, since their labor was vital to the operations of the facility.[85] They detailed the poor treatment they received, came up with a list of seven grievances and resolutions, and hoped that using work stoppage as a tool of protest would get the authorities' attention.

First, the strikers affirmed that guards created an inhumane environment that caused psychological and physical distress.[86] They were concerned that the heat of the Imperial Valley resulted in heat exhaustion and heatstroke. Prisoners slept inside air-conditioned barracks, but guards did not allow them indoors until nightfall. Cliff Rogers, deputy director at El Centro, admitted that "detainees stay[ed] outside after the morning meal until they line[d] up for dinner about 4:30 pm [and then went] into the barracks." Rather than acknowledge that the Imperial Valley was treacherously hot, reaching up to 120 degrees during summer months, Rogers justified this practice as commonplace. He said, "Keeping the inmates outside in the shaded recreational areas is no different than conditions imposed on local workers who have to work out in the heat during the day. You can look out your window and see highway crews working on highway 86 during the hottest days."[87] Rogers suggested that migrants should not complain because the heat impacted the entire workforce in the valley. Although immigration detention was not defined as a punishment for a crime, Rogers's discussion of the heat depicts how the men at El Centro were compelled against their will and subject to inhumane conditions nonetheless. Rogers argued that the facility had a shaded outdoor space. The area he referenced, however, was covered with small pebbles, a strategic choice made by local INS officials to prevent prisoners from running fast enough to escape.[88]

In addition to the unbearable weather, detained migrants listed the poor quality and inadequate amount of food they were served as further examples of insufficient care and punishment. One of the strikers claimed that meals consisted of powdered eggs, beans, and Kool-Aid and that to have access to this food, they had to line up outdoors in the sun two hours before serving time in case meals ran out.[89] Demonstrators demanded access to greater nourishment, accommodations for vegetarians, and vitamins to compensate for the lack of nutritious foods.[90] Given the fact that one of the prisoners' main grievances was the poor quality of the food, it was not surprising that they chose to stop eating as their form of protest. Correctional institutions, including immigration detention centers, provided food with little nutritious value as a money-saving decision, making the prisoner hunger strike that much more symbolic. For instance, Erika Camplin has argued, "It is the obligation of the state to keep the prisoner alive and at least minimally nourished. . . . Food is a powerful tool in coercion within prison, and the hunger strike is an excellent paradigm of that."[91] The hunger strike, as one of many forms of protest, shows how migrants defied guards who used food as a means for extracting compliance inside the detention center.[92]

Graciela Zavala claimed that one doctor on staff provided prisoners with poor medical treatment. Aspirin was his prescription for all ailments.[93] Michelle Crawford, a staff attorney for California Rural Legal Assistance, told reporters, "These people are not even getting the level of treatment that is required of criminals, once they have been convicted in prison."[94] As the letter prisoners wrote indicates, when they complained about a cold, fever, or pain from the beatings guards inflicted, immigration authorities ignored them.[95] One prisoner told reporters that they often shared quarters with people suffering from venereal disease and tuberculosis.[96] Strikers insisted that authorities correct this issue immediately.

A less life-threatening yet important concern for the migrant men was the lack of entertainment inside the facility, which added to their psychological distress. The El Centro Immigration Detention Center had a recreational area where prisoners played soccer, but it was poorly maintained. Broken glass and stones were scattered throughout the grassless field. Protesters asked INS officials to open a library with newspapers and connect a television or radio. They requested greater access to legal resources because they were expected to advocate for themselves. Since migrants were held on civil grounds, they were not entitled to legal counsel unless they paid for it or it was provided pro bono.[97] During the 1980s various legal organizations—such as the San Francisco Lawyers Committee, the Central American Refugee Committee, the Lawyers Committee for Human Rights, and the Imperial Valley Immigration Project—attempted to assist people inside immigration detention centers, but the detention facilities' isolation made it challenging for attorneys to communicate with potential clients.[98] So, in 1985, detained migrants took matters into their own hands by requesting a copy machine, pencils, and access to typewriters. Another demand was that their private mail remained confidential.[99]

Last, prisoners emphasized the physical abuse, psychological intimidation, solitary confinement, and threats guards used to expedite deportation proceedings.[100] Noe Arnaldo Celaya, one of the main organizers of the strike, felt strongly about this claim. At only thirty-two years of age, Celaya had escaped death threats in El Salvador. He was in El Centro while he waited for his political asylum application to be processed. In detention, he suffered from heat exhaustion, malnutrition, and verbal and physical harassment. On one occasion a guard told him, "Why don't you go back where you came from. You're not wanted here. Why don't you go to a country where they speak Spanish?"[101] The verbal abuse Celaya experienced revealed the racism of the guards. The guards treated Spanish-speaking migrants as foreigners who did not belong in the United States. Celaya helped to organize the hunger strike because of the mistreatment he experienced. He believed guards abused him to encourage him to self-deport. Celaya told reporters that this mistreatment was common. For instance, guards often referred to a Cuban prisoner as a scarecrow and called him by that name.[102] A man told Cynthia Anderson of the Central American Refugee Center that "a guard whacked [his] friend in the mouth while he was standing in line for food and knocked out three of his teeth."[103] Solitary confinement was also frequently used to isolate prisoners. Eduardo Antonio Evora testified that he was placed in isolation for two days after being beaten so badly by a guard that his arm was broken.[104] Stories like these were abundant in 1985.

Yet immigration officials seemed puzzled by these grievances. Regional INS commissioner Harold Ezell told the press: "This is our best operation. We follow the same standards [as those] maintained by the American Correctional Association. We are proud of our operation here."[105] Ezell's remark revealed that despite the law, the INS conceived of immigration detention centers as prisons. The strikers challenged INS claims that detention simply functioned as an administrative holding site. They knew firsthand that INS employees made detention unnecessarily difficult. For example, Emiliano Javier Flores, a Honduran migrant and one of the leaders of the hunger strike, mentioned that he got involved because he did not think it was right to hold people for nine months in such subpar conditions.[106] Flores and his fellow protesters were angry and frustrated at being incarcerated and having the INS violate their rights. Immigration officers insisted that they provided detained migrants with the necessary care, but this paternalist logic did not include listening to them. It was this shared experience of rightlessness within the carceral system that fostered solidarity among the detained men.[107]

State Repression and Solidarity Beyond the Detention Fence

Strikers at El Centro organized across nationalities. They negotiated with INS officers to get what they needed for subsistence during the demonstration.[108] For example, the protesters agreed to line up for the daily head count in exchange for materials such as bedsheets. They used the sheets to sleep outdoors and as makeshift banners to list the names of their home countries. Collaborating was essential for the men to organize and make their grievances heard.

Solidarity, central to the emergence of transnational migrant politics, manifested across various nationalities and even beyond the detention fence. While the hunger strikers occupied the outdoors near the fence, immigrant activists and church groups from Los Angeles, Yuma, and Imperial County, such as El Rescate and the Central American Refugee Center, gathered on the opposite side to protest in solidarity with the hunger strikers.[109] The United Farm Workers sent a group of volunteers to support the strike.[110] Activists from the outside talked to the prisoners through the fence, and one of them showed a striker the newspaper coverage of the event to keep the men motivated.[111] Chicano activists from San Diego supported the Mexican migrants inside El Centro, but they also recognized the injustice of confining Central American asylum seekers. For instance, organizations such as Chicanos in Solidarity with the People of Central America (CHISPA) and Union del Barrio protested U.S. involvement in Central America at the Fifteenth Annual Chicano Moratorium in Los Angeles, shortly after the hunger strike had taken place.[112]

On Wednesday, May 29, 1985, four of the strikers met with the facility's acting supervisor, Robert C. Rolls. The protesters gave him one final opportunity to respond to their demands. Rolls concluded that regional INS officials could not do anything about their requests, because they were responsible for enforcing rather than altering immigration policy.[113] He refused to take responsibility for the guards' actions and local detention conditions, although local INS officials, agents, and guards had a history of exerting their power to make the law when it was to their benefit.[114] Rolls's deflection suggested that immigration authorities did not value the experiences of migrants. That night the strikers heard trucks in the distance and saw guards running around the facility. José Israel Murillo reported that the strikers were afraid and discussed what action they would take if the INS attacked. He said, "We decided that we should respond with no resistance."[115]

When local INS officials called the El Centro Tactical Intervention and Control Unit (TIAC), a local component of the Border Patrol Tactical Unit (BORTAC), to help relocate the protesters, the strikers sat down with their arms crossed.[116] BORTAC was formed in 1984 as an "elite, special forces team" for the INS. Trained in riot control, surveillance, counterterrorism, advanced weapon skills, and foreign law enforcement, they were charged with responding to riots and disturbances inside INS detention centers.[117] At six in the morning on May 31, they entered the demonstration site with riot gear and batons. They violently forced the fifty-six remaining protesters to relocate indoors. During the removal, protesters were hit on the head and ribs, handcuffed, kicked, and forcibly dragged inside the building by their hands and feet.[118] Strikers suffered bruises and injuries to their wrists and backs.[119] At this point in the strike, the men were weak from lack of food and from being outdoors for so many days. Guards took some of the protesters to the infirmary, tied them up with plastic wires, and placed them face down on the floor for hours before putting them in solitary confinement.[120]

The repression of the INS crushed the strike. On June 1 the number of strikers had dwindled to eight: Oscar Hernandez from Cuba, Walter Chu from China, Emiliano Javier Flores from Honduras, Antonio Caraza from Peru, Rex Singh from Guyana, and Noe Arnoldo Celaya, José Hilario Martínez, and José Alberto Ramírez Flores from El Salvador.[121] Four of the strike leaders had criminal backgrounds, and they told the Imperial Valley Immigration Project that they had abandoned the hunger strike because INS officials insisted that their protest would ruin their immigration cases.[122] Walter Chu told the press that guards mocked them for not eating. He said, "Each day, we were taken to the dining room and made to sit in front of a plate full of food."[123] This tactic demonstrates the psychological abuse that the INS unleashed to maintain its authority.[124] Yet INS officials framed their actions in a different light. Bob Mandgie, INS assistant district director, said, "We've got rules regarding a hunger strike. . . . We have to take them, put a plate of food in front of them for 10 minutes and only if they refuse to eat can we certify them as hunger strikers."[125] The strike ended on Monday, June 3, 1985, when the INS released the final demonstrators on bail. Alex William Koski, a local Lutheran pastor involved with the Imperial Valley Immigration Project, paid Murillo's $1,500 bond because he felt that the beating the latter had received warranted his release.[126] Koski then used his life savings to bail out the remaining strikers, at the cost of $26,750, right before guards attempted to force-feed the men.[127]

The released demonstrators held a press conference in the home of Reverend Koski. When reporters from *La Voz* interviewed José Hilario, he said he understood why people ended the strike earlier than he did. He said, "It is not easy. I had already participated in other actions of this type in the past."[128] Although sources indicate that the detained strikers were experienced organizers and politically conscious, INS officials attempted to delegitimize the hunger strike and the credibility of the strikers' claims. Harold W. Ezell, a regional commissioner of the INS, asserted, "Their so-called demands are really so much baloney. . . . The conditions at the center have been inspected over and over [and] have been found to be perfectly good. The inmates are living in a correctional facility [not] the Conrad Hilton." Ezell's response suggested that immigration authorities believed conditions inside the El Centro Immigration Detention Center were acceptable and that they viewed detainees as prisoners, even though they were held for administrative and not criminal proceedings. James B. Turnage Jr., INS district director, told reporters that the strikers did not maintain their fast because they obtained food from the facility's vending machines.[129] He claimed that guards found hundreds of candy bar wrappers near the recreational area.[130]

Rather than engaging with the strikers' demands, INS officials disputed the commitment of the protesters and the legitimacy of their grievances.

INS officials accused Graciela Zavala of conspiring to turn the strike into a revolt.[131] Ezell and Turnage told news reporters that they "feared outside agitators could whip up a riot at the desert facility." Turnage did not believe that the detained migrants were capable of organizing on their own. He claimed, "This certainly is not a spontaneous demonstration. . . . This has been stage managed by outsiders, and it appears that mainly Legal Aid attorneys opposed to U.S. policy in Central America are involved here."[132] Immigration officials blamed people outside of the facility, mainly immigrant rights activists and the people involved in the Sanctuary Movement, for initiating the strike. By blaming outside agitators, the INS denied the strikers' agency. In response to accusations by the INS, Zavala stressed that her clients planned the strike and that she had limited involvement. She merely ensured that the demonstration remained peaceful.[133] Ezell blamed Zavala for the strike and filed a complaint with the State Bar of California and the Board of Immigration Appeals to bar her from the facility.[134] Turnage and Ezell described Zavala as a member of a group of attorneys who "formed the nucleus of a band of outside agitators."[135] Zavala responded by stating that Central American immigrants were sophisticated and experienced political actors. She said, "People from Central America [are] politically astute. The[y] organized in their own countries. They [are] *guerrilleros* and they [know] that they [have] certain human rights."[136]

The hunger strikers were persistent and outspoken about their rights, precisely because many had organized within the context of war and revolution. For instance, hunger strike leader Noe Arnoldo Celaya was a member of Ande, a group that advocated for democratic reform and human rights in Nuevo Guadalupe, El Salvador. It was his activism that forced him to flee, as death squads had killed over three hundred Ande members. He was next on the kill list, forcing him to leave El Salvador. He told reporters that the men organized the strike because they could no longer tolerate the conditions.[137] INS officials used immigration advocates as scapegoats to divert attention from the charges prisoners brought forth, but incarcerated migrants did not need outside encouragement to protest the grim conditions. As historian Maria Cristina Garcia has argued of advocacy networks, detained migrants and their allies "used a variety of tactics learned from other social movements around the world," particularly the politics of the 1960s.[138] Their protests emerged from struggles that surpassed the detention center's fences and took place beyond the nation's borders.

FIGURE 10 By the El Centro Immigration Detention Center fence, 1985 (photo by Robert Gumpert). Robert Gumpert Photograph Archive, The Bancroft Library, University of California, Berkeley (BANC PIC 2016.033). Used by permission of Robert Gumpert.

Immigration officials responded to the hunger strike of 1985 by strategically isolating the demonstrators. Consequently, attorneys from the Central American Refugee Center, the National Center for Immigrants' Rights, the Legal Aid Foundation of Los Angeles, the National Lawyers Guild, and the American Civil Liberties Union filed an injunction against the INS challenging this retaliatory action.[139] Immigration authorities abruptly cut off migrants' access to legal counsel. Advocates stated that the INS did so "in retaliation, and without justification."[140] ACLU attorney Mark Rosenbaum claimed that the "INS broke the strike by intimidation and by transferring most of their leaders to other detention centers in Denver, San Diego and Inglewood."[141] Bob Mandgie admitted that the prisoner population was reduced during the strike, with INS agents removing ninety-three inmates.[142] The INS shuffled the migrant population as a tactic to challenge the demonstration, a practice that immigration officers had often used to smash dissent at El Centro.[143] Immigration officials borrowed the strategy of separating detained migrants from prisons.[144] Decades earlier the INS could not move migrants from state to state because there was not enough detention space, but the expansion of detention centers throughout the 1980s allowed for this new approach. INS policy allowed officials to transfer prisoners from one center to another, or from a local jail to an immigration detention center, as a form of discipline or because their appeal required longer detention.[145]

Following the strike California representative Howard Berman, Matthew G. Martinez, and Esteban Torres investigated conditions inside the detention facility. They created a congressional delegation that consisted of church representatives, civil rights groups, and government officials from the Los Angeles and San Diego regions. This included Church Women United, Friends of Rescate, Interfaith Peace Center, Church of the Brethren, UCLA students, CISPES, CRECEN, El Rescate, School of Theology of Claremont, National Center for Immigrant Rights, Laverne Church of the Brethren, Comite Nacional Contra Represion, Interfaith Task Force on Central America, and the LA Equal Rights Congress. They requested that the INS be held accountable for their actions toward strikers during the demonstration.[146] Delegation members inspected the facility and found major overcrowding.[147] Cynthia Anderson, a representative with the church-based Southern California Interfaith Task Force on Central America, said, "The conditions at El Centro are abhorrent. Salvadorans are housed like criminals without basic tools needed to even help out in their own legal cases."[148] INS Commissioner Alan Nelson asserted that the delegations' allegations were unfounded. He said, "Like all detention facilities, it is clean, well-kept and there is good food," but "you must remember this is a detention facility."[149] Nelson did not acknowledge the experiences of the migrants. He suggested that the INS did not have the responsibility to provide noncitizens with humane conditions. After the 1985 hunger strike, INS officials began to allow prisoners to remain indoors during the day, and in 1986 they opened a library inside the facility.[150] The Mexican government came to the aid of detained migrants because the U.S. government was abusive and neglectful. They funded a large part of the library. The Mexican consulate donated Spanish-language books and magazines, including titles such as *Romeo and Julieta*, *Crónica de una Muerte Anunciada*, *Don Quijote de la Mancha*, and *El Viejo y el Mar*.[151]

Immigration Detention in El Centro
after the 1985 Hunger Strike

After the 1985 hunger strike, INS authorities stressed that conditions had improved inside the El Centro Immigration Detention Center, suggesting that conditions did in fact need altering. Allen W. Hausman, assistant director of the Office of Immigration Litigation for the INS, insisted that the center included telephones from which detained migrants could make collect calls, as well as a television with HBO. Officer Atunez added, "Hunger-strikers complained about the bread ration in the past. . . . But no one can complain about that anymore."[152]

Yet, in 1988, Leslie Johnson, the attorney who replaced Zavala after the strike, described the facility in eerily similar ways. She told reporters that when she first interviewed a nineteen-year-old Salvadoran client, he was shaking and crying. Johnson asserted, "Refugees from El Salvador who claim to fear persecution at the hands of guerillas face slightly better prospects of winning asylum than the larger number of Salvadorans who say they are threatened by right-wing death squads." Asylum seekers from Central America continued to face low chances of gaining political asylum, regardless of their background. From October to December 1987, the INS granted only 8 out of 5,800 Salvadoran asylum petitions across the United States. As reporter Mark Thompson wrote, "The immigration detention center in El Centro is almost always just a legal way station on the road back to the war zone."[153] It was rare for a migrant to escape these circuits of violence. It was not until the end of the Cold War in 1991 that the U.S. government admitted its role in discriminating against Central American asylum seekers in the *American Baptist Churches v. Thornburgh Settlement Agreement*, known as the ABC lawsuit.[154] INS agents could not deport eligible Guatemalans and Salvadorans until they obtained the benefits of the Settlement Agreement, which included participating in a new asylum interview based on the 1990 asylum regulations.[155]

Yet the people still faced with detention encountered a regime that had rapidly expanded. As a response to increasing strikes, in 1987 the Department of Justice created a national *Detention Officer Handbook*. It established procedures for how to respond to a hunger strike, such as force-feeding prisoners with nasogastric tubes and gastric lavage stomach pumping.[156] Violent conditions and INS repression continued to plague detention facilities. A press statement from 1990 by members of the American Friends Service Committee's US/Mexico Border Program emphasized how little conditions had changed. After receiving several complaints about abuse from Mexican and Central American migrants, the organization asserted, "We have not seen any improvements or attempts to control the abuses to date. . . . Unfortunately, victims and witnesses are afraid to come forward with their complaints for fear of retaliation."[157]

During the 1980s the federal government developed a powerful regime within the context of mass incarceration and the expansion of immigration detention. The U.S. government influenced the migration of Central Americans through its policies but then imprisoned them when they attempted to find refuge in the United States. The El Centro Immigration Detention Center was one of several punitive spaces intended to push out these excluded populations. Yet the men refused to let their experiences go unnoticed. Salvadoran asylum seekers, in particular, showed the rest of the world that immigration authorities mistreated them and violated their human rights a couple of years before the infamous Atlanta prison riots of 1987, when Cuban prisoners in Atlanta, Georgia, and Oakdale, Louisiana, took control of the prisons. Although the 1985 protest did not result in substantive policy changes at El Centro, its expression of transnational migrant politics sparked further manifestations of such politics. It was a harbinger of resistance to come.

Protesters used their bodies as tools to challenge a system that was never strictly administrative but instead policed their physical movement and threatened their livelihood.

PART III | Liminal Punishments

CHAPTER SIX

Secreted Spaces of Antimigrant Violence

> The shifting visibility and invisibility of these prisons are
> emblematic of penality's relationship to the law's deepest secret,
> its own violence.
>
> —MICHELLE BROWN, 2009

> To engage in war and refugee studies, then, is to listen to
> "fragmentary testimonies, to barely distinguishable testimonies,
> to testimonies that never reach us"—that is, to write ghost stories.
> As tellers of ghost stories, it is imperative that we always look for
> the "something more" in order to see and bring into being what is
> usually neglected or made invisible or thought by most to be dead
> and gone.
>
> —YÊN LÊ ESPIRITU, 2014

I found a photograph buried in the archival records of Mexico City's Secretariat of Foreign Affairs that captures the moment a Border Patrol agent apprehended Jesús Reyes Mondragon. His parents took the photo to document the arrest. On July 17, 1990, the family members of Reyes Mondragon showed up at the Mexican consulate in Calexico, California, to see if they could assist in investigating the Border Patrol's aggressive apprehension of their son at their home in Indio, California. The INS agent trespassed into their home and beat Jesús into submission before handcuffing him and taking him away. The Mondragons told the Mexican consulate that the agent did not explain why he beat and arrested Jesús. "They just took him," lamented his mother.[1] Jesús was transported to the El Centro Immigration Detention Center. The violence used by the INS to remove Jesús from his family is indicative of the physical force used in all aspects of immigration enforcement. In the experiences of the Mondragon family it becomes clear that hidden within the histories of immigration enforcement, physical violence is a central strategy of the apprehension, detention, and deportation process.

INS guards carried out physical violence against detained migrants inside the El Centro Immigration Detention Center and the Eclectic Communications, Incorporated (ECI) facility for unaccompanied minors located three miles north of El Centro in the city of Imperial.[2] The following testimonies of migrant pain occurred between 1986 and 1994. They uncover the connections between immigrant detention, punishment, and gender. Punishment and surveillance are gendered practices. Gender is constructed through relationships of power, and punishments categorize behaviors "along lines of difference."[3] Dominant discourses about masculinity shaped life inside detention, a part of larger administrative regimes, where racial and gendered cruelty was weaponized against migrants.

The following testimonies of detained men and children highlight one of the larger functions of immigration detention centers, which was to inflict violence on migrant bodies. The 1987 federal INS *Detention Officer Handbook* emphasized that detention was not intended to serve as a form of punishment but rather to "ensure the alien's availability for deportation proceedings or expulsion."[4] Yet, the following testimonies and government sources suggest that punishment was the main way guards attempted to maintain order. The immigration detention center was and continues to be a racialized and gendered administrative regime of punishment.[5]

Centering migrant voices illuminates a hidden history of abuse and historicizes their vulnerability and pain.[6] The detention center included men who expressed, imagined, and performed various types of masculinity.[7] Not only was violence "hidden from view" and "secreted away," but, as the following testimonies reveal, guards used particular sites inside detention centers to inflict pain.[8] The mapping of state violence reveals that immigration authorities transformed particular areas into liminal spaces, where migrants not in prison yet were treated like prisoners, to physically hurt migrants with impunity.

The bathrooms inside the El Centro Immigration Detention Center and the punishment room at ECI were specific locations where violence against detained migrants was more likely to occur, engendering a type of geography of violence.[9] These sites display the punishment and pain experienced by migrants and the prevalence of state violence in detention. Five decades had passed since the immigration facility first opened in El Centro, and yet violence continued to structure everyday life for the men held within its walls.

Codifying Race, Criminalization, and Culpability

In 1990 the INS could detain a total of fourteen thousand people per day across the United States.[10] The expansion of detention spaces arose from government legislation that increased the avenues for policing migration and further marked migrants as criminals. For instance, on November 6, 1986, President Ronald Reagan signed the Immigration Reform and Control Act (IRCA). This legislation is remembered largely for its granting of amnesty, yet IRCA did not just create a path for legalization. IRCA increased border enforcement and encouraged detention, consequently increasing apprehensions along the border.[11] This legislation also framed migrants along a dichotomy, between the slightly more deserving and the criminal. It called for the "expeditious deportation of convicted aliens" and the creation of new detention sites.[12] The discursive link between migration and crime racialized migrants as lawbreakers.

Narcotics legislation passed in the 1980s and early 1990s further enabled INS agents to police migrants. The Anti-Drug Abuse Act of 1986 established mandatory minimum sentences for drug trafficking crimes and drug possession and increased the number of drug offenses that made a noncitizen deportable or excludable.[13] Then, in 1988, the INS created the Alien Criminal Apprehension Program (ACAP) and the Institutional Removal Program (IRP), in an effort to make the "criminal alien" removal process more efficient. A "criminal alien" was defined as "any deportable or excludable alien who ha[d] been convicted of a crime," and these programs provided the government with the resources to identify, process, prosecute, and remove such people.[14] This same year the Anti-Drug Abuse Act of 1988 was updated to include "aggravated felonies" as grounds for deportation. This included "murder, drug trafficking, and illicit traffic in firearms."[15] Explicitly associating migrants with crime made them more vulnerable, as immigration authorities viewed them as culpable, regardless of whether they simply overstayed a visa, which was not a crime, or crossed the border without legal authorization, which was a crime if prosecuted. This discourse shaped detention policy and practice, including daily and intimate occurrences inside of immigration detention centers.

The INS *Detention Officer Handbook* of 1987 mandated that immigration employees, including Border Patrol agents, airplane pilots, deportation and detention officers, guards, investigators, attorneys, and supervisory officers, be trained to respond to prisoner threats. The meticulous detention instructions suggest that whoever passed through a detention center was viewed as inherently dangerous and culpable. The INS handbook concluded that the best method of stamping out potential threats was by enforcing discipline. It defined discipline as "the instruction, training, correction, guidance and supervision of individuals with respect to behavior, which results in a continuing orderly acceptable way of life." Prisoners were categorized into various sorts of "problem-aliens." The list ranged from men labeled "indifferent, lazy, shy, physically or mentally sick" to "irritable, stubborn, conceited, suspicious, selfish, aggressive, impatient, stupid, hysterical, [or] sneaky." Detention staff were instructed to interview migrants as soon as they were brought into an INS facility. They evaluated the migrant's past, "including escapes and assaultive behavior, narcotics use, alcoholism, theft, mental capacity, emotional disturbance, educational level, and religious interests."[16] If an official suspected that a prisoner was dangerous or escape-minded or that required additional security measures, he was required to make a note on his I-203, or the notice to detain or release. Also, prisoners might be separated in secure quarters with additional locks. This detention center policy suggests that INS officials were trained to look for signs of dissent and deviance because the detained men were prone to such behaviors.

Guards used discipline as a preventative measure to keep migrants in line, and punishment if migrants disobeyed or challenged their authority. They demanded that prisoners remain orderly and report signs of misconduct by fellow prisoners. Detention staff hoped the men would help with surveillance by exposing potential conflict. Guards turned off facilities' lights at the same time every evening, ensured that prisoners did not talk to anyone who had not been authorized, and focused on identifying potential leaders. According to the *Detention Officer Handbook*, guards were instructed "not to wait for trouble to start," and "if trouble [arose], [they should] determine the cause [and segregate] the troublemakers."[17] Furthermore, they were instructed to use oral reprimands for minor offenses and solitary confinement for more serious threats. The handbook states that discipline and punishment were "absolutely necessary for the purpose of effective administration of [the] processing center."[18] INS employees routinely used physical violence to assert their authority inside immigration detention centers.

As a response to the rampant violence against detained migrants, in 1990 the El Centro Asylum Project, Centro de Asuntos Migratorios, Esperanza para los Niños, the American Friends Service Committee's U.S.-Mexico Border Program, and the Southwest Refugee Rights Project took more forceful measures to call out this abuse. At a press conference, representatives from these organizations claimed that they knew of at least twenty-four people, including children, who had been beaten by immigration authorities inside the El Centro Immigration Detention Center and ECI.[19] Legal defense officers and advocacy groups from El Centro and San Diego came together to condemn this system on October 9, 1990, when fifteen Latin American refugees and the Center for Human Rights and Constitutional Law in Los

Angeles filed a claim in federal court.[20] Represented by attorney Peter Schey, the plaintiffs sought $15 million in damages for the physical violence they experienced at El Centro and ECI. Schey argued that "his clients' [sic] testimony reveal[ed] a persistent pattern of brutality and abuse" enacted by INS guards.[21] Scholars have pointed out that detention centers can be viewed as spaces where the state performs the expulsion of migrant bodies, but examining the testimonies of these plaintiffs suggests that the detention center was not just a step in the removal process.[22] Centro de Asuntos Migratorios, El Centro Asylum Project, Esperanza para los Niños, and the Southwest Refugee Rights Project collected testimonies of the plaintiffs and concluded that a pattern of violence shaped their everyday experience. The incidents that the men and young boys recounted took place between September 8, 1989, and August 13, 1990, indicating that their statements unearthed a much deeper and more prevalent issue.[23] The experiences of the plaintiffs make up a large part of this chapter's sources. As scholar Naomi Paik asserts, "Testimonies of rightlessness contest the nationalism and racism behind camp-thinking. The testimonial act contains within it a call for social change."[24] Detained adults and children without the protections of U.S. citizenship were willing to make themselves vulnerable to challenge their violent confinement.

One of the main functions of immigration detention was punishment. A report published by the National Center for Immigrants' Rights in 1986 found that INS employees used violence to coerce asylum seekers to give up on their asylum case and agree to deport. The document reads, "Those who refuse are often subjected to verbal and physical intimidation," and at El Centro "refugees are regularly placed in solitary confinement [where] beatings of prisoners have been documented."[25] Guards sought to teach prisoners a lesson by inflicting violence against their bodies. The plaintiffs showed that they were "beaten, denied adequate medical care, handcuffed and frequently placed in an isolation cell, known as *el hoyo* (the pit), for punishment."[26] The INS adopted this isolation strategy from prisons. The purpose of solitary was to "break close emotional ties, to segregate all natural leaders [and] to prohibit group activities that [did] not fit brainwashing objectives." Communication between migrants was particularly threatening because it could result in solidarity, conspiracy, or dissent.

The American Friends Service Committee's U.S.-Mexico Border Program (AFSC-USMBP) documented INS abuse throughout Southern California.[27] Roberto Martínez, the director of the AFSC-USMBP, said, "The system is flawed at its core, leaving INS officers completely unaccountable [and] such a system has permitted the INS to engage in a systematic, nationwide pattern and practice of depriving people of their civil and human rights. The inmates in INS custody have no meaningful redress and are punished if they complain."[28] The stories of the detained migrant men and unaccompanied minors reveal that state violence was not an irregularity but a norm inside immigration detention centers. Giorgio Agamben argues that the state of exception "inaugurates a new juridical-political paradigm in which the norm becomes indistinguishable from the exception." Hence, the inhabitants of such spaces of exception "moved in a zone of indistinction between . . . exception and rule, licit and illicit, in which the very concepts of subjective rights and juridical protection no longer made any sense."[29] Violence in all its forms became a tool for the INS with which to punish and discipline confined migrants.

Unaccompanied Minors

The Department of Health and Human Services is currently responsible for managing unaccompanied migrant children, but during the 1980s and early 1990s, the INS was charged with their apprehension and confinement as they waited for deportation proceedings. Staff and immigration attorneys determined if the minors would be released to a sponsor or family member, deported, or continue to be detained. If the latter option was chosen, the children remained in immigration custody until they turned eighteen years of age or agreed to voluntary deportation. Before the 1980s immigration agents frequently released unaccompanied minors rather than hold them in detention. But within the context of civil war throughout Central America and increased migration, the federal government argued that placing children in its custody was a protection measure.[30] In 1985 thirteen-year-old Alma Cruz, fifteen-year-old Jenny Flores, and sixteen-year-old Dominga Hernandez and Ana Martínez filed a class action suit against the INS. *Flores et al. v. Meese et al.* took over two decades to develop, and during this time the plaintiffs argued that the INS should not detain minors simply based on not having a parent or legal guardian take custody over them.[31] This suit exposed the many challenges that unaccompanied minors faced inside of immigration facilities.

Minors dealt with the same immigration system as adults regardless of how unfamiliar they were with the legal procedures. They were expected to pay for a lawyer and fend for themselves. Immigration officials insisted that keeping minors in detention protected them from nonverifiable guardians, but keeping them in the custody of the INS was also dangerous, as the following testimonies show. INS employees were often brought into facilities for minors to serve as the office disciplinarians of unauthorized and unaccompanied youth.[32] A settlement was finally reached in 1997, in which the Supreme Court upheld the right of the federal government to detain minors in "secure facilities" and for "unspecified and prolonged periods."[33] But the ruling also called for the creation of federal detention standards specific to unaccompanied minors, which were to include balanced meals, education, counseling, medical services, and recreation. *Flores v. Meese* was a significant case because it shed light on the plight of unaccompanied minors. Yet the suit did not help children without family members or guardians able to claim them, and so they remained in detention.[34]

Carmen Mejia-King, a representative with Centro de Asuntos Migratorios (CAM), denounced the practice of excluding and removing children from the United States. She recounted the experience of Edwin Gutiérrez, a sixteen-year-old boy held at ECI in Imperial. She said: "He hardly talks about his family at all. . . . He is longing for a home. He last saw his mom when he was 5 years old and was taken from Nicaragua to Guatemala by his father. Two years later his father was kidnapped by guerillas. He has no family ties in either country."[35] Gutiérrez's experience highlights the unrealistic expectation of merely releasing minors to parents or close relatives in the context of war and rampant death. Children, especially from Central America, were escaping violence and poverty, and many did not have family ties in the United States. They traveled north in search of safety and protection after fleeing traumatic situations, only to face similar mistreatment in the United States.

During the 1980s and 1990s, immigration officials did not have the proper infrastructure in place to take care of growing rates of unaccompanied minors. It was also difficult for children to navigate the detention and deportation regime because they could be held in numerous jails run by various counties or cities, INS contracted facilities, shelters, or group homes, all with separate policies and procedures.[36] INS agents constantly transferred unaccompanied minors from facility to facility, making the detention experience confusing and frightening.[37] The testimonies of unaccompanied minors held inside ECI suggest that children did not escape the punitive experience of immigration detention. Immigration authorities contracted out with ECI and trusted their treatment of minors. ECI staff members maintained strict security and disciplinary measures inside the facility, which was surrounded by a tall razor-wire fence. They counted the minors several times a day, and if the latter did not follow the rules they castigated them.

On July 5, 1990, INS guards beat three seventeen-year-old boys from El Salvador and Mexico. The staff accused Ramos, Linares, and Calderón of plotting to escape from the facility and called in INS employees to handle the situation. They took the boys into separate rooms. Ramos was taken into an office building, where he was thrown against the wall, and Linares was banged into a building headfirst.[38] They deported Calderón to Mexico before he could make a statement on the matter, but Ramos claimed that he also saw Calderón taken into a room. The boy's statements indicate that the INS used physical abuse to discourage escape and political asylum. Linares wrote, "The short, muscular INS agent told me that he would personally see to it that I was beaten and would make my life miserable when I turned 18 years old and was transferred to the *Corralòn* (adult detention center)." Staff used threats such as inflicting more harm when a youth aged out, physical violence, and accelerated deportation to maintain order at ECI. On August 6, 1990, Carmen Mejìa-King met with INS officials Nathan C. Davis, Hector Nàjera, and Robert Mange to discuss the treatment of the three boys.[39] She showed them the declarations, and the officers said they would follow up with the Office of the Inspector General. Although this office was known for ignoring similar accusations, they agreed to forward the case to the Civil Rights Division of the U.S. Department of Justice. But in the end, the officer in charge concluded that the Department of Justice would not prosecute the officers involved.[40] The boy's non–U.S. citizenship status meant that violence against their bodies occurred with impunity and that INS staff and guards did not see them as children or gendered as masculine.

ECI staff used what youth called the "punishment room" whenever a detained child broke a rule. On August 2, 1990, staff members placed four boys inside the room. They had attempted to get out, and, as a response, they were beaten and handcuffed. One of the boys explained, "This is not the first time that immigration officials have come to ECI and physically and verbally abused me. The experience humiliates me and frightens me."[41] Jorge Ivan Ortega Linares, a seventeen-year-old Honduran, was one of the boys hurt that evening. He needed to use the bathroom, and, when he was not permitted, he vocalized urgency. Staff members called in detention staff, who proceeded to punch Linares in the stomach. Officer Vásquez shouted, "Does it hurt?" When Linares did not respond, Vásquez provoked him and asked,

"How macho are you?" Like the men held at the El Centro Immigration Detention Center, the young boys were expected to tough out these beatings to prove they were real men. Linares also witnessed the beating of his companions. Guards insulted and hit Julio Cesar Villa Gamez, a fifteen-year-old Honduran, for suggesting that he wanted to run away from ECI. He was beaten so badly that he started to cry. Linares disclosed, "I felt like crying too when I heard him crying."[42] Immigration advocates used these stories to expose the mistreatment of unaccompanied minors in detention. Attorney Lynn Marcus said, "This culture of violence . . . has to stop," suggesting that the physical abuses inflicted on minors and adults were not isolated incidents but part of the everyday tactics used by the INS in enforcing immigration laws.[43]

Investigations conducted by the National Council of La Raza in the 1990s revealed that INS abuse of unaccompanied minors was an everyday occurrence at ECI. A typical tactic was to force the young boys to stand in place for as long as one hour.[44] Sometimes they were also required to run outside in the heat. A sixteen-year-old boy from El Salvador recounted how ECI staff obligated all of them to run laps, sometimes fifty, but up to one hundred, when someone broke a rule.[45] It did not matter which rule. If someone used the bathroom without asking for permission, they would have to run.

One of the reprimands the boys feared the most was being placed inside the punishment room. There was a range of reasons for ending up in this place, but they all boiled down to challenging or dismissing authority. A young boy explained, "One time I ended up there because I left the building looking for a mop, another time I wanted to exchange pants with another detainee but I guess that was not allowed."[46] One of the young men was placed in the punishment room for three days because he did not understand English or Spanish.[47] His primary language was Quechua, yet staff expected him to understand their English instructions. Punishing children for not knowing English reveals the larger racial and xenophobic processes that unfolded inside detention. Migrants were treated like racial enemies so routinely that the detention system could not exist without racial cruelty. The punishment room functioned as a liminal zone where INS employees could hurt the detained children, although they were not legally allowed to do so. This practice was a spatial tactic of state violence.

Rumors also served to instill fear among the detained boys. Staff threatened to call the INS, or "the men in black," as the children referred to them. The boys circulated information about how the men in black beat children.[48] Unfortunately, this was not just gossip. INS employees physically harmed detained minors. In one instance a staff member put a young man into a chokehold and dragged him about forty feet into a back room after a verbal disagreement.[49]

The boys at ECI were required to wear a hat every day. On one occasion a young man asked for a new hat, and staff members became upset. They transferred him to the El Centro juvenile hall. In his written testimony the young man wrote, "I was handcuffed on three separate occasions at ECI. I was treated like an animal, not a person."[50] A young man from Honduras mentioned that one of the most common reasons they got in trouble was for forgetting to wear their hats. "If you do not wear your hat or are late to the headcount you have to wash the bathroom for seven days or sit in the punishment room," he said. Staff forced detained youth to clean when they broke a rule or talked back to a staff member, and they also disciplined the children if they did not participate in the facilities programming. For instance, a young boy wrote: "When I was brought to ECI I was given a list of rules. I read them and agreed to them. However, these rules did not say that I had to wear a hat at all times, that I would be forced to play and run laps, or that I would be punished for accidentally kicking the soccer ball over the fence."[51] Staff punished minors for almost anything at ECI. The widespread use of physical punishment at ECI indicates that punishment was used as a fundamental form of maintaining order.

ECI staff and immigration employees humiliated and mocked the incarcerated youth. On one occasion, after hearing rumors that a few boys wanted to escape, the ECI director handcuffed three migrants to one another by the ankles. He forced them to walk about the facility, stumbling from place to place, for two hours.[52] ECI staff also used labor to keep the young men busy and under control. They asked them to renovate the sidewalks and soccer field at ECI. In exchange for their labor, minors were promised a small amount of money, soda, or extra food.[53] But the boys claimed that they did not always receive what they were promised, and, when they did, money earned could be taken away as a form of punishment.[54] ECI staff used food as an incentive to get minors to work, but also as castigation. Sugar, biscuits, salt, salsa, and bread could all be taken away from children if they disobeyed.[55]

One of the main reasons ECI staff punished minors was to encourage deportation. A seventeen-year-old boy from Guatemala disclosed that a staff member told him he should request voluntary deportation since it would take seven months to hear about his asylum application and that he would not win.[56] Another boy revealed: "The atmosphere at ECI is oppressive.

I am extremely depressed here. Some others are so depressed that they have decided to request deportation rather than proceed with their cases, although they do not want to be sent back to their countries."[57] As these stories illustrate, punishment and discipline were a central part of life at ECI. The ages of the young boys did not protect them from the violence of the detention and deportation regime. Scholar Susan J. Terrio explains, "The suspension of national and international norms premised on the detention of children is acceptable only because it applies to undesirable subjects. A situation that would be considered intolerable if it were applied to white middle-class U.S. citizen children is accepted because of the perceived threat they pose as 'illegal aliens.'"[58]

Policing Sex and Gender at El Centro

Immigration officers were trained to look for gender and sexual variance inside immigration detention centers and to regulate a prisoner's most intimate life. The federal INS *Detention Officer Handbook* of 1987 stressed that "violations against the law or public morality, including murder, stealing, forgery, sodomy, bestiality, homosexuality, drug peddling, drunkenness, gambling, and subversion," would result in legal penalties or discipline inside the detention center.[59] In the 1970s detention staff put saltpeter, or potassium nitrate, commonly used in making gunpowder and preserving meat, in the prisoners' food under the impression that it would prevent sexual arousal.[60] The focus on policing gender and sexuality is reiterated throughout the detention handbook. It classified a "sex deviant" as someone who was "sexually inadequate or abnormal," including prisoners who used "abnormal object[s] for sexual satisfaction" or "an abnormal means for sexual satisfaction." The manual defined "sex deviants" as psychologically immature and warned that such "inversions" and "perversions" could be triggered in anyone. Guards were trained to watch out for men who were "extra affectionate, acted in a feminine way or acted out to attract attention." The handbook indicates that this behavior was concerning because it could result in rivalries from same-sex relationships and threaten the work officers put into making the facility a disciplined space. It further stresses that "it [was] the duty of the detention officer not only to protect the detained alien during the period of custody but also to protect the alien from other detained aliens who may damage, weaken, coerce, or otherwise destroy his moral fiber."[61] If a guard suspected that a prisoner fit the definition of a sex deviant, he was required to keep the prisoner under surveillance and segregate him if necessary.

This isolation practice can be viewed as what scholar Brett Story calls "a spatial tactic" used by immigration officials to maintain heteronormative order in a homosocial environment.[62]

INS employees were also charged with making sure that so-called deviant prisoners had limited access throughout the facility. Migrants with "poor cleanliness, skin diseases, unattractive outward disabilities, [and] communicable illnesses," as well as "homosexuals" were not allowed to work in food services.[63] This segregation contributed to the way that detention staff viewed the prisoners. When migrants walked into the detention center, the INS already viewed them as criminal, culpable, and morally deviant, which helped justify INS abuse. One of the main reasons the INS instituted these gender and sex hierarchies was to manage power relations inside the facility.[64]

The mistreatment of the men held inside the El Centro Immigration Detention Center suggests that immigration authorities viewed them as inherently guilty. Archival stories found across the United States and Mexico evidence that a pattern of systematic violence unfolded inside immigration detention centers. On January 31, 1990, Pablo Delgadillo, held at the El Centro Immigration Detention Center, filed a complaint with the Mexican Secretariat of Foreign Affairs against an INS guard by the name of Haley. He claimed that the guard beat him in detention, and he had statements from witnesses backing up his assertion.[65] Delgadillo explained that Haley entered the barracks and violently dragged him outside without an explanation. "He threw me against the wall [and] hurt me so hard that the windows shook and the wall trembled," he stated.[66] Delgadillo reported the incident to the INS supervisor, but his claim was not taken seriously.

Detention staff like Haley trusted that they could get away with the mistreatment of detained migrants.[67] Delgadillo spoke up against the violence he experienced even if he had limited resources. He understood the importance of having witnesses and asked fellow migrants to submit evidence on his behalf. Risking potential retaliation, including deportation, several men came forward and submitted statements verifying Delgadillo's claims. Abelardo Cruz Jimenez wrote, "I saw when the officer asked Delgadillo to get out of the barracks and from the window I saw him grab him from the neck and hit him in the face."[68] Humberto Villaseñor asserted that he heard a body being slammed into the wall when Delgadillo was sent outside.[69] Witness José Sautos Tellez added that he heard Haley talk to two guards about the event. Haley joked about the beating and claimed that next time he would kick Delgadillo in the rear. The men framed their testimony as a struggle between prisoners and INS employees, and their claims exposed the various ways in which gender was performed at El Centro. Scholar Carolyn Newton has argued that "the ideal of dominance and power which are part of the definition of masculinity is not equally available to men. Those at the bottom of the hierarchies have limited access to many masculine statuses, and thus their sense of masculinity may be more precarious."[70] Challenging or "rejecting hegemonic masculinity" by fighting back with their voices instead of their fists, the detained men expressed their frustration at being victimized by exerting alternative forms of masculinity through solidarity and demanding that detention staff be held accountable for their acts.[71]

The Bathroom as a Space of Liminal Punishment

INS guards used specific locations, mainly the facilities' bathrooms, to enact violence against prisoners. Emerging scholarship on the bathroom emphasizes its function as a violent place that "accentuates otherness."[72] Sheila L. Cavanagh argues that the bathroom has been used as "a site for gender-based hostility [and] discipline, anxiety, fear, desire, and unease" through "gendered codes of conduct and [its] hygienic and panoptic design."[73] For example, police have historically used the bathroom as a place to surveil gay men.[74] Hegemonic attitudes about public health, morality, propriety, hygiene, and gender division helped transform the bathroom into a place of difference and policing. Although the information on the sexual orientation of the migrants is not available, the following sources suggest that detention staff imposed their heterosexist views on the incarcerated men.

In ten out of fifteen instances, guards attempted to hide their violent acts inside the facility's bathrooms. Guards and INS officials transformed the bathroom into a liminal space for INS employees within the facility to enact violence on the bodies of the prisoners.[75] Guards often sent migrants inside the bathroom, where they could mistreat them with impunity. Maintaining a degree of secrecy ensured that the perpetrator's actions would have no consequences. Consequently, not only did INS employees live a middle-class life in the Imperial Valley, but they also had access to commit violence with impunity.

On November 29, 1989, two INS guards entered the El Centro Immigration Detention Center and dragged Herbert Ruìz-Pocasangre, a Salvadoran migrant, off of his bed. They yanked his hair and twisted his arms as they took him outside.[76] The guards banged Ruìz-Pocasangre's face against a fence and jabbed their knees against his ribs. INS officer Munoz, known among prisoners for committing such acts, took him into one of the facility's bathrooms and shoved him into a wall.[77] Officer Munoz challenged Ruìz-Pocasangre to fight. Being beaten and broken down was extra humiliating and shameful for the detained men, as it made them seem weak and challenged their masculinity.[78] Guards wanted to elicit a reaction from them to justify their beatings, making the bathroom a space of competing masculinities. For the INS, inflicting violence over detained migrants was viewed as a way of performing masculinity. But the detained migrants often responded in alternative expressions of masculinity by calling out their abuse. For instance, Ruìz-Pocasangre reported the incident to the assistant district director of the INS. The case was then forwarded to the Office of the Inspector General, but officials there concluded that the allegation was "unsubstantiated."[79] The violence committed by INS officials and guards went unchallenged by the government. Sometimes guards used violence as a response to an incident, but, as this case demonstrates, prisoners were also randomly abused. Officer Munoz took Ruìz-Pocasangre to the bathroom to keep the mistreatment secret. The bathroom became a place of violence within the confines of an already punitive facility. As Bernard Tshumi theorizes, "There is no architecture without violence. . . . Architecture is linked to events in the same way that the guard is linked to his prisoner, the police to the criminal, the doctor to the patient, order to chaos."[80] Detention staff used the bathroom as a space to conceal violent acts, even though they operated inside a place that was already deeply invisible.

In 1987 Juan Antonio Ramírez-Cruz left El Salvador for the United States to escape military persecution. Two years later INS agents apprehended Ramírez-Cruz and transported him to El Centro. Ramírez-Cruz waited to hear back on his political asylum application for months.[81] In January 1990 he mocked a guard, and, as a response, he was sent to a bathroom, where guards proceeded to beat him. One of the men wore a black uniform. He belonged to the El Centro Tactical Intervention and Control Unit (TIAC).[82] The TIAC officer locked Ramírez-Cruz inside the bathroom for hours.[83] The guards kept him alone and bloody as a form of punishment. Ramírez-Cruz endured the violence that he hoped to avoid by fleeing El Salvador and migrating to the United States.

A few months later Moris Anibal Gonzàlez Centeno, a twenty-year-old Salvadoran political asylum applicant, arrived late to the daily head count. This angered Officer Espinoza, who demanded that Centeno meet him in the bathroom. Officer Espinoza insulted Centeno and punched him in the mouth, shoulders, ribs, and testicles before throwing him against the wall. This mistreatment left Centeno's face bloody and his arms immobile. When Centeno attempted to report the incident to the facility supervisor, he was accused of fabricating the story and placed in solitary confinement for twenty-four hours.[84] Centeno told the AFSC-USMBP, "There are many like me who are mistreated but they say nothing out of fear of reprisals from guards."[85] These testimonies illustrate the frequency and degree of mistreatment that occurred inside immigration detention centers. While immigration officials routinely claimed that detention was not intended to be punitive, these examples demonstrate that those in detention were not listened to. The immigration system does not view migrants as worthy to be heard.[86] The INS defined immigration detention facilities as administrative places necessary to process deportations, yet they also functioned as spaces entrenched with punitive violence.

INS employees found various ways to harass prisoners. When they found out that Rigoberto Cabezas, a Nicaraguan migrant, was speaking with an immigrant rights attorney, they locked him inside a bathroom. They accused Cabezas of being a troublemaker and repeatedly punched him in the stomach. He testified: "They tried to provoke me [by saying] 'Come on . . . hit me.' I believe [the officer] was punching me in soft spots as to not leave bruises. He continued to punch me several times more when I suddenly slipped on some water and fell on the floor. He left me on the floor."[87] Cabezas's testimony illustrates how racial and gender regimes shaped detention conditions. Guards believed that real men fought back when provoked. Weak men avoided violence. In other words, the testimony of these men illustrates the gendered nature of the state, as enacted by detention staff. Violence was used to cause fear and obedience inside detention centers regularly.[88] The bodies of detained brown men inhabited a space of continued violence. These incidents were not new to migrants, as many of the men who ended up at El Centro had already experienced the violence of the U.S. empire.[89] They waited inside detention centers, hoping to avoid deportation, yet the price they paid was marred with brutality that was inflicted on them with impunity. The detention bathroom could have evoked a feeling of privacy and protection for the detained migrants, but the guards transformed this place into a space of vulnerability, where those confined were exposed to secret violence and pain. The detention bathrooms were places with no cameras to document and evidence abuse; they were a display of liminal punishment.

Continued Violence

INS employees frequently targeted prisoners who expressed dissent inside detention centers.[90] On December 12, 1989, six Salvadorans and two Guatemalan protesters participated in a hunger strike. They protested their pending deportation and argued that they would be persecuted if returned to Central America.[91] Guards verbally and physically harassed the strikers. Officer Cox took Carlos Morales Jordan, a thirty-two-year-old Guatemalan, into a bathroom and proceeded to beat him. The man was beaten so badly that he was sent to the El Centro Regional Medical Center after having a seizure. Carmen Mejía-King filed a report with Assistant Officer Hector Nájera, but in the end no one was suspended, fired, or prosecuted.[92] Instead, the INS relocated some of the hunger strikers to Florence, Arizona.[93]

Most of the prisoners had come to the United States to escape war, including torture and death, yet faced similar cruelties inside U.S. immigration detention centers. Salvadorans encountered security forces and an army that frequently targeted, tortured, and imprisoned presumed political dissenters. The torture they experienced included beatings, water immersion, electric shock, burns, sexual violations, threats, and isolation.[94] They continued to face a type of torture when they migrated to the United States. Being abused in Central America looked eerily similar to life inside a U.S. detention center.

INS officers harmed prisoners with frequency and impunity. After 1986 the INS gained more resources to police migration, and as government legislation emphasized the criminalization of migrants, violence became a normalized part of everyday life inside detention centers. Federal immigration detention center policies reveal that the violence the men and boys experienced inside the El Centro Immigration Detention Center and ECI was not the result of a broken system or unfortunate exceptions but that the centers were created to enforce immigration law through discipline and punishment. Migrants experienced brutality regardless of their age. The lives of children were not respected or treated with care and dignity, because brown boys were viewed and treated without worth. They were treated the same as the adult men held at the El Centro Immigration Detention Center. The violence the state exerted was also shaped by hegemonic notions of masculinity, as exemplified by the actions of the detention guards. Yet migrants responded to this abuse by expressing alternative masculinities that included being vulnerable, showing solidarity toward fellow prisoners, and making claims on the state.

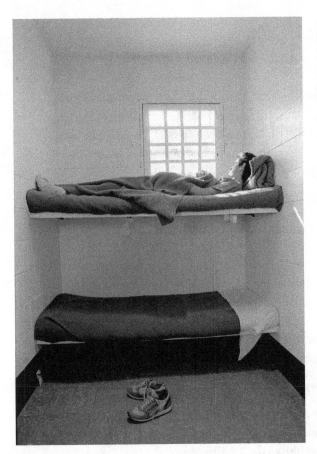

FIGURE 11 A cell at the El Centro Immigration Detention Center, 1985 (photo by Robert Gumpert). Robert Gumpert Photograph Archive, The Bancroft Library, University of California, Berkeley (BANC PIC 2016.033). Used by permission of Robert Gumpert.

As shown by what occurred inside the El Centro Immigration Detention Center bathrooms and the punishment room at ECI, violence was built into the fundamental definition of migrant detention. Although unpalatable, this structural understanding of the functions of detention makes activists' struggles to abolish migrant prisons more meaningful and pressing. The final chapter explores the ultimate loss in this system: migrant death.

CHAPTER SEVEN

Migrant Deaths and Unmarked Graves

> Finally, the complete destruction of a corpse constitutes the most complex and durable form of necroviolence humans have yet invented. The lack of a body prevents a "proper" burial for the dead, but also allows the perpetrators of violence plausible deniability.
>
> —JASON DE LÉON, 2015

On July 21, 1983, immigration agents apprehended Alfredo Serrano Martínez at a Border Patrol checkpoint in San Clemente, California. They transported him 165 miles southwest to the El Centro Immigration Detention Center. Three days later an official informed Martínez's family of his release. But the INS official followed up the next day and told them that Martínez had hung himself. Shortly before Martínez committed suicide, guards injected him with a sedative.[1] Fourteen days after Border Patrol agents apprehended Alfredo Martínez, they detained a man by the name of Fidencio Martínez traveling on a Greyhound bus to the same checkpoint. They removed him from the bus and asked that he sign a voluntary departure form. When Martínez refused, the agents took him inside a restroom, where they proceeded to beat and torture him.[2] They hurt him to the point that an ambulance had to transport him to the Tri-City Hospital.

Tragic incidents such as these permeate the history of immigration enforcement. Examples of injury, declining health, and death exist at the hundreds of places migrants are detained. As the history of detention in El Centro shows, the immigration detention center has always been a place of state violence, surveillance, and policing. By 1994 the INS operated nine Service Processing Centers, contracted out six facilities with private corporations, held about six hundred thousand people in local and state jails, operated a joint criminal alien contract facility with the Bureau of Prisons, and held migrants with mental health conditions at a Public Health Service hospital.[3] The number of people caught within this system grew at an unprecedented rate. As government officials thought of ways to detain more people at a cheaper cost, migrants were figured into their equations only as numbers and not as people, further rendering them disposable.

Between 2003 and 2017 Immigration and Customs Enforcement (ICE) officials documented 172 in-custody deaths, including 21 suicides, but, as the preceding cases show, these figures are misleading, as data for migrant death decades past does not exist.[4] Antimigrant violence has been an integral part of controlling migration to the United States. The following examples of migrant suffering occurred within a larger context of xenophobia and anti-immigrant policies.[5] This chapter shows the prevalence of migrant death between 1994 and 2018 and that such losses could have been avoided if not for punitive government policies. Death and injury occurred while crossing the border, during apprehension, in detention, or once deported and within the context of a larger system based on inhumane conditions and neglect.

The Crossing

Mexican migration to the United States increased during the 1990s with the passage of the North American Free Trade Agreement (NAFTA), an agreement signed by leaders in Canada, the United States, and Mexico, effective on January 1, 1994.[6] The goals of this trade deal were to end tariffs and trade restrictions and improve business between the three countries. Yet NAFTA led to the privatization of Mexico's collective farms, which displaced rural populations and forced many to migrate north.[7] NAFTA provided protections to corporations across national borders at the same time that the INS surveilled people attempting to cross these same places. As scholar Peter Andreas argues, NAFTA contained no regulations addressing migrant labor, which resulted in a "borderless economy and a barricaded border."[8]

Within a context of heightened anti-immigrant rhetoric and debates over the passage of California's Proposition 187, which would prevent undocumented migrants from receiving social services, the INS amplified the militarization of the U.S.-Mexico border. Migrant crossings became more difficult and dangerous throughout the 1990s.[9] In 1994 the Clinton administration implemented Operation Gatekeeper, a measure aimed to reduce the number of unauthorized border crossings near the San Diego region and modeled after Operation Hold the Line, started in El Paso, Texas, a year prior. Gatekeeper called for increasing the number of Border Patrol agents, doubling the INS budget to $800 million, and constructing more fences believed to deter crossings.[10] The installation of new fencing and sensors along the border made crossing it more difficult, but it did not reduce migration. Instead, migrants chose entry points farther east, in more isolated and mountainous regions. This shift resulted in more deaths due to the terrain and to conditions such as hypothermia. In 1994 "fewer than 30 migrants died along the border," but "by 1998 the numbers had risen to 147" and to "477 by 2012."[11]

Border Patrol violence against migrants escalated along the U.S.-Mexico border. Deported migrants spoke out against "border justice" inflicted by agents who went out of their way to chase them.[12] This included enduring verbal harassment and being kicked, stepped on, shoved, and hit with agents' fists, flashlights, and billy clubs. Often Border Patrol agents saw the injuries they caused or the results of the migrants' treacherous journey north, and they neglected to provide aid or care. On October 8, 1994, a deported migrant living in Tijuana reported that when he attempted to cross, he saw a Border Patrol officer on horseback chase a woman while she was holding a child. "He nearly trampled them," he said.[13] As a result, the women's leg was cut by the hoof of the horse.

After the passage of Operation Gatekeeper, the number of dead bodies found throughout the deserts and mountains along the U.S.-Mexico border increased. Between 1994 and 2017 more than eleven thousand migrants perished while trying to cross.[14] Operation Gatekeeper increased migrant reliance and dependence on coyotes, or smugglers, who "underplay[ed] [the] dangers [of crossing the border] when they ma[de] their pitch to the migrants," such as detailing a journey that would take up to four days across rough terrain and in extreme climate conditions.[15] If migrants fell behind the group, coyotes often left them. In 1995 Terrace Park Cemetery in Holtville, California, became a burial place for hundreds of nameless migrants.

The cemetery, which opened in the 1930s, lies eleven miles east of the El Centro Immigration Detention Center. Holtville is a small town with about six thousand residents.[16] Most of the migrants' bodies brought here died from thirst or heat-related conditions or drowned in the All-American Canal while attempting to cross the U.S.-Mexico border. Deterrence was the goal of Operation Gatekeeper, but rather than reduce migration, it increased migrant death. A Border Patrol memo from 1994 reads, "Illegal entrants crossing through remote, uninhabited expanses of land and sea along the border can find themselves in mortal danger. . . . The prediction is that with traditional routes disrupted, illegal traffic will be deterred, or forced over more hostile terrain, less suited for crossing."[17] If death was the goal, then this policy was successful. In 1998 alone twenty-one migrants died from hypothermia in the Tecate Mountains and Mount Laguna, forty-six died from heat stress near the Salton Sea, and fifty-two drowned in the All-American Canal.[18]

In 2009 the dirt lot behind Terrace Park Cemetery held 280 migrants whose families could not pay for a gravesite and 240 migrants whom the coroner could not identify.[19] Visitors to the cemetery pointed out the sharp difference between the treatment of migrants with documents and those without. The burial sites of anonymous migrants include a brick with the words "John Doe," "Jane Doe," or "Baby Doe." In 2009 the last migrant was buried there.[20] Since then unidentified bodies have been cremated and their ashes scattered at sea, to save the county $555 per person.[21] Immigrant rights activists have argued that cremation is disrespectful because the majority of the dead were Catholic, a religion that frowns on such a practice. Groups such as Border Angels, a nonprofit organization that advocates for migrant human rights, pointed out that cremation inhibits future DNA testing of the yet unidentified bodies. Enrique Marones, founder and director of Border Angels, said, "Even in death they are marginalized."[22] Members of Border Angels and volunteers visit the unmarked migrant graves. Besides coordinating religious services, they have attempted to bring dignity to the migrants by placing wooden crosses with the words "Not Forgotten" on the burial sites.[23]

Although we have a sense of migrant death, it is harder to comprehend migrant injury. Migrant testimonies suggest that Border Patrol agents were often negligent when encountering migrants. As the following example shows, migrants did not always die, but they were often confronted with life-threatening hazards. Esther Morales migrated from Oaxaca, Mexico, to the United States in 1989. Throughout the 1990s she crossed back and forth, and although these crossings were not easy, she was able to avoid serious repercussions.[24] But in 2008 ICE agents deported her to Mexico after she served five years at the California Rehabilitation Center in Norco and the Valley State Prison for Women in Chowchilla, California.

During an attempt to reunite with her daughter Elsa in September 2008, Esther came across a swamp. She got stuck and thought she was going to die. Immigration agents who had spotted her watched her struggle from a distance.[25] They pulled her out as she was moments away from drowning. When they dragged her out by using a log, Morales was saturated with mud and covered in green critters.[26] The Border Patrol agents took her to a hospital. Morales felt ill and had a fever due to the vaginal infection she developed while absorbing the muddied water. She was then transferred to the privately run Western Region Detention Facility in San Diego, California. During her six-month stay, fellow prisoners spread rumors that she had been hospitalized because she had contracted a disease. Although doctors had given her medication, the infection did not go away. They concluded that it was best to burn and remove her clitoris. Morales was held at a private facility, but migrants faced similar conditions whether they spent months or a few hours inside a federal or private detention center.

Detention

Overcrowding is a frequent complaint of people held at short-term migrant holding facilities near the U.S.-Mexico border. Migrants mention having to sit on the floor next to piles of trash. On occasion, guards blasted the air conditioner and limited the number of blankets allocated to prisoners. A migrant disclosed that when he was in INS custody, detention staff forced him to take off his clothes and stand under the air vent.[27] They proceeded to mock him as he shivered in place. Immigration employees routinely called migrants offensive names, from *cabrones* (shitheads) to *pinches putos* (fucking sons of whores). Often, they also used physical force as a form of amusement. ICE guards woke up prisoners with kicks. One migrant declared, "Patean y pegan por gusto [they kick and hit for the fun of it]."[28] Some INS officers denied detained migrants access to basic resources such as water. The only source of water inside short-term detention cells came from the hand-washing sinks, which had a strange odor. Two women testified that when they requested water, the agent said, "We are not running a restaurant."[29]

In 1996 the El Centro Immigration Detention Center was overcrowded with migrants from Mexico, Central America, South America, the Caribbean, and Southeast Asia.[30] Overcapacity resulted in amplified tensions.[31] On one March night in 1998, guards stormed into one of the sleeping quarters to search for drugs. A Jordanian prisoner recalled, "When they do a search, we lose legal paperwork, pictures of our families, phone books. They throw them in the trash."[32] One of the migrants had enough that night. The INS responded to his protest with quick and militant action. A group of protesters refused to step out of the barracks, prompting INS officials to call in the tactical intervention team. Dressed in black and equipped with riot helmets, ski masks, pepper spray, billy clubs, and guns with wooden bullets, they closed in on the prisoners.

When FBI crisis negotiators arrived to deescalate the situation, they wrote down the strikers' grievances and assured them they would investigate further. Yet the FBI did not follow up, as the detained men made clear during a hunger strike started to protest the lack of response. The men wrote a memo addressed to "El Centro INS Detention Staff / and Media TV" from "The Whole Detention Camp." It reads, "The officers dressed in army fatigues . . . along with 3-feet wide batons . . . indiscriminately came in numbers of dozens and started hitting inmates in this facility in the face, head, and body . . . without any type of justification." The men ended the memo by inquiring why the FBI did not conduct a proper investigation into the incident.[33] This event reveals how quickly the INS attempted to repress dissent inside detention facilities, but it also highlights that immigration officials neglected to address protester grievances.

Death also lingered inside detention centers. In May 2007 immigration agents arrested twenty-three-year-old Victoria Arellano during a routine traffic stop. They sent Arellano, a transgender Mexican migrant, to the ICE Detention Center in San Pedro, California. During her initial intake, Arellano informed the staff that she had AIDS and would need access to medication. The clinical director of the facility did not allow her to get lab work done and refused to prescribe medication for an entire month, claiming that there was a prohibition on lab tests for thirty days, which was "a violation of ICE medical guidelines and medical ethics."[34]

Despite knowing the importance of medication in helping to prevent opportunistic infection for people diagnosed with HIV and AIDS, medical staff did not make an exception. Arellano's health worsened. She became weak and complained about a cough and fever. Within two months blood appeared in her vomit and urine. Yet medical personnel continued to ignore her and suggested she take Tylenol and drink lots of water along with the antibiotics they prescribed. Arellano died of meningitis while in ICE custody on July 20, 2007. The very next year ICE reported that denying detained migrants' treatment authorization requests saved them $129,713.62 on HIV-related treatments.[35] Detained migrants who were HIV-positive faced similar situations at places such as the Krome detention facility in Miami, Florida. Migrant deaths, including suicides, occurred within an environment that bred state-sanctioned violence.

On April 28, 2013, Elsa Guadalupe-Gonzales, a twenty-four-year-old Guatemalan migrant, hung herself in a cell at the Eloy Detention Center in Arizona. The Corrections Corporation of America–operated facility had opened in 1994. About a month before committing suicide, Guadalupe-Gonzales entered the United States near Sasabe, Arizona, after which Border Patrol agents apprehended her. They transferred her to the Eloy facility on March 20, 2013, where they assigned her to the Bravo housing unit for women, cell 206. During the initial processing, immigration officers allowed Guadalupe-Gonzales to keep her shoes, which included laces. Despite the nurse's report that claimed she was in good health and did not have any mental health problems, various prisoners thought otherwise.[36]

ICE officials scheduled the removal of Guadalupe-Gonzales for April 2, and, to avoid deportation, she applied for asylum. On April 26 Guadalupe-

Gonzales participated in a fifty-minute credible fear interview as part of her asylum application. During the meeting, she disclosed that her family "was involved in a violent property dispute in Guatemala, which caused her to fear for her life." Prisoners reported that Guadalupe-Gonzales had very mixed feelings on that day. She was ecstatic because ICE was to release her husband from the Florence Correctional Facility but also troubled after the interview. One of the women she confided in reported that Guadalupe-Gonzales was afraid of deportation and also worried that, if given the choice, she would not be able to afford bail. She also missed her son, who lived in Guatemala. After Guadalupe-Gonzales's death, several prisoners revealed that they had told her that ICE would deport her regardless of how well her credible fear interview had gone.[37] This demonstrates the dangers of making migrants recount their traumatic experiences as part of the asylum process.

On the day that Guadalupe-Gonzales took her own life, her sadness was clear. She skipped breakfast and morning recreation. During lunch, she did not eat. She told a fellow prisoner this was her last meal. After lunch, the officer in charge asked her why she was washing her shoelaces. Guadalupe-Gonzales said they were dirty, and she proceeded to clean them. During dinner, Guadalupe-Gonzales told the officer in charge that she was going to skip the meal. She stayed in her cell with the door locked, as was protocol. After dinner one of the detained women approached cell 206 and proceeded to scream. The officer in charge ran to the cell, where she found Guadalupe-Gonzales hanging from the bunk bed by a pair of shoelaces. By the time the officer untied her and lowered her body, Guadalupe-Gonzales did not have a pulse. The paramedics arrived at 5:45 p.m. but were unable to revive her. They declared Elsa Guadalupe-Gonzales dead twenty-one minutes later. The acting field office director of the Phoenix Enforcement and Removal Operations (ERO) mailed her husband a letter informing him of her death four days later.[38]

Removal

The activism and advocacy of immigration lawyer Claudia E. Smith illuminate how difficult crossing the U.S.-Mexico border became during the 1990s. Shortly after the passage of Operation Gatekeeper, Smith and Roberto Martínez, director of the American Friends Service Committee's U.S.-Mexico Border Program, traveled to immigration checkpoints in San Ysidro, Otay, and Mexicali, Mexico, to interview migrants released from

INS custody. They wrote, "Everywhere we heard the same litany of complaints. All too often the interview ended with: 'nos tratan como perros' [they treat us like dogs]."[39] Mistreatments included being transported in handcuffs and chains despite having no criminal record and denied food and water while en route to the border. Smith and Martínez also found that after 1994 many immigration agents started to separate family members by busing them to different locations.[40]

On February 23, 1995, Smith interviewed people on bus number 2005 in Mexicali, Mexico. The bus contained thirty-eight men whom the INS had picked up in Stockton, Fresno, Bakersfield, and Los Angles, California. Several of the men carried gallons of water that they purchased along the way because the INS did not provide them with any.[41] On March 22, 1995, Border Patrol officers apprehended Antonio Gomez in Stockton.[42] A few days before his apprehension, medical personnel treated Gomez for a gunshot wound in his torso. Gomez was still in pain on that day, and he needed frequent bandage changes. Yet the Border Patrol agents on duty refused to provide him with a clean dressing and painkillers. The driver allowed Gomez to buy aspirin in Chowchilla, but only after several of the men on the bus demanded it.[43] By the time Gomez reached Mexico, his bandage was soiled, and he needed medical attention.

After a year of advocacy from immigration lawyers such as Smith, the INS created the Western Regional Detention and Deportation Transportation System Plan. The guidelines attempt to address what the INS considered oversights. The plan was written to clarify and create new policies about the transportation of migrants in INS custody. The document emphasizes the importance of "protecting the lives, safety and welfare of our officers, the general public, and those in INS custody." The guidelines include requiring drivers to complete a bus training program, where they learned responsibilities such as inspecting the vehicles, ensuring prisoners were transported safely, operating vehicles prudently, obeying traffic laws, and protecting the vehicles and occupants. The plan states that migrants should be treated humanely and safely but also specifies that security is a top priority. For instance, in regard to seating assignments, the document indicates that "restraining equipment [would] be utilized on any person identified as a high-security risk." Drivers were encouraged to carry extra pairs of handcuffs, flex-cuffs, cutters, batons, pepper spray, and a Taser. These guidelines verify that INS employees had not always followed policy, as "detainees with identified medical problems [should have been] situated in areas that accommodate[d] their medical conditions" or provided with alternative transportation arrangements.[44] Last, INS policy required drivers to provide migrants with meals and plenty of water during all bus transfers, as well as snacks if they were held longer than six hours.

Six months after the plan was published, Smith found that the rules continued to be ignored. Bus drivers often transported migrants in unsafe conditions. Prisoners complained of being forced to sit three to a seat or to stand. Some drivers drove so recklessly that deportees arrived in Mexico covered in bruises after being thrown around.[45] On the weekend of the Fourth of July 1997, Smith interviewed migrants in Mexicali. Despite the summer heat, Border Patrol agents did not provide the migrants with water. She also witnessed that "109 people got off an INS bus with a maximum passenger capacity of 64."[46] These violations were not simply difficult to enforce. Deep-rooted racist ideas about migrants' lack of worth and value shaped how INS agents treated them.

These views were revealed when Smith started receiving hate mail for her activism. An anonymous Border Patrol agent wrote, "I was so repulsed at your sympathetic liberal, multi-culturalist, anti-American hogwash hatched in hell" toward "dishonest, disgusting, filthy, ignorant, racist, ungrateful, vile, violent people internationally recognized as Mexicans, locally referred to as wets, and, in my occupation, affectionately termed as 'tonks.'" The writer concluded by asking Smith if she inquired whether the deported migrants "[came] over with the intent to commit crimes. Or to fraudulently submit paperwork for the plethora of social hand-outs?"[47] These stereotypes were based on the presumption that Mexican migrants were nonwhite, non-American, and nonlegal and hence undeserving of the privileges that come with such identities and statuses. As Lisa Marie Cacho argues, "Certain bodies and behaviors are made transparently criminal while privileged bodies and their brutal crimes are rendered unrecognizable as criminal or even as violent."[48] Hence, the letter writer viewed migrants as criminals without examining his or her own complicity.

Deportation

The passage of the Antiterrorism and Effective Death Penalty Act (AEDPA) and the Illegal Immigration Reform and Immigrant Responsibility Act (IIRIRA) in 1996 helped to expand immigration control in the United States. IIRIRA mandated that individuals classified as national security risks be detained and called for the apprehension of "criminal aliens," defined as noncitizens guilty of a criminal offense. These offenses included aggravated felonies or criminal convictions with sentences of five years or more, controlled substance violations, drug trafficking, and crimes of moral turpitude.[49] IIRIRA also required the indefinite detention of noncitizens who could not be deported to their home countries. It increased the number of people deemed detainable and deportable by making these laws retroactive.[50] By the year 2000, the number of people held under this policy grew to five thousand nationwide.[51]

AEDPA legalized the detention and deportation of legal permanent residents convicted of a crime, including minor offenses. Daniel Jauregui Mariz was one of the numerous people affected by this new policy. He had lived in the United States since the age of three, and although he was a permanent resident, ICE deported him to Tijuana, Mexico, in 2014 based on his criminal record. Mariz lamented, "All my friends who have been deported have either died or committed suicide because they just can't find a way of life over here."[52] Speaking to the difficulties of being deported and then forced to acclimate to a new and unfamiliar country, Mariz highlights the physiological effects of such a process. In apprehending and deporting people who spent most of their lives in the United States, immigration agents uprooted a new generation of deportees, many of whom faced isolation as a result of these policies.

In 2006 ICE agents deported Emma Sanchez de Paulsen to Tijuana, forcing her to leave her husband and three children in the United States. In 2013 Paulsen's husband was scheduled to undergo open-heart surgery. She requested special permission to visit him in the hospital, but ICE officials rejected her appeal. Her husband added, "Dying, she could come and bury me, but she couldn't come to visit me during a major operation of open heart surgery." Paulsen continued to press immigration authorities for permission to be with her husband. She requested humanitarian aid at the San Ysidro crossing but was told that she could cross only if her husband was dead or a few hours from dying.[53] Paulsen expressed the frustration of being separated from loved ones, particularly when the immigration system did not account for the human experiences of aging and illness.

Jessica Nalbach also discussed the toll that deportation takes on one's mental health. One evening ICE agents showed up at her home and apprehended her husband on the basis that he had a criminal record from ten years prior. Even though he had served time for the crime, immigration agents deported him to Mexico. Nalbach took her two kids and moved to be close to him. Already suffering from postpartum depression, she was extremely frustrated and upset at the circumstances. Within the first six months of trying to make a new life in Mexico, Nalbach attempted suicide three times.[54] Nalbach's distress shows that the effects of policing migration did not end once the migrants were deported.

Deportation might have been the final step for immigration enforcement authorities, but for deported migrants, this was one of several threats. ICE agents deported Gerardo Sánchez Pérez to Tijuana after he had lived in the United States for twelve years. They apprehended him during a work raid and transported him to a short-term detention facility. When Pérez was deported, he lived on the streets because he did not know anyone in Tijuana, and he did not have money or resources. He recounts the tremendous loneliness of being separated from his family in an unfamiliar place. Like many other deportees, Pérez was a casualty of the War on Drugs. In 2017 he was caught in the crossfire of a narco shootout on the streets of Tijuana. Pérez was shot and killed while simply trying to get by working at a homeless shelter.[55] Antimigrant violence continued after immigration agents removed deportable migrants.

Jesús Trevino, a deported migrant living in Tijuana, described the detention and deportation system as an apparatus of death. "It's like sudden death," he said about the apprehension process. "You never imagine that being in the US, this misfortune can happen to you," he clarified. Trevino went on to discuss the weight of deportation by revealing how much solitude he felt. Being confined to a new city and a new country and starting over is not only logistically challenging but connected with feelings of fear, isolation, depression, and precarity. Trevino's contemplation on migration and death illuminates a system created to manage migration even when the cost includes death. Although anti-immigrant violence has deep roots in the United States, the racist and xenophobic discourse of the 1990s shaped the policing of migration. Calls for free trade and nativism resulted in policies such as Operation Gatekeeper, which created an environment that made migrant death probable.

The El Centro Immigration Detention Center would continue to play a large role in the greater system of violence as immigration enforcement until 2014, when its doors officially closed. If the ghosts who have haunted the Imperial Valley for decades are to be vanquished, it is essential that we understand the function of placing migrants inside detention centers. The system cannot be reformed, because violence is at the core of its essence. Confronting the ghost, the dark history of migrant detention in the United States might allow us to imagine and work toward a world without cages.

Conclusion

During the early history of the El Centro Immigration Detention Camp, detained migrants constantly escaped from the facility to flee a system of exploitation and forced labor. By the 1970s immigration officials transformed the camp into a service processing center. The history of detention in the Imperial Valley changed over time, especially as government funding and resources increased, but contestations between detained migrants and INS/ICE employees remained constant. The stories I highlight throughout this study expose how detained migrants organized against their incarceration and challenged detention conditions. They came together to make claims on the state throughout various decades and across nationalities.

Historicizing immigration detention reveals its function and consequences. Immigration officials increasingly turned to detention as a form of regulating and deterring future unauthorized migration but also as a form of punishing people awaiting a deportation hearing. Detention was not just a step toward deportation but a significant site of exploitation, discipline, and abuse. Some of the consequences of this system included the separation of families, the racial marking of Latin American migrants as inherently criminal and subversive, and the rise of a profitable system for corporations.

The El Centro Immigration Detention Center was operational throughout eight decades, and although migrants had attempted to protest its horrid conditions throughout the years, many of the region's residents came to associate the facility as a key place of employment and a way of maintaining a middle-class lifestyle. In 2014 rumors spread that the facility was going to close because it had the "highest capitated rate" or "the highest cost per day per inmate."[1] City council members rationalized that it cost so much to maintain this facility precisely because it was old and outdated. Detention staff worried that closure would result in job loss. For instance, Jaime Platt, an ICE detention officer in El Centro, said, "It's what I know and have done for 15 years."[2] This feeling was so common throughout the Imperial Valley that it resulted in a rally of ICE employees and their supporters in May 2014. They claimed that up to five hundred people could lose their jobs, and children held signs that read, "Our parents need a job."[3] In the end the El Centro Immigration Detention Center was closed, and many employees were not rehired at the Imperial Regional Detention Facility. The reaction of residents is significant, however, because it reveals their personal ties to the facility. Dependent on the larger carceral state, these protesters did not mention the violent treatment that often took place inside the detention center. They separated their need to pay bills, and perhaps their political views on migration, from their complicity in the larger detention and deportation regime. This estrangement is part of the larger uncanny feeling that envelops the Imperial Valley and other regions that rely on the carceral state for employment.

When the Imperial Regional Detention Facility opened, changes within detention operations were immediately apparent. Immigration hearings now take place largely over televideo, where asylum seekers are forced to plead their case by recounting their migration experiences to a judge in San Diego over videoconference. Although immigration officials have argued that the use of televideo is an effective and efficient procedure, immigration lawyers have spoken out against the practice. In 2016 ACLU attorney Bardis Vakili asserted that limited physical contact between an immigration judge and a migrant made the process more dehumanizing and affected the mental state of migrants, who were forced to recount traumatic experiences, such as being tortured, to a television screen. Vakili said, "This process takes out humanity [from] the courtroom."[4] It is my hope that the voices I highlight throughout this book provide a deeper context than the one represented on the news or by the protest of ICE officers pleading to keep their jobs.

When I first started to research the El Centro Immigration Detention Center it was still operational. Throughout the course of my investigations on its history, INS officials shut it down. I grappled with its absence. The stories I have documented here might have never been written, leaving a void in the knowledge about the countless people affected. Yet, immigration enforcement is so entrenched in the United States that the operations in El Centro were simply moved 17 miles southeast to Calexico. The experiences of the incarcerated migrants contained in this book are now mirrored throughout the country. Life inside the El Centro Immigration Detention Center points to the continuity of antimigrant violence, that like a ghost lingers on decade after decade.

Notes

Abbreviations in Notes

ACLUNCR	American Civil Liberties Union of Northern California Records, California Historical Society, San Francisco, California
ACLUSCR	American Civil Liberties Union of Southern California Records, Special Collections, Charles E. Young Research Library, University of California, Los Angeles
AFSCUSMBPR	American Friends Service Committee—United States-Mexico Border Program Records, Mandeville Special Collections, University of California, San Diego
AIJR	Americans for Immigrant Justice Records, Rubenstein Library, Duke University, Durham, North Carolina
Baca Papers	Herman Baca Papers, Mandeville Special Collections, University of California, San Diego
CASA	Centro de Acción Social Autónomo Papers, Department of Special Collections, Stanford University, Stanford, California
CSPC	Claudia E. Smith Private Collection
ERHA	El Rescate Historical Archives, Los Angeles, California
Galarza Papers	Ernesto Galarza Papers, Department of Special Collections, Stanford University, Stanford, California
GZPC	Graciela Zavala Private Collection
IPS	Investigaciones Politicas y Sociales, Instituciones Gubernamentales: Epoca Moderna y Contemporanea, Administracion Publica Federal S. XX, Archivo General de la Nación, Mexico City, Mexico
KLHCBPRP	Kelly Lytle Hernández Collection of Border Patrol Research Papers, Chicano Studies Research Center, University of California, Los Angeles
LACPFBC	Los Angeles Committee for the Protection of the Foreign-Born Collection, Southern California Library, Los Angeles, California
LHC	Liberty Hill Collection, Southern California Library, Los Angeles, California
Martínez Papers	Roberto Martínez Papers, Mandeville Special Collections, University of California, San Diego
NCLRR	National Council of La Raza Records, Department of Special Collections, Stanford University, Stanford, California
PAC	Protección y Asuntos Consulares, Secretaría de Relaciones Exteriores, Mexico City, Mexico

RINS	Records of the Immigration and Naturalization Service, Record Group 85, U.S. National Archives, Washington, DC
RRPL	Ronald Reagan Presidential Library, Simi Valley, California
SDUTPC	San Diego Union-Tribune Photograph Collection, San Diego Historical Society, San Diego, California
USCISHL	U.S. Citizenship and Immigration Services Historical Library, Washington DC
USMC	U.S. Marshal Collection, Center for Southwest Research, University of New Mexico, Albuquerque, New Mexico
Yellen Papers	Ben Yellen Papers, Mandeville Special Collections, University of California, San Diego

Prologue

1. Mackey, INS *Annual Report* (1951), 55.

2. Cohen, *Braceros*, 8.

3. Dicochea, "Environmental Injustices," 1, 34, 41.

4. Andres, *Power and Control*, 8, 68, 82, 93; Dicochea, "Environmental Injustices," 37, 39, 42. The Spanish referred to the Imperial Valley as the Colorado Desert; Mendez, "Cheap for Whom?," 33.

5. In 1910 the Imperial Valley was run by three corporations that focused on water, transportation, and land; Mendez, "Cheap for Whom?," 33. Elizabeth Hinton defines the carceral state as composed of law enforcement, judicial employees, and people in charge of handling people convicted of a crime. In this context, immigration agents charged with policing migration also made up part of the carceral state; Hinton, *From the War on Poverty*, 2; CIVIC, "Immigration Detention Map and Statistics."

6. Harrison, INS *Annual Report* (1944).

7. Miller, INS *Annual Report* (1949).

8. Castillo, INS *Annual Report* (1978).

9. Dowling and Inda, *Governing Immigration through Crime*, 16; CIVIC, "Immigration Detention Map and Statistics." Immigration officials used various sites as detention spaces, including service processing centers, local jails, and holding rooms inside Border Patrol sectors. This study focuses on the El Centro Immigration Detention Center because it was one of the most important detention facilities in California, but my sources suggest that detained migrants were mistreated during apprehension and at various sites of detention. See "Deadly Force and Human Rights Violations against Undocumented Workers in California," June–December 1985, box 1, folder 3, AFSCUSMBPR.

10. D. Hernandez, "Detained in Obscurity," 59.

11. Williams, *Ultimate Guide*, 272–73.

12. Elizabeth Lopez, phone interview with author, March 22, 2016.

13. The El Centro Immigration Detention Center only held men; Bureau of Immigration and Customs Enforcement, *Detainee Handbook: Service Processing Center, El Centro, California*, 2003,1. (Hereafter cited as ICE, *Detainee Handbook*.)

14. "Trickle to Flood: Wetback Influx Termed Greatest Peace Invasion," *Imperial Valley Press*, February 18, 1954, 1.

15. ICE official, Guided Tour, El Centro Service Processing Center, El Centro, CA, April 2, 2014; ICE, *Detainee Handbook*, 2.

16. D. Hernandez, "Pursuant to Deportation," 40.

17. ICE, *Detainee Handbook*, 4, 37.

18. ICE, *Detainee Handbook*, 4.

19. ICE official, Guided Tour, El Centro SPC, April 2, 2014.

20. Cortez, "Broken Mirrors," 4, 74–76, 85, 98; C. Garcia Hernandez, "Migra in the Mirror," 891; Correa and Thomas, "Rebirth of the U.S.-Mexico Border," 239–54.

21. Letter from Michael J. Bracken to Ralph Cordova Jr., Development Management Group, Inc., in *Final Report of Findings: Economic Impact Analysis for the El Centro SPC*, April 16, 2014, 2.

22. Gordon, *Ghostly Matters*, 8, 63.

23. Stoler, *Haunted by Empire*, xiii, 2. See also Derrida, *Specters of Marx*.

24. The name of the detention facility was changed to the El Centro Service Processing Center in 1974.

25. Development Management Group, *Final Report of Findings*, 1. Costs included labor (wages and benefits), material purchases (operational consumables and detainee food) and detainee healthcare.

26. Development Management Group, Inc., *Final Report of Findings*, 5. The 21 percent rate is based on data from 2014.

27. Development Management Group, *Final Report of Findings*, 7.

28. Tatiana Sanchez, "ICE Immigration Center in El Centro Closes," *Desert Sun*, October 1, 2014.

29. Development Management Group, *Final Report of Findings*, 5. The $38.5 million contract expired on June 30, 2014.

30. Anonymous immigration attorney, interview with author, January 9, 2016. The term "deportation regime" describes a government system that restricts people's movement and migration; De Genova and Peutz use the term in their book *Deportation Regime*.

Introduction

1. Quoted in Sheryl Gay Stolberg, "Ocasio-Cortez Calls Migrant Detention Centers 'Concentration Camps,' Eliciting Backlash," *New York Times*, June 18, 2019.

2. Agamben, *Homo Sacer*, 171.

3. Dow, *American Gulag*, 9.

4. Coolman et al., *No Refuge Here*, 4.

5. Luis A. Ogilvie, testimony, January 14, 2000, box 4, Krome Affidavits, AIJR, 1.

6. Hartney and Glesmann, *Prison Bed Profiteers*, 7.

7. Florida Immigrant Advocacy Center, "Dying for Decent Care: Bad Medicine in Immigration Custody," February 2009, box 15, AIJR, 13, 18–19.

8. Bureau of Immigration and Customs Enforcement, *Detainee Handbook*, 1. Hereafter cited as ICE, *Detainee Handbook*.

9. Wong, *Rights, Deportation, and Detention*, 2. The concept of an immigration industrial complex is used by Deepa Fernandes, Robert Koulish, and Tom K. Wong.

10. Similar to Dylan Rodriguez, I consider the detention and deportation of migrants to be part of the larger prison regime: "a dynamic state-mediated practice of domination and control, rather than a reified 'institution' or 'apparatus;'" see Rodriguez, *Forced Passages*, 40.

11. ICE, *Detainee Handbook*, 15.

12. Angela Davis and Ruth Wilson Gilmore center intersectionality in their work on incarceration, while earlier scholars such as Michel Foucault failed to do so. See Davis, "Race, Gender, and Prison History"; Gilmore, *Golden Gulag*; and Foucault, *Discipline and Punish*.

13. Juanita Diaz-Cotto defines the state as a "series of administrative, legal, bureaucratic, and coercive organizations and relationships" in *Gender, Ethnicity, and the State*, 1. A limitation of this book is the restricted discussion on sexuality inside detention. While I hoped that my sources would have allowed me to examine this topic in greater detail, I was unable to access historical information on the sexual lives and identities of the people confined in El Centro. This theme is incredibly significant, and it is my hope that future scholarship is able to center this topic.

14. Foucault, *Discipline and Punish*.

15. Overmyer-Velazquez, *Beyond la Frontera*, xxxi; Mae M. Ngai, "How Grandma Got Legal," *Los Angeles Times*, May 16, 2006.

16. Ngai, *Impossible Subjects*, 18.

17. Golash-Boza, *Immigration Nation*, 33; E. Lee, *At America's Gates*, 155. Lee further argues that the Chinese Exclusion Act was justified in the name of national sovereignty and empire building.

18. Kelly Hernández, *City of Inmates*, 64.

19. E. Lee, *At America's Gates*, 47.

20. Kelly Hernández, *City of Inmates*, 78; Cannato, *American Passage*, 62.

21. E. Lee, *At America's Gates*, 75.

22. Kelly Hernández, *Migra!*, 92; Macías-Rojas, *From Deportation to Prison*, 17; Ngai, *Impossible Subjects*, 60; Immigration Act of 1929, March 4, 1929, 45 Stat. 1551, sec. 2, amended June 4, 1929, Pub. L. No. 21, 71st Congress.

23. Kelly Hernández, *City of Inmates*, 138–41; Memo to Carl Robe White from Wagner White, re: Immigration Station Galveston, Texas, October 1, 1931, entry 9, 55599/137A, box 7539, Record Group 85, RINS.

24. Clark, *Deportation of Aliens*; Kanstroom, *Deportation Nation*; Baldarrama and Rodriguez, *Decade of Betrayal*; De Genova and Peutz, *Deportation Regime*; Wilsher, *Immigration Detention*; Kanstroom, *Aftermath*; Golash-Boza, *Deported*.

25. Golash-Boza, *Immigration Nation*; Macías-Rojas, *From Deportation to Prison*; K. Hernández, *City of Inmates*. Others include Escobar, *Captivity beyond Prisons*; D. Hernandez, "Pursuant to Deportation"; Shull, "Nobody Wants These People"; Loyd and Mountz, *Boats, Borders, and Bases*; Dow, *American Gulag*; E. Lee, *Angel Island*; Welch, *Detained*; Wong, *Rights, Deportation, and Detention*; and Hamm, *Abandoned Ones*.

26. Golash-Boza, *Immigration Nation*; Kahn, *Other People's Blood*; Escobar, *Captivity beyond Prisons*; Lindskoog, *Detain and Punish*; Loyd and Mountz, *Boats, Borders, and Bases*.

27. Gordon, *Ghostly Matters*; Cho, *Haunting the Korean Diaspora*; DuComb, *Haunted City*; Young, *Haunting Capital*; Schwab, *Haunting Legacies*; Stoler, *Haunted by Empire*; Freed, *Haunting Encounters*; Derrida, *Specters of Marx*; Epiritu, *Body Counts*.

28. Freed, *Haunting Encounters*, 4, 18, 69–70.

Chapter One

1. Mackey, INS *Annual Report* (1952), 48.

2. Walter I. Welden, Secretary of the Imperial Valley Central Labor Council, to George Meany, President of the American Federation of Labor, telegram, March, 3, 1954, folder 3, box 50, Galarza Papers, 1; R. K. Sessions to George Meany, March 4, 1954, folder 3, box 50, Galarza Papers, 1.

3. Ernesto Galarza to Eugénio V. Pesquería, El Consul de Mexico in Calexico, March 3, 1954, folder 3, box 50, Galarza Papers, 1; Kelly Hernández, *Migra!*, 175.

4. Pesquería to Galarza, re: Detained Mexicans at a border camp in El Centro, March 5, 1954; Galarza to Pesquería, March 3, 1954, both in folder 3, box 50, Galarza Papers, 1; Kelly Hernández, *Migra!*, 175.

5. Childs, *Slaves of the State*, 44.

6. See Lichtenstein, *Twice the Work*; Tibbs, *Black Power*; LeFlouria, *Chained in Silence*; Haley, *No Mercy Here*; Herivel and Wright, *Prison Nation*; and Gilmore, *Golden Gulag*.

7. Childs, *Slaves of the State*, 2; C. Robinson, *Black Marxism*; Kelley, "What Did Cedric Robinson Mean?"; Haley, *No Mercy Here*, 3.

8. Perry M. Oliver from W. H. Wagner, memo, re: "Enlargement of Detention Station at El Centro into a Permanent Facility," October 1, 1945, Subject: El Centro, California Detention Camp, entry 9, 56125/160, box 18527, Record Group 85, RINS, 1; Ivan Williams, Officer in Charge in Santa Fe, N.M., to Los Angeles District Director, memo, December 18, 1944, Subject: El Centro, California Detention Camp, entry 9, 56125/160, box 18527, RINS, 1.

9. McBride, "Internment of *SS Columbus* Crew," 9–10; Reg: Kurt Hincsh, memo for file, January 17, 1940, entry 9, 56035/28A, box 16840, RINS, 6.

10. McBride, *Interned*, 3, 15.

11. Herbert L. Webb to Heinz Schepelmann, memo, January 12, 1940, entry 9, 56035/28A, box 16840, RINS, 2.

12. San Francisco District Director to INS Commissioner Houghteling, memo, January 19, 1940, entry 9, 56035/28A, box 16840, RINS, 1.

13. San Francisco District Director to Houghteling, March 5, 1940, entry 9, 56035/28A, box 16840, RINS, 1.

14. "Nazis at Angel Island Camp," *Examiner*, March 8, 1940, entry 9, 56035/28A, box 16740, RINS, 1.

15. San Francisco District Director to Houghteling, March 5, 1940, entry 9, 56035/28A, box 16840, RINS, 2.

16. Grover C. Wilmoth, El Paso District Director, to William F. Kelly, Chief Supervisor of Border Patrol, memo, November 19, 1941, entry 9, 56035/28A, box 16840, RINS, 1.

17. Reg: Kurt Hincsh, memo for file, January 17, 1940, entry 9, 56035/28A, box 16840, RINS, 4, 3.

18. San Francisco District Director to Houghteling, memo, March 21, 1940, entry 9, 56035/28A, box 16840, RINS, 2.

19. McBride, *Interned*, 24.

20. Eddie E. Adcock to Wilmoth, June 22, 1941, entry 9, 56035/028, pt. 2, box 16741, RINS, 1.

21. Marshall E. Dimock to District Director I. F. Wixon, memo, January 30, 1941, entry 9, 56035/028, pt. 1, box 16740, RINS, 2.

22. Lemuel B. Schofield, Special Assistant to the Attorney General, and Kelly, Chief Supervisor of Border Patrol, to Wilmoth, memo, January 30, 1941, entry 9, 56035/028, pt. 1, box 16740, RINS, 1.

23. McBride, *Interned*, 38.

24. Martínez-Matsuda, "Making the Modern Migrant," 111–12.

25. McBride, *Interned*, 54, 57, 65–66, 68.

26. McBride, "Internment of SS Columbus Crew," 107; McBride, *Interned*, 48.

27. McBride, *Interned*, 74.

28. Adcock to Wilmoth, memo, June 22, 1941, RINS, 1.

29. Schofield to the Attorney General, memo, June 25, 1941, entry 9, 56035/028, pt. 2, box 16741, RINS, 1.

30. Adcock to Wilmoth, memo, June 22, 1941, RINS, 2–3.

31. Wilmoth to the INS Commissioner of Washington, D.C., memo, February 26, 1941, entry 9, 56035/028, pt. 2, box 16741, RINS, 1.

32. Memo from Wilmoth to the Border Patrol Chief Supervisor, February 17, 1942, entry 9, 56035/028, pt. 4, box 16742, RINS, 1.

33. Schofield, INS *Annual Report* (1942), 23.

34. Fox, *America's Invisible Gulag*, 5; Krammer, *Undue Process*, 32.

35. Fox, *America's Invisible Gulag*, xvii–xviii; Earl G. Harrison, Commissioner of the INS, U.S. Department of Justice, 'Civilian Internment: The American Way," Record Group 85, Subject and Policy Files, 1893–1957, entry 9, box 18468, RINS, 2.

36. Commissioner Earl G. Harrison and Kelly to El Paso District Director, memo, December 8, 1942, entry 9, 56035/028, pt. 5, box 16742, RINS, 1.

37. Wilmoth to the INS Commissioner of Washington, D.C., memo, February 9, 1942, entry 9, 56035/028, pt. 4, box 16742, RINS, 1. The men who escaped included Alexander Boettjer, Robert Grobleben, Oswald Henning, Hans Kraus, Herbert Meyer, Willy Michel, Hans Rathje, Otto Rayhofer, and Irwin Siewert.

38. Krammer, *Undue Process*, 54; Akashi, *Betrayed Trust*, 261; McBride, *Interned*, 82; McBride, *Fort Stanton Marine Hospital*, 99; McBride, *Interned*, 94.

39. McBride, "Internment of SS Columbus Crew," 123.

40. McBride, "Internment of SS Columbus Crew," 131.

41. Culley, "Santa Fe Internment Camp," 66; McBride, *Interned*, 82.

42. Kelly, Assistant Commissioner for Alien Control, to Ammon Tenney, Officer in Charge of Fort Stanton, memo, December 19, 1944, entry 9, 56125/133, box 18523, RINS, 1.

43. Akashi, *Betrayed Trust*, 259.

44. Culley, "Santa Fe Internment Camp," 64.

45. "Confinement in the Land of Enchantment: Japanese Americans in New Mexico during World War II." Public Lands History Center, Colorado State University, http://csurams.maps.arcgis.com/apps/MapJournal/index.html?appid=7b919435 f0f848581a7062fcc18a2; For scholarship on the internment of Japanese Americans, see Ng, *Japanese American Internment*; Okihiro, *Encyclopedia*; G. Robinson, *Tragedy of Democracy*; and E. Lee, *Making of Asian American*.

46. Akashi, *Betrayed Trust*, 260.

47. Visit to the Internment Camp, Fort Stanton, Mr. M. Metraux, April 20, 1945, entry 9, 56125/133, box 18523, RINS, 2.

48. Mary E. Parrish, Financial Officer, to Felipe Sanchez y Baca, U.S. Marshal, memo, March 29, 1944, folder 18, box 13, USMC.

49. Tenney to Sanchez y Baca, August 3, 1942, folder 5, box 14, USMC; Tenney to Sanchez y Baca, memo, September 6, 1942, folder 5, box 14, USMC.

50. Payroll, INS, Fort Stanton, New Mexico, December 26, 1943–January 1, 1944; January 10, 1944–January 15, 1944; February 6, 1944–February 12, 1944, all in folder 5, box 31, USMC.

51. Krammer, *Undue Process*, 156.

52. Ivan Williams to Kelly, Assistant Commissioner for Alien Control, memo, September 14, 1945, entry 9, 56035/028, pt. 8, box 16744 RINS, 1.

53. Akashi, *Betrayed Trust*, 273, 277.

54. Office in Charge of Terminal Island to M. H. Scott, Officer in Charge of Fort Stanton Internment Camp, memo, September 20, 1945, entry 9, 56125/133, box 18523, RINS, 1. The men the INS transferred included Sanae Paul Akashi, Heinrich Fassbender, Tsutomi Higashi, Mitsuo Hirashima, Nobuichi Honda, Herbert Jabs, Kintoku Kge, Shigeru Matsuda, Kanji Nomura, Gentaro Ono, Edward Akira Osugi, Kogi Saito, Paul Schmidt, Ernest Arthur Schumacher, Akira Shimizu, Shunichi Shishido, Yuki Tabuchi, Zenshiro Tachibana, Jitsushige Tsusha, Isamu Uchida, and Kenji Wada.

55. Taylor, *Mexican Labor*, 2. Several people contributed, including African Americans, Native Americans, Hindus, Filipinos, Japanese, and Mexicans. Dicochea, "Environmental Injustices," 54.

56. Taylor, *Mexican Labor*, 5, 6, 7.

57. Mendez, "Cheap for Whom?," 39.

58. Taylor, *Mexican Labor*, 8, 17, 18, 26.

59. Thomas C. Brown, Secretary of the International Longshoremen's and Warehousemen's Union to Frances Perkins, Secretary of Labor, memo, May 6, 1940, entry 9, 55854/100-B, box 12982, RINS, 1.

60. Houghteling to Perkins, memo, May 16, 1940, entry 9, 55854/100-B, box 12982, RINS, 1.

61. Regina Raglia, Executive Secretary of the Hollywood League, to Perkins, memo, April 30, 1940, entry 9, 55854/100-B, box 12982, RINS, 1.

62. Houghteling to Perkins, memo, May 16, 1940, entry 9, 55854/100-B, box 12982, RINS, 2; William A. Carmichael, Los Angeles District Director, to INS Commissioner, May 1, 1940, entry 9, 55854/100-B, box 12982, RINS, 1–3.

63. Carmichael to INS Commissioner, May 1, 1940, RINS, 1–3.

64. Richard L. Williams, Patrol Inspector, statement, April 23, 1940, entry 9, 55854/100-B, box 12982, RINS, 1.

65. Mendez, "Cheap for Whom?," 60.

66. H. J. Walls to Perry M. Oliver, memo, re: Expansion El Centro Detention Camp, September 27, 1945, Subject: El Centro, California Detention Camp, entry 9, 56125/160, box 18527, RINS, 2.

67. Carusi, INS *Annual Report* (1945), 27, 46.

68. Albert Del Guercio to the Director of Personnel, memo, August 21, 1945, Subject: El Centro, California Detention Camp, entry 9, 56125/160, box 18527, RINS, 1–2.

69. Harrison, INS *Annual Report* (1944), 20.

70. Del Guercio to the Commissioner, memo, re: Detention Camp at El Centro, CA, January 18, 1945, Subject: El Centro, California Detention Camp, entry 9, 56125/160, box 18527, RINS, 1.

71. To Del Guercio and C. E. Waller, memo, January 11, 1945, General Subject File: Advice of Allotments for Field and Detention Facilities, 56195/878-A, box 19680, RINS, 1; Del Guercio to the Director of Personnel, memo, August 21, 1945, RINS, 1; Report from George L. Townsend and Kelly, Subject: Construction of Border Patrol Sub-District Headquarters Buildings, Los Angeles District, December 15, 1944, 55912/899, RINS, 1; Del Guercio to the Commissioner, memo, January 18, 1945, RINS, 1.

72. Del Guercio to the Commissioner, memo, January 18, 1945, RINS, 1.

73. Kelly to Los Angeles District Director, memo, July 14, 1945, re: El Centro Detention Camp, Subject: El Centro, California Detention Camp, entry 9, 56125/160, box 18527, RINS, 1.

74. Bern Berard to S. A. Diana, memo, re: Recommendation to Close El Centro Detention Facility, November 17, 1949, entry 9, 56251/1, box 20374, RINS, 2.

75. "Roundup of Wet Mexicans No 'Drive in Valley,'" *Imperial Valley Press*, October 11, 1946, 8.

76. Schofield, INS *Annual Report* (1942), 16.

77. Memo to W.F. Kelly, Assistant Commissioner for Alien Control from N. D. Collaer, Chief, Detention and Deportation Sector: El Centro, re: Expansion of Detention Station at El Centro, June 17, 1946, Subject: El Centro, California Detention Camp, entry 9, 56125/160, box 18527, RINS, 1.

78. J. E. Riley to T. B. Shoemaker, memo, re: Confidential Report from the Federal Bureau of Investigation, October 7, 1947, folder 13, box 4, KLHCBPRP, 5. For additional information on the use of detainee labor, see Shoemaker to Carmichael, memo, re: Alleged Irregularities in Operations of Border Patrol in the El Centro Sector, October 15, 1947, folder 13, box 4, KLHCBPRP.

79. Shoemaker to Carmichael, memo, October 15, 1947, folder 13, box 4, KLHCBPRP.

80. Del Guercio to the Director of Personnel, memo, August 21, 1945, RINS, 1.

81. Carusi, INS *Annual Report* (1946), 6.

82. Mr. Lewis to Diana, memo, re: El Centro and Camp Elliott Detention Facilities, October 8, 1948, entry 9, 56251/1, box 20374, RINS, 1.

83. Carmichael to Philadelphia Commissioner, memo, re: Proposed Patrol Unit Office and Living Quarters in Jacumba, Calif., October 14, 1947, entry 9, 56188/47, box 19553, RINS, 1.

84. Carmichael to Philadelphia Commissioner, memo, October 14, 1947, RINS, 1.

85. Report transcribed by Theraon F. Culp, "Camp Elliott," August 25, 1947, folder 13, box 4, KLHCBPRP, 1. For literature on other examples of paternalism, see Soss, Fording, and Schram, *Disciplining the Poor*, and Cashin and Eskew, *Paternalism in a Southern City*.

86. Culp, "Camp Elliott," August 25, 1947, KLHCBPRP, 1.

87. Culp, "Camp Elliott," August 25, 1947, KLHCBPRP, 2, 3.

88. Riley to Shoemaker, memo, October 7, 1947, KLHCBPRP, 1.

89. Theron F. Culp and Richard H. Wells, interview, August 28, 1947, folder 13, box 4, KLHCBPRP, 2.

90. Riley to Shoemaker, memo, October 7, 1947, KLHCBPRP, 2.

91. Culp and Joseph W. Alexander, interview, August 27, 1947, folder 13, box 4, KLHCBPRP, 2, 3.

92. Haley, *No Mercy Here*, 4, 27; Childs, *Slaves of the State*, 25.

93. Riley to Shoemaker, memo, October 7, 1947, KLHCBPRP, 2.

94. Riley to Shoemaker, memo, October 7, 1947, KLHCBPRP, 2.

95. Culp and Charles E. Wilson, interview, August 26, 1947, folder 13, box 4, KLHCBPRP, 5.

96. Riley to Shoemaker, memo, October 7, 1947, KLHCBPRP, 5. For additional information on the use of detainee labor, see Shoemaker to Carmichael, memo, October 15, 1947, KLHCBPRP.

97. Riley to Shoemaker, memo, October 7, 1947, KLHCBPRP, 5.

Chapter Two

1. Ramiro Cortez Martínez, interview with the author, Oakley, CA, April 25, 2015.

2. Martínez, interview with the author, Oakley, CA, April 25, 2015.

3. Cockcroft, *Outlaws in the Promised Land*, 15.

4. Chacon and Davis, *No One Is Illegal*, 78, 140.

5. Bender, *Run for the Border*, 123.

6. Chacon and Davis, *No One Is Illegal*, 140.

7. Galarza, *Strangers in the Fields*, 18.

8. Gonzalez, Price, and Salinas, *Harvest of Loneliness*; Gretchen Laue, interview with the author, El Centro, CA, January 8, 2016; Minan, *Undocumented Lives*, 86.

9. G. C. Wilmoth, El Paso District Director, INS Border Patrol Training School, El Paso, Texas, Lecture on Immigration Border Patrol Officers' Duties and Authority to Act, March 29, 1944, entry 9, 56192/582, box 19647, RINS, 1; Mendez, "Cheap for Whom?"

10. Calavita, *Inside the State*, 28; Cockcroft, *Outlaws in the Promised Land*, 69; Mize and Swords, *Consuming Mexican Labor*, xxii; Mendez, "Cheap for Whom?"

11. Galarza, *Strangers in the Fields*, 27.

12. Chacon and Davis, *No One Is Illegal*, 78, 146; Kelly Hernández, *Migra!*, 113, 135; Ngai, *Impossible Subjects*, 148.

13. Mendez, "Cheap for Whom?,", 103.

14. Kelly Hernández, *Migra!*; Ngai, *Impossible Subjects*, 58.

15. Laue interview.

16. De Genova, *Working the Boundaries*, 8.

17. Mendez, "Cheap for Whom?," 59; Molina, *Fit to Be Citizens*, 58; Flores, *Grounds for Dreaming*, 22.

18. Steve Velásquez, "Isidoro Ramírez," Bracero History Archive, Item No. 142, http://braceroarchive.org/items/show/142 (accessed June 12, 2019).

19. H. Anderson, *Bracero Program in California*, 11.

20. Loza, "Unionizing the Impossible," 23.

21. Flores, "Town Full of Dead Mexicans," 132; Flores, *Grounds for Dreaming*, 53-54.

22. Cohen, *Braceros*, 102.

23. Letter from Hank Anderson to Ernesto Galarza, May 9, 1958, box 17, folder 3, Galarza Papers, 1.

24. Letter from Hank Anderson to Ernesto Galarza, November 18, 1958, box 17, folder 3, Galarza Papers, 2.

25. Quoted in Cohen, *Braceros*, 56.

26. Salinas, *Managed Migrations*, 7.

27. "America's Misplaced Millions: Mexican Worker-Victims of Mass Deportations by US Immigration Authorities," February, 7, 1953, folder 12, box 1, LACPFBC, 2. In 1951 Congress extended the labor program under Public Law 78. The Mexican government had helped to monitor the treatment of Mexican workers in previous years, but after the program became law, the U.S. Department of Labor became responsible for managing all bracero contracts; see Chacon and Davis, *No One Is Illegal*, 142-43.

28. Montejano, *Anglos and Mexicans*, 197.

29. Hank Anderson to Ernesto Galarza, May 9, 1958, 2.

30. Mckiernan-González, *Fevered Measures*, 15.

31. Flores, *Grounds for Dreaming*, 47; Mitchell, *They Saved the Crops*, 84; Cohen, *Braceros*, 96.

32. Velásquez, "Isidoro Ramírez."

33. Mize and Swords, *Consuming Mexican Labor*, 10; Flores, *Grounds for Dreaming*, 46.

34. McCallum, *Military Medicine*, 100.

35. Molina, *Fit to Be Citizens*; Stern, "Buildings, Boundaries, and Blood," 41-81.

36. Kinkela, *DDT and the American Century*, 3, 28.

37. Charles Hillinger, "El Centro Called Home of Voluntary Repatriates," *Los Angeles Times*, August 26, 1959, Box 18, Folder 1, Galarza Papers, 8.

38. Manuel Acosta Meza, *El Imparcial*, May 10, 1948, Tijuana Baja California, translated June 25, 1948, entry 9, 56251/1, box 20374, RINS, 1.

39. Mays, *Women in Early America*, 371.

40. Letter from the District Director of Los Angles, to M. H. Scott, Officer in Charge, Camp Elliott, re: Receiving Aliens: Camp Elliott Detention Facility, June 23, 1948, entry 9, 56251/1, box 20374, RINS, 2.

41. W. A. Carmichael to Immigration Commissioner, memo, re: Processing of Alien Detainees at Camp Elliott Detention Facility, June 29, 1948, entry 9, 56251/1, box 20374, RINS, 1.

42. Letter to the District Director of Los Angeles from M.H. Scott, June 23, 1948, 2.

43. Mendez, "Cheap for Whom?," 97–98.

44. Acting Commissioner to Paul J. Reveley, Division of Mexican Affairs, October 13, 1948, entry 9, 56251/1, box 20374, RINS, 1.

45. Molina, *Fit to Be Citizens*; Mckiernan-González, *Fevered Measures*.

46. David H. Carnahan, Regional Southwest Commissioner, to Frank H. Partridge, Assistant Commissioner of Enforcement, memo, re: Parasitic Infestation: Detention Facilities, March 8, 1957, folder 3, box 6, KLHCBPRP, 1, 2.

47. Partridge to Carnahan, memo, March 12, 1957, KLHCBPRP, 1.

48. "How the Meek Inherit the Earth," June 1, 1959, folder 2, box 1, Yellen Papers, 1.

49. "Newsletter from Dr. Ben Yellen: It Is Not True!," February, 23, 1962, folder 5, box 1, Yellen Papers, 1; Letter to the Human Rights Commission of the United Nations from the Committee for the Protection of Mexican Workers, November 4, 1959, folder 5, box 3, Yellen Papers, 1.

50. H. Anderson, *Bracero Program in California*, 23.

51. Camplin, *Prison Food in America*, 11.

52. Letter to the Human Rights Commission, Yellen Papers, 1.

53. Cohen, *Braceros*, 125; Gamboa, *Bracero Railroaders*, 92.

54. "Newsletter from Dr. Ben Yellen," Yellen Papers, 1.

55. Camplin, *Prison Food in America*, 17.

56. Galarza, *Strangers in the Fields*, 41.

57. "INS Bid, February 1, 1947, El Centro, CA," entry 9, 56125/255, RINS, 1.

58. Letter to the Human Rights Commission, Yellen Papers, 1.

59. Galarza, *Strangers in the Fields*, 37. Two dollars in 1941 was equal to about thirty-five dollars in 2019.

60. Galarza, *Strangers in the Fields*, 22–23, 35.

61. Cohen, *Braceros*, 119.

Chapter Three

1. Albert Del Guercio, Los Angeles District Director, to Philadelphia Commissioner, memo, re: David Calderón-Cisneros, Subject: El Centro, California Detention Camp, June 20, 1945, entry 9, 56125/160, box 18527, RINS, 1; Chief Patrol Inspector of El Centro to Los Angeles District Director, memo, re: Investigation: David Calderón-Cisneros, Subject: El Centro, California Detention Camp, June 14, 1945, entry 9, 56125/160, box 18527, RINS, 1; interview of Leo L. Lewis by Richard Wells, June 22, 1945, 56125/160, box 18527, Record Group 85, entry 9, RINS, 2.

2. Del Guercio to Philadelphia Commissioner, memo, re: David Calderón-Cisneros, June 20, 1945, RINS, 1–2; interview of Leo L. Lewis by Richard Wells, RINS, 1–2; interview of Findlay J. Postles by Richard Wells, 56125/160, box 18527, RINS, 1, 3.

3. "The History of the INS Border Patrol," folder 5, box 6, KLHCBPRP, 3–4.

4. Del Guercio to the Philadelphia Commissioner for Alien Control, memo, re: Security Measures at El Centro Detention Facility to Prevent Escapes, General Subject File: Attempted Escape of Alien Enemies from Detention Camps, May 23, 1945, entry 9, 56125/80A, box 2428, RINS, 1; Del Guercio to the Philadelphia Assistant Commissioner for Alien Control, memo, re: Escape from Detention Facility at El Centro, General Subject File: Attempted Escape of Alien Enemies from Detention Camps, July 20, 1946, entry 9, 56125/80A, box 2428, RINS, 1. The number of detainee escapes from the El Centro Immigration Detention Camp may have been be higher, but this is the number I was able to find in the archives.

5. Chief Patrol Inspectors in El Paso and Alpine, TX, to Senior Patrol Inspector in Charge of Crew at Fort Stanton, NM, memo, Preliminary Plan for Handling Possible Escape of Crewmen, March 29, 1941, 56035/28, pt. 2, box 16741, Record Group 85, entry 9, RINS, 1–3; Memo for Major L. B. Schofield, from Director John Edgar Hoover, February 10, 1942, 56035/28, pt. 4, box 16742, Record Group 85, entry 9, RINS, 2; Memo to Commissioner Harrison, from Wilmoth, November 3, 1942, 56035/28, pt. 4, box 16742, Record Group 85, entry 9, RINS, 2.

6. Memo to District Director of the INS from Ammon M. Tenney, Officer in Charge, November 20, 1942, 56035/28, pt. 4, box 16742, Record Group 85, entry 9, RINS 5; Memo to Commissioner Harrison, from Wilmoth, November 3, 1942, 56035/28, pt. 4, box 16742, Record Group 85, entry 9, RINS, 2.

7. INS, Fort Stanton Hearing, November 6, 1942, 56035/28, pt. 4, box 16742, Record Group 85, entry 9, RINS, 1; Carusi, INS *Annual Report* (1945), 29; 18 U.S. Code § 752, Instigating or assisting escape, https://www.law.cornell.edu/uscode/text/18/752.

8. Carusi, INS *Annual Report* (1945), 30, 29.

9. 18 U.S. Code § 752.

10. Kelly Hernández, "Entangled Bodies and Borders," 78, 97–99, 102–3.

11. Chief Patrol Inspector at El Centro to Del Guercio, memo, re: Escape of Aristeo Castañeda-Agredano, Subject: El Centro, California Detention Camp, June 14, 1945, entry 9, 56125/160, box 18527, RINS, 1; Memo from District Director of Los Angeles to W. F. Kelly, Assistant Commissioner of Alien Control, June 2, 1945, 56125/160, box 18527, Record Group 85, entry 9, RINS, 1.

12. Del Guercio to the Philadelphia Commissioner for Alien Control, memo, re: Escape from El Centro Detention Camp, Subject: El Centro, California Detention Camp, January 29, 1945, entry 9, 56125/160, box 18527, RINS, 1.

13. Del Guercio to the Philadelphia Commissioner, memo, January 29, 1945, 56125/160, box 18527, Record Group 85, entry 9, RINS, 2; Del Guercio to the Philadelphia Commissioner, May 23, 1945, 56125/160, box 18527, Record Group 85, entry 9, RINS, 2.

14. El Centro Chief Patrol Inspector to the Los Angeles District Director, memo, re: Escape: El Centro Detention Camp, Subject: El Centro, California Detention Camp, January 26, 1945, entry 9, 56125/160, box 18527, RINS, 1; Del Guercio to Philadelphia Commissioner, May 23, 1945, RINS, 1.

15. Del Guercio to a Philadelphia Assistant Commissioner for Alien Control, memo, May 6, 1945, entry 9, 56125/160, box 18527, RINS, 2; Philadelphia Commissioner to Del Guercio, memo, re: Escape of Aristeo Castañeda-Agredano, July 19, 1945, Sub-

ject: El Centro, California Detention Camp, entry 9, 56125/160, box 18527, RINS, 1; Del Guercio to Philadelphia Commissioner, RINS, 1; INS Investigation of the Escape of Aurelio Luna-Vertiz, April 19, 1945, Subject: El Centro, California Detention Camp, entry 9, 56125/160, box 18527, RINS, 1. Escapes continued to occur, as evidenced by the escape of Salvador Aguilar-Montanes and Alfonso Hurtado-Velasques on May 11, 1945, and of José Garcia-Vega and José Torres-Valle on May 21, 1945.

16. C. Robinson, *Black Marxism*. For additional scholarship that addresses confinement and escape, see LeFlouria, *Chained in Silence*; Myers, *Race, Labor, and Punishment*; Mancini, *One Dies, Get Another*; and Chavez-Garcia, *States of Delinquency*.

17. C. Robinson, *Futures of Black Radicalism*, 3.

18. Del Guercio to the Philadelphia Commissioner from, memo, May 8, 1945, Attempted Escapes of Aliens, 56125/80a, Record Group 85, entry 9, RINS, 1.

19. Del Guercio to the Philadelphia Commissioner for Alien Control, memo, re: Oscar Bermudez-Fimbres, Escape from Detention Facility at El Centro, General Subject File: Attempted Escape of Alien Enemies from Detention Camps, May 6, 1945, entry 9, 56125/80A, box 2428, RINS, 1; Richard H. Wells to the Chief Patrol Inspector of El Centro and the District Director of Los Angeles, memo, re: Oscar Bermudez-Fimbres, file 1600-1995, General Subject File: Attempted Escape of Alien Enemies from Detention Camps, May 4, 1945, entry 9, 56125/80A, box 2428, RINS, 1; interview of Guard Leland J. Shanks by examining officer Richard H. Wells, at El Centro, CA, May 3, 1945, Attempted Escapes of Aliens, 56125/80a, Record Group 85, entry 9, RINS, 1–4.

20. Chief Patrol Inspector to Los Angeles District Director, memo, April 23, 1945, re: Oscar Bermudez-Fimbres, Attempted Escapes of Aliens, 56125/80a, Record Group 85, entry 9, RINS, 1.

21. Del Guercio to Philadelphia Commissioner, May 6, 1945, RINS, 2.

22. Del Guercio to Philadelphia Commissioner, May 8, 1945, RINS, 2.

23. Del Guercio to Philadelphia Commissioner, May 6, 1945, RINS, 2; Del Guercio to Philadelphia Commissioner, May 23, 1945, RINS, 2.

24. Memo to the Employees at the El Centro Detention Camp and the Chief Patrol Inspector at El Centro from the Assistant Commissioner for Alien Control, re: Instructions to Guards at the El Centro Detention Camp, May 15, 1945, Subject: El Centro, California Detention Camp, entry 9, 56125/160, box 18527, RINS, 1, 2.

25. Memo to the Employees at the El Centro Detention Camp and the Chief Patrol Inspector at El Centro from the Assistant Commissioner for Alien Control, May 15, 1945, RINS, 3.

26. Dubrofsky and Magnet, *Feminist Surveillance Studies*, 7.

27. Andrea Smith, "Not-Seeing," in Dubrofsky and Magnet, *Feminist Surveillance Studies*, 21.

28. Memo to Los Angeles District Director from Chief Patrol Inspector of El Centro, May 19, 1945, 56125/160, box 18527, Record Group 85, entry 9, RINS, 1–2.

29. Memo to W. F. Kelly, Assistant Commissioner for Alien Control, from N. D. Collaer, Detention and Deportation Chief, June 27, 1945, Subject: El Centro, California Detention Camp, entry 9, 56125/160, box 18527, RINS, 1.

30. Memo to W. F. Kelly from N. D. Collaer, Chief Detention and Deportation Section, June 21, 1945, 56125/160, box 18527, Record Group 85, entry 9, RINS, 1.

31. LeFlouria, *Chained in Silence*, 134.

32. Carmichael, Los Angeles District Director, to Washington Commissioner, memo, re: Escape of Andres Silva-Sanchez and Ramon Ochoa-Duran from Detention Facility at El Centro, CA, September 13, 1949, entry 9, 56251/1, box 20374, RINS, 1.

33. Carmichael to Washington Commissioner, September 13, 1949, RINS; interview of James C. Dean by Fred H. Voight, investigating officer, August 21, 1949, 561251/1, box 20374, Record Group 85, entry 9, RINS, 3.

34. Interview between Investigating Officer Fred H. Voight and Respondent George S. Chapman, United States Department of Justice, INS Report of Investigation of Escape of Andres Silva-Sanchez and Ramon Ochoa-Duran, August 21, 1949, entry 9, 56251/1, box 20374, RINS, 6.

35. Carmichael to Washington Commissioner, September 13, 1949, RINS, 2; interview of Jesus Alcala-Camarillo by Patrol Inspector John J. Mitchell, August 22, 1949, 561251/1, box 20374, Record Group 85, entry 9, RINS, 1–3.

36. Memo to Fred H. Voight from Chief Joseph F. Smith, re: Statement of Chief Security Officer Joseph F. Smith, Relative to Facts Surrounding Escape of Ramon Ochoa-Duran and Andres Silva-Sanchez, August 22, 1949, entry 9, 56251/1, box 20374, RINS, 1.

37. Kelly Hernández, "Entangled Bodies and Borders," 135–36.

38. Mackey, INS *Annual Report* (1953), 46–47.

39. Mackey, INS *Annual Report* (1953), 46.

40. U.S. Department of Justice, Immigration and Naturalization Service, *Manual of Instructions for Detention Officers*, 1955), JV 6414DE9m, USCISHL, 1-3, 2-7, 4-4.

41. Manion, *Liberty's Prisoners*, 24; Chavez-Garcia, *States of Delinquency*.

42. Mancini, *One Dies, Get Another*, 65–68; Myers, *Race, Labor, and Punishment*, 28; Haley, *No Mercy Here*, 202–3.

Chapter Four

1. Memo to Washington Commissioner from W. A. Carmichael, re: Mexican Border Situation, October 28, 1949, entry 9, 56251/1, box 20374, RINS, 1; Memo to W. F. Kelly, Assistant Commissioner, from S. A. Diana, re: Recommendations to Close El Centro, November 18, 1949, entry 9, 56251/1, box 20374, RINS, 1; Memo to S. A. Diana from Bern Berard, re: Recommendations to Close El Centro Detention Facility, November 17, 1949, entry 9, 56251/1, box 20374, RINS, 2–3.

2. Memo to Diana from Berard, November 17, 1949, 1. During the 1940s detainees spent as long as forty-five days inside camps, and INS officials hoped that placing migrants closer to an immigration judge might speed up their proceedings.

3. Memo to Washington Commissioner from W. A. Carmichael, re: Mexican Border Situation, 1; Memo to W. F. Kelly from S. A. Diana, re: Camp Elliott Detention Facility, February 3, 1950, entry 9, 56251/1, box 20374, RINS, 1; Memo to W. F. Kelly from S. A. Diana, re: Recommendations to Close El Centro Detention Facility, November 18, 1949, entry 9, 56251/1, box 20374, RINS, 1; Memo to Diana from Berard, November 17, 1949, 3; Carusi, INS *Annual Report* (1947), 20, 28.

4. Memo to Washington Commissioner from H. R. Landon, re: Closing of Detention Camp at El Centro, January 18, 1950, entry 9, 56251/1, box 20374, RINS, 1; Memo to INS Commissioner from H. R. Landon, re: SF Position Description, Camp Elliott, December 23, 1949, entry 9, 56251/1, box 20374, RINS, 1.

5. M. H. Scott, Office in Charge, Camp Elliott, August 25, 1947, box 4, folder 13, KLHCBPRP, 1.

6. Mendez, "Cheap for Whom?," 7, 17.

7. Mackey, INS *Annual Report* (1951), 55.

8. Lindskoog, *Detain and Punish*; Golash-Boza, *Immigration Nation*.

9. Herbert Brownell Jr., Address at Naturalization Ceremonies, New York, November 11, 1954, 5–6.

10. "Reds Pouring into U.S.? Rep McDowell Says They're Streaming in via Mexico," *Washington Daily News*, May 22, 1947, box 50, folder 1, Ernesto Galarza Collection, Stanford Special Collections, 1.

11. "Mexican Airlift Begins from IV: Aliens Being Returned to Mexico by Airlines from Air Stanton," *Imperial Valley Press*, June 1, 1951, box 50, folder 5, Galarza Papers, 1.

12. Report in the *Los Angeles Daily News*, February 19, 1951, box 50, folder 1, Galarza Papers, 1.

13. "U.S. Inaugurates 'Wetback Airlift': Planes Flying Illegal Border-Crossers Deep into Mexico to Stem Alien Influx," *San Diego Union*, June 2, 1951, box 50, folder 5, Ernesto Galarza Papers, 1.

14. Mackey, INS *Annual Report* (1951), 1–2, 39–40.

15. Mackey, INS *Annual Report* (1951), 35.

16. Cohen, *Braceros*, 30.

17. Chacon and Davis, *No One Is Illegal*, 194.

18. Mackey, INS *Annual Report* (1953), 1.

19. Mackey, INS *Annual Report* (1950), 3.

20. Mackey, INS *Annual Report* (1953), 40.

21. Mackey, INS *Annual Report* (1953), 52; Swing, INS *Annual Report* (1954), 30.

22. Quoted in "Trickle to Flood: Wetback Influx Termed Greatest Peace Invasion," *Imperial Valley Press*, February 18, 1954, 1.

23. "Trickle to Flood," 1.

24. "Trickle to Flood," 1.

25. "Trickle to Flood," 1.

26. Patricia Morgan, "Shame of a Nation: A Documented Story of Police-State Terror against Mexican Americans in the U.S.A.," 3, Los Angeles Committee for Protection of Foreign Born, September 1954, box 24, folder 8, ACLUSCR; Mize and Swords, *Consuming Mexican Labor*, 25.

27. "Trickle to Flood."

28. "Valley Ready for History's Greatest Wetback Roundup: Border Task Force Starts Next Week," *Imperial Valley Press*, June 11, 1954.

29. "Station History," Sector Portfolio, Border Patrol Museum, 1, box 6, folder 7, KLHCBPRP; "First Day's Alien Roundup Tops 2 Thousand Captures," *Imperial Valley Press*, June 18, 1954; Swing, INS *Annual Report* (1954), 31.

30. Swing, INS *Annual Report* (1954), 36.

31. Kelly Hernández, "Crimes and Consequences," 421.

32. "Mexican Aliens Sentenced for Grapefruit Theft," *Imperial Valley Press*, May 11, 1954.

33. "Calexico Crime Rate Vanishes in 'Wet' Roundup," *Imperial Valley Press: Morning Post*, June 15, 1954.

34. "Camp for Wetbacks Set at Brownsville," *Corpus Christi Caller-Times*, June 17, 1952, 9.

35. "Camp for Wetbacks Set at Brownsville," 9.

36. "Camp for Wetbacks Set at Brownsville," 9.

37. Mackey, INS *Annual Report* (1953), 48.

38. Memo for File, May 7, 1953, box 6, folder 3, KLHCBPRP, 2.

39. Anexo 1, May 27, 1953, PAC T27-29 Campo de Detencion, PAC, 1; Raymond Brooks, "Wetback Death March Policy Bared by Paper," *American-Statesman*, June 7, 1953, PAC T27-29 Campo de Detencion, PAC, 1.

40. Memo to Consul General de Mexico from Secretaria de Relaciones Exteriores, Lic. José T. Delgado, August 11, 1955, re: Reclamacion ante Gobierno de Estados Unidos, III-2228-2 Part 1, Muerte de Resendiz Casareo, PAC, 1; Memo to Consul General de Mexico from Secretaria de Relaciones Exteriores, Embajador Manuel Tello, March 7, 1956, re: Caso de trabajador Cesareo Resendez, III-2228-2 Part 1, Muerte de Resendiz Casareo, PAC, 1; Memo from Secretaria de Relaciones Exteriores, Direccion General de Relaciones Exteriores, re: Caso de Cesareo Resendez, August 17, 1954, III-2228-2 Part 1, Muerte de Resendiz Casareo, PAC.

41. Letter from the Secretary of the State to Don Manual Tello, Ambassador of Mexico, February 24, 1956, III-2228-2 Part 1, Muerte de Resendiz Casareo, PAC, 1.

42. Memo to Frank H. Partridge, Special Assistant to the Commissioner, from Einar A. Wahl, Chief Border Patrol Officer, re: Operation of McAllen Detention Facility, January 3, 1955, box 4, folder 11, KLHCBPRP, 1–2.

43. Memo to San Antonio District Director from SW Region Commissioner, re: Inspection Report: San Antonio District, November 15, 1955, box 4, folder 11, KLHCBPRP, 1. One hundred fifty women and children were held at the McAllen Camp at this time.

44. Mackey, INS *Annual Report* (1951), 56.

45. "Behind Barbed Wire: Some Facts on an American Concentration Camp," box 7, folder, 8, LACPFBC, 1–2, 4–5.

46. Testimony of James V. Bennett before the Subcommittee on Appropriations of the U.S. House of Representatives, June 15, 1954, box 3, folder, 18, LACPFBC, 1, 6.

47. Memo to Assistant Commissioner of Enforcement Division to David H Carnahan, Regional Commissioner, re: In-Service Training, June 5, 1956, box 6, folder 1, KLHCBPRP, 1–2.

48. Memo to T. L. Ball, Acting Chief Patrol Inspector, from Joseph G. Maskornick, Patrol Inspector, re: Apprehension of false claims to citizenship, May 15, 1956, box 6, folder 1, KLHCBPRP, 1; Memo to Lt. General J. M. Swing, Commissioner, from David H. Carnahan, Regional Commissioner, re: Incident at Harlingen, TX, June 5, 1956, box 6, folder 1, KLHCBPRP, 1.

49. Memo to Lt. General Swing from Carnahan,, re: Incident at Harlingen, TX, June 5, 1956, 1.

50. U.S. Department of Justice, INS, "Service Processing Center Design Guide," November 17, 1992, JV6414.DE9F21d, 20, USCISHL.

51. Castillo, INS *Annual Report* (1978), 31; Chapman, "Illegal Aliens," 15; De Genova, "Illegal Production," in Dowling and Inda, *Governing Immigration through Crime*, 49; Massey, "Racial Formation," 12–26.

52. Massey and Pren, "Unintended Consequences," 1–29.

53. Garcia, *Seeking Refuge*, 32.

54. Chapman, "Illegal Aliens," 15.

55. L. Chavez, *Latino Threat*, 121.

56. La Feber, *Inevitable Revolutions*, 5.

57. W. Thompson, "A New Alien Detention Facility at El Centro," 25.

58. Frankel, "INS Research and Development Programs," 33.

59. Letter to Leonard F. Chapman, Jr., from Albert R. Garcia, President of the Mexican American Association, December 28, 1973, Border Patrol "La Migra" abuses, Baca Papers, 1–2.

60. Letter to Albert R. Garcia from L. F. Chapman, INS Commissioner, January 24, 1974, Border Patrol "La Migra" abuses, Baca Papers, 3.

61. Jesus Saldana, "La Tragedia de los Braceros," *Heraldo de Mexico*, July 24, 1972, DGIPS Caja 1675B, Exponiente 10, IPS.

62. Letter to Albert R. Garcia from L. F. Chapman, January 24, 1974, 3.

63. Frank del Olmo, "Alien Detention Center at El Centro Stirs Up Criticism," *Los Angeles Times*, February 24, 1974.

64. Frank del Olmo, "Alien Detention Center at El Centro Stirs Up Criticism," *Los Angeles Times*, February 24, 1974.

65. "Incoformidad Absoluta de Mexico," *El Heraldo de Mexico*, June 20, 1974, DGIPS Caja 1676A E3, IPS.

66. Miguel Lopez Saucedo, "Miles de Hambrientos en Campos de Detencion de EU," *El Excelsior*, July 9, 1974, DGIPS Caja 1676A E3, IPS.

67. Santiago Gonzalez Natall, "Jaulas de Oro, 'Asoleaderos' para Braceros Detenidos en EU," *Sol de Mexico*, February 19, 1976, DGIPS Caja 1676C, Exponiente 9, IPS; D. Martínez, "Alien Detention Facilities," 32.

68. Quoted in D. Martínez, "Alien Detention Facilities," 32.

Chapter Five

1. Anonymous immigration attorney, interview with author, El Centro, California, January 9, 2016.

2. The migrants were from various regions in Latin America, Tahiti, Tonga, Fiji, Bulgaria, Pakistan, China, Hungary, Canada, South Africa, Vietnam, Iran, and Portugal; "Refugee Hunger Strikers Confront INS," *San Diego Newsline* 8, no. 34 (June 11, 1985). The exact number of detainee who went on strike is unknown because news sources reported different numbers. H. G. Reza, "Aliens Planning Hunger Strike at Detention Center," *San Diego Union*, May 27, 1985, Local, B3; H. G. Reza, "300 Aliens on

Hunger Strike at El Centro INS Detention Center," *Los Angeles Times*, May 28, 1985, A8; letter to Graciela Zavala from detained clients, "Re: Formal Complaint against the I.N.S.," n.d. GZPC.

3. Reza, "Aliens Planning Hunger Strike," B3; Reza, "300 Aliens on Hunger Strike," A8; Marshall Ingerson, "As Debate Stirs over Immigration Policy, Detained Illegals Wait," *Christian Science Monitor*, February 20, 1985, GZPC, 6; "Refugee Hunger Strikers Confront INS."

4. Letter to Graciela Zavala, GZPC; Reza, "300 Aliens on Hunger Strike," A8; "Hunger Strikers Claim INS Guards Beat Them in Center," *San Jose Mercury News*, June 1, 1985, Local, 7b.

5. "Refugee Hunger Strikers Confront INS."

6. Orantes-Hernandez v. Smith, 541 F. Supp. 351 (C.D. Cal. 1982), June 2, 1982, https://law.justia.com/cases/federal/district-courts/FSupp/541/351/2289102/.

7. Dowling and Inda, *Governing Immigration through Crime*, 24; Paik, *Rightlessness*.

8. Refugee Act of 1980, Pub. L. No. 96-212, 94 Stat. 102 (1980). The act defined a refugee in two new ways:as a person "who [was] unable or unwilling to return to [their home country] because of well-founded fears of persecution on account of race, religion, nationality, membership in a particular social group, or political opinion" or in the special circumstances "[that] the President [declared] a well-founded fear of persecution"; Tempo, *Americans at the Gate*, 9.

9. Capó, "Queering Mariel," 92.

10. Tempo, *Americans at the Gate*, 167.

11. Memo from William P. Clark and William French Smith to President Reagan, January 20, 1982, re: Contingency Planning for a Cuban boatlift, Roger Fontaine Files, box 6, Cuba/Refugees, RRPL; Helton, "Imprisonment of Refugees," 133.

12. Capó, "Queering Mariel," 91.

13. "Immigration and Naturalization Service FY 1985 Congressional Inquiries," Box 36, Folder 4, NCLR, 3; Memo to Michael Guhin from David Hiller, re: Immigration Emergency Act, April 15, 1982, Michael Guhin Files, Box 2, Immigration Legislation, Ronald Reagan Presidential Library, 6.

14. 47 FR 30045, July 9, 1982; Supplemental Appropriations Act, September 10, 1982, Pub. L. 97-257 Congressional 97th Session, 823; 47 FR 46494, October 19, 1982; James D. Cockcroft, "Mexican Migration, Crisis, and the Internationalization of Labor Struggle," *Contemporary Marxism*, no. 5 (August 1982): 1, Baca Papers.

15. Dow, *American Gulag*, 8; Supplemental Appropriations Act 1982; Louis v. Nelson (1982), 544 F Supp. 973,982 District Court Southern District of Florida, 3; Memo to Interested Lawyers and Legal Organizations, from Arthur C. Helton, re: Representation of detained asylum seekers (February 1, 1984), box 4, folder 6, 1984, AFSCUSMBPR, 1.

16. Quoted in Steve Weinstein, "Inside El Centro," *Los Angeles Reader*, June 7, 1985, GZPC.

17. Laurie Becklund, "Conditions Assailed: Salvadoran Men Languish in INS Center in Desert," *Los Angeles Times*, February 20, 1985.

18. Mark Thompson, "Between War and Asylum," *California Lawyer*, April 1988, carton 106, folder 1337, Public Information Subject Files, Immigration/Alien Rights, ACLUNCR, 42.

19. Human Rights Watch / Americas, *Brutality Unchecked: Human Rights Abuses Along the US-Border with Mexico*, May 1995, 56.

20. Joan Mullen, Kent John Chabator, and Deborah M. Carrow, U.S. Department of Justice, National Institute of Justice, "Issues and Practices: The Privatization of Corrections," February 1985, Charles Smith Papers, series III, box 2, RRPL, 67.

21. Federal Detention Plan, September 1990, JV6414.DE9f, USCISHL, 5, 6, 10.

22. Sellers, *History and Politics*.

23. Sellers, *History and Politics*, 17; The President's Private Sector Survey on Cost Control: Chronology, January 15, 1984, Michael E. Banoody Collection, OA 11228, PPSSCC Press Kit, RRPL, 1.

24. President's Private Sector Survey on Cost Control, 46.

25. Mullen, Chabator, and Carrow, "Issues and Practices," 4–5.

26. Cushing N. Dolbeare, "Detention of Undocumented Aliens: Actions by the INS prior to Adoption of the Immigration Reform and Control Act of 1986," October 1990, folder 24, box 49, AFSCUSMBPR, 33.

27. "José Medina Fight Highlights Struggle of Undocumented Workers," *Black Panther*, February 5, 1977, 6; "José Medina Fights Deportation," *Workers World*, October 22, 1976.

28. Frank del Olmo, "Alien Detention Center at El Centro Stirs Up Criticism: New Director Says He's Trying to Remedy 'Some Difficulties,'" *Los Angeles Times*, February 24, 1974; D. Martínez, "Alien Detention Facilities," 34.

29. Letter from the Committee for the Defense of José Jacques Medina to the Liberty Hill Foundation, September 10, 1976, 2–3, box 4, folder 6, José Medina Defense Committee, LHC.

30. Timothy F. Harding, Affidavit in Support of José Jacques Medina's Claim for Political Asylum to the INS, February 9, 1977, Committee for the Defense of José Jacques Medina, box 4, folder 6, José Medina Defense Committee, LHC, 5.

31. Poniatowska, *Massacre in Mexico*, 203.

32. "José Medina Fights Deportation," October 22, 1976.

33. Harvey, *Brief History of Neoliberalism*, 98.

34. José Jacques y Medina, *De mojado a diputado: Memoria gráfica y documental* (Mexico City: Movimento Migrante Mesoamericano "No nos vamos," 2009), 19.

35. Harding, Affidavit in Support of José Jacques Medina's Claim, 9.

36. Antolin Gomez, "José Medina Fights for Political Asylum," *La Voz de el Congreso de UC Santa Barbara*, 6, box 34, folder 5, CASA.

37. "Human Rights for José Jacques Medina Political Asylum Now!," 1976, box 27, folder 7, Baca Papers, 1–2; Jocelyn Y. Steward, "A Strange Twist for a Resolute Radical," *Los Angeles Times*, May 13, 2000; Letter from the Committee for the Defense of José Jacques Medina, 2–3.

38. "Human Rights for José Jacques Medina," 1–2.

39. Bill Steiner, National Lawyers Guild Board Member, "Labor Organizer Charged as 'Illegal Alien,'" box 4, folder 6, José Medina Defense Committee, LHC, 6–7; "FBI Harass CASA Members," *Sin Fronteras*, April 1976, box 35, folder 10, CASA, 3.

40. "FBI Harass CASA Members," 3.

41. "Human Rights for José Jacques Medina," 1–2.

42. Medina's Testimony of Events, box 35, folder 4, CASA, 9–10.

43. Medina's Testimony of Events, 10, 12.

44. Gilda Rodriguez, Comité Nacional de Defensa para José Medina, July 13, 1977, box 34, folder 11, CASA, 1–3.

45. "José Medina: My Struggle Represents Millions," *Guardian*, March 23, 1977.

46. Letter from the Committee for the Defense of José Jacques Medina, 2–3; "FBI Harass CASA Members," 3.

47. Joyce Betries, "Demand Political Asylum for José Medina!," *Workers World*, December 31, 1976, 3; Arleen Eisen, "Jan 8: Day of Solidarity with José Medina," *Guardian*, January 5, 1977.

48. Betries, "Demand Political Asylum for José Medina!," 3.

49. Letter from the Committee for the Defense of José Jacques Medina, 1.

50. Pulido, *Black, Brown, Yellow, and Left*, 174–75.

51. "Milwaukee Demonstration Demands Political Asylum for José Medina!," Committee for the Defense of José Jacques Medina, box 4, folder 6, José Medina Defense Committee, LHC.

52. Report from the José Jacques Medina Defense Committee to the Liberty Hill Foundation, May 11, 1977, box 4, folder 6, José Medina Defense Committee, LHC, 2–3.

53. Department of State, James L. Carlin, letter to Joseph Sureck, re: José Jacques Medina, February 23, 1977, box 34, folder 12, CASA.

54. Harding, Affidavit in Support of José Jacques Medina's Claim, 3–4.

55. Rodolfo Acuna, "Affidavit in Support of José Jacques Medina's Claim for Political Asylum to the INS," February 11, 1977, Committee for the Defense of José Jacques Medina, box 4, folder 6, José Medina Defense Committee, LHC, 2, 4.

56. Kahn, *Other People's Blood*, 17.

57. Weinstein, "Inside El Centro"; Paula D. Pearlman, "Monthly Report: Imperial Valley Immigration Project," June–September 1984, American Friends Service Committee, U.S./Mexico Border Program, press statement, folder 16, box 45, AFSCUSMBPR, 2.

58. Rene Adan Contreras-Aragon in Deportation Proceedings, box 4, folder 6, 1984, AFSCUSMBPR.

59. Bell and Castillo, "Minorities and Women in the INS," 2–3.

60. "Guatemala: Between the Lines—A Publication of the Guatemala Information Center," vol. 2, no. 1, January–February 1982, box 16, folder 3, LHC.

61. Rene Ernesto Torres Garcia, Detention Testimonies, October 1981, ERHA.

62. Flores interview with author, April 30, 2018.

63. Flores interview.

64. Flores interview.

65. Cunningham, *God and Caesar*; Garcia, *Seeking Refuge*.

66. National Center for Immigrants' Rights, 1982 Call to Action, Press Statement, folder 1, box 1, AFSCUSMBPR.

67. Schoultz, "Central America," 190.

68. Orantes-Hernandez v. Smith, 541 F. Supp. 351 (C.D. Cal. 1982), June 2, 1982, https://law.justia.com/cases/federal/district-courts/FSupp/541/351/2289102/.

69. Orantes-Hernandez v. Smith.

70. Ecumenical Project for Immigration Counseling, "El Centro: Detainees," ERHA.

71. Ingerson, "As Debate Stirs over Immigration Policy," 7.

72. "Stop the Death Flights Flyer," Folder 9, Box 15, LHC.

73. Michael P. Roth, "Liberty or Death," *Los Angeles Reader*, May 11, 1984, ERHA.

74. Kahn, *Other People's Blood*, 41; Roth, "Liberty or Death."

75. Becklund, "Conditions Assailed"; Roth, "Liberty or Death."

76. Quoted in Roth, "Liberty or Death."

77. Hamilton and Chinchilla, *Seeking Community*, 119.

78. Declaration of José Santos Lemus, June 7, 1983, ERHA, 1; Declaration of Jaime Ulises Gonzalez-Flores, n.d., ERHA, 2.

79. Declaration of José Santos Lemus, 2; Declaration of Jaime Ulises Gonzalez-Flores, 2.

80. Declaration of José Santos Lemus, 3.

81. "Refugee Hunger Strikers Confront INS."

82. Letter to Graciela Zavala, 6–7.

83. W. Thompson, "A New Alien Detention Facility at El Centro," 25.

84. Arthur Golden, "Attorneys Blamed for Alien Strike," *San Diego Union*, May 29, 1985, Local, B1. The *Los Angeles Times* reported that there were 300 strikers; the *San Diego Union* claimed the number was closer to 175. The figures Graciela Zavala reported were also a lot higher than the statistics provided by the INS; Reza, "300 Aliens on Hunger Strike," A8; Gina Lubrano and Michael Abrams, "Detention Center Hunger Strike Dwindles; 8 Hold Out," *San Diego Union*, May 31, 1985, Local, B3, 5; Human Rights Watch / Americas, *Brutality Unchecked*, 57.

85. Church World Service Immigration and Refugee Program, 7–8.

86. Letter to Graciela Zavala, 4.

87. Quoted in Virginia Horn, "100 Striking Aliens Given Support by Right Backers," *Imperial Valley Press*, May 28, 1985, A2.

88. Gracela Zavala, phone interview with author, April 16, 2014.

89. "Refugee Hunger Strikers Confront INS."

90. Letter to Graciela Zavala, 4.

91. Camplin, *Prison Food in America*, 34, 60.

92. Madrigal, "We Are Human!," 254.

93. Reza, "300 Aliens on Hunger Strike," A8; Zavala interview.

94. Reza, "Aliens Planning Hunger Strike," B3.

95. Letter to Graciela Zavala, 4–5.

96. Becklund, "Conditions Assailed."

97. Becklund, "Conditions Assailed," 5.

98. Imperial Valley Immigration Project, "Monthly Report," May 1984, Press Statement, folder 16, box 45, AFSCUSMBPR, 1.

99. Letter to Graciela Zavala, 5–6.

100. Letter to Graciela Zavala, 5–6.

101. "Refugee Hunger Strikers Confront INS."

102. "Refugee Hunger Strikers Confront INS."

103. Weinstein, "Inside El Centro."

104. Ecumenical Project for Immigration Counseling, "El Centro: Detainees."

105. Becklund, "Conditions Assailed."

106. "Refugee Hunger Strikers Confront INS."

107. Paik, *Rightlessness*.

108. Zavala interview.

109. "Refugee Hunger Strikers Confront INS."

110. Zavala interview; Horn, "100 Striking Aliens," 1; Virginia Horn, "7 Still Strike: INS 'Force' Alleged," *Imperial Valley Press*, May 31, 1985, 1.

111. Zavala interview.

112. *Union del Barrio Newsletter*, September–October 1985, box 12, folder 9, AFSCUSMBPR.

113. Virginia Horn, "Aliens Said Being Deported to Hurt Strike," *Imperial Valley Press*, May 30, 1985, 1.

114. Kang, *INS on the Line*; Salyer, *Laws Harsh as Tigers*.

115. "Refugee Hunger Strikers Confront INS."

116. "Refugee Hunger Strikers Confront INS."

117. "Border Patrol Tactical Unit (BORTAC)," U.S. Customs and Border Protection, https://www.cbp.gov/sites/default/files/documents/Border%20Patrol%20Tactical%20Unit.pdf; Dunn, *Militarization*, 52, 59.

118. William Polk, "INS Accuses Imperial Valley Attorney of Instigating Strike," *San Diego Evening Tribune*, May 31, 1985, A-12; "Hunger Strikers Claim INS Guards Beat Them 7B.

119. Arthur Golden, "Candy Wrappers Hint Hunger Strikers didn't Starve," *The San Diego Union*, June 1, 1985, Local B3; Virginia Horn, "Doctor: Striker Is Injured," *Imperial Valley Press*, June 3, 1985, 1.

120. Zavala interview; Edward J. Boyer, "3 Congressmen Seek Investigation of INS," *Los Angeles Times*, June 7, 1985.

121. Golden, "Candy Wrappers," B3; Jaime Olivares, "Liberan a 8 Huelguistas de Hambre de Centro de Detención del INS," newspaper source unknown, GZPC.

122. Virginia Horn, "Hunger Strikers Claim INS Guards Beat Them," 7b; Olivares, "Liberan a 8 Huelgistas de Hambre de Centro de Detención del INS."

123. Virginia Horn, "Strikers Claim INS Beatings, But No Outside Influence," *Imperial Valley Press*, June 5, 1985, A2.

124. "Psychotherapy and Counseling Project by the National Center for Immigrants' Rights, Inc.," January 1986, folder 5, box 1, AFSCUSMBPR.

125. "Refugee Hunger Strikers Confront INS."

126. Golden, "Candy Wrappers," B3; Zavala interview.

127. "Hunger Strike Ended by El Centro Aliens," *San Diego Evening Tribune*, June 4, 1985, A-16; Horn, "Doctor: Striker Is Injured," A2.

128. Olivares, "Liberan a 8 Huelguistas de Hambre de Centro de Detención del INS."

129. Golden, "Attorneys Blamed for Alien Strike," B1.

130. Golden, "Candy Wrappers," B3.

131. Zavala interview.

132. Golden, "Attorneys Blamed for Alien Strike," B1.

133. Zavala interview.

134. Polk, "INS Accuses Imperial Valley Attorney," A-12; Zavala interview; Golden, "Attorneys Blamed for Alien Strike," B1.

135. Polk, "INS Accuses Imperial Valley Attorney," A-12.

136. Zavala interview.

137. "Refugee Hunger Strikers Confront INS."

138. Garcia, *Seeking Refuge*, 5.

139. A federal district judge ruled that the INS had to inform the families and attorneys if detainees were transferred.

140. Lubrano and Abrams, "Detention Center Hunger Strike Dwindles 8," B3: 5; H. G. Reza and Bill Farr, "INS Says Lawyer Incited Alien Hunger Strike, Asks to Bar Her," *Los Angeles Times*, May 31, 1985, A3.

141. Leonard Greenwood and Bill Farr, "Immigrants on Hunger Strike Drop to 7—Hearing Set on Tactics of INS," *Los Angeles Times*, June 1, 1985, OC26.

142. Horn, "7 Still Strike," A2.

143. Raul Amilcar Rodriguez Prado, Detention Testimonies, September 1981, ERHA.

144. H. Thompson, *Blood in the Water*, 24.

145. Dolbeare, "Detention of Undocumented Aliens," 34.

146. "The Los Angeles and San Diego Delegation to El Centro Detention Facility," GZPC.

147. Martin Hill, "The Thin Line, Part III," *San Diego Magazine*, July 1986, folder 20, box 16, AFSCUSMBPR; Zavala interview.

148. Becklund, "Conditions Assailed," 1.

149. Dan Weikel, "Detention: INS Holding Sites Draw Heavy Criticism," *Orange County Register*, February 1, 1987.

150. Human Rights Watch / Americas, *Brutality Unchecked*, 58; Ingrid Greenberg, "UN Inspector Visits INS El Centro Center," August 20, 1985, newspaper source unknown, GZPC; "Refugee Hunger Strikers Confront INS."

151. Letter from Fernando Gonzalez Santoyo, Mexican consulate, Secretary of Foreign Relations, to Mr. Robert Roll, August 27, 1987, CAI-4-6, Histórico Genaro Estrado, Secretaria de Relaciones Exteriores, Mexico City, 1–2.

152. Mark Thompson, "Between War and Asylum," April 1988, California Lawyer, Carton 106, Folder 1337, Public Information Subject Files, Immigration/Alien Rights, American Civil Liberties Union of North California Records, California Historical Society, San Francisco, 44.

153. M. Thompson, "Between War and Asylum," 44, 41.

154. Lilia S. Velasquez, interview with author, January 4, 2016, San Diego, California.

155. U.S. Citizenship and Immigration Services, "American Baptist Churches v. Thornburgh (ABC) Settlement Agreement," https://www.uscis.gov/laws/legal-settle ment-notices/american-baptist-churches-v-thornburgh-abc-settlement-agreement.

156. U.S. Department of Justice, INS, *Immigration Detention Officer Handbook*, 1987, 10–81, 10–83. (Hereafter cited as INS, *Detention Officer Handbook*.)

157. American Friends Service Committee, U.S./Mexico Border Program press statement, folder 4, box 38, AFSCUSMBPR, 1.

Chapter Six

1. Registro de Casos de Protección, Mexican consulate in Calexico, Exponiente 73.6, CAL-15-26, Secretaría de Relaciones Exteriores, Mexico City.

2. Carlos Holguin, Peter A. Schey, James Morales, and Paul Hoffman, US District of Court of Appeals for the Ninth Circuit, Jenny Lissette Flores v. Edwin Meese, III, NCLRR, box 402, folder 13, 1; 8 U.S.C. (1252); "Concerns regarding Current Detention Conditions and Release Policies for Unaccompanied Minors INS Custody," Working Group on Minors in INS Detention, January 22, 1990, NCLRR, box 403, folder 9, Stanford University, 3.

3. McCorkel, "Embodied Surveillance," 201–2; Carrabine and Longhurst, "Gender and Prison Organization," 245–49; Manion, *Liberty's Prisoners*, 1.

4. INS, *Detention Officer Handbook*, 7-1.

5. McCorkel, "Embodied Surveillance," 201; Davis, "Race, Gender, and Prison History," 36.

6. Ogletree and Sarat, *Punishment in Popular Culture*, 3.

7. I use the term "masculinities" to express what Carolyn Newton refers to as "a belief that genders are not homogenous entities." Carolyn Newton, "Gender Theory," 236.

8. Morin and Moran, *Historical Geographies of Prisons*, 2.

9. Tyner, *Space, Place, and Violence*, ix; Agamben, *State of Exception*, 1, 50; Agamben, *Homo Sacer*, 171.

10. "Federal Detention Plan," September 1990, JV 6414.DE9f1992-1996, USCISHL, 1.

11. Cooper and O'Neil, "Lessons," 3.

12. Immigration Reform and Control Act of 1986, Pub. L. No. 99-603, November 6, 1986.

13. "Federal Detention Plan," September 1990, 1–4.

14. Immigration and Naturalization Service, *Criminal Alien Program Procedures Manual*, May 1, 1988, JV 6414.G87c 1988c2, 2–3, USCISHL.

15. Macias-Rojas, *From Deportation to Prison*, 59; "Federal Detention Plan," September 1990, 1–4.

16. INS, *Detention Officer Handbook*, 9-1–9-2, 9-6, 10-6.

17. INS, *Detention Officer Handbook*, 10-4.

18. INS, *Detention Officer Handbook*, 9-8–9-9.

19. Letter from Lynn Marcus and the Tucson Ecumenical Council Legal Assistance (TECLA) to Congressman Morris K. Udall, September 14, 1990, box 2, folder 1, AFSCUSMBPR; press statement, Lynn Marcus, n.d. box 13, folder 5, AFSCUSMBPR.

20. Press statement, Lynn Marcus, n.d., 2.

21. Tracy Wilkinson, "*LA Times*: Refugees Claim Mistreatment by INS Guards," October 10, 1990, folder 6, box 1, Martínez Papers.

22. Escobar, "Neoliberal Captivity," 17; Wilsher, *Immigration Detention*, xix.

23. Press Packet on INS Abuse at Detention Facilities in El Centro, CA (September 6, 1990) (hereafter cited as Press Packet), folder 5, box 47, AFSCUSMBPR.

24. Paik, *Rightlessness*, 17.

25. National Center for Immigrants' Rights, Inc., "Psychotherapy and Counseling Project," January 1986, box 1, folder 5, AFSCUSMBPR.

26. Wilkinson, "*LA Times*: Refugees Claim Mistreatment."

27. "Complaints of Abuse on the U.S. Mexico Border and in the San Diego Region by Local and Federal Enforcement Agencies: AFSC-USMBP's 2000 Abuse Report," folder 1, box 15, AFSCUSMBPR, 21; "Press Conference News Release: Immigration Officers Beat Detainees, Group Charges, U.S. Congressmen Decry Alleged Abuses," September 6, 1990, folder 4, box 38, AFSCUSMBPR.

28. "Press Conference News Release: Immigration Officers Beat Detainees."

29. Agamben, *Homo Sacer*, 170.

30. Terrio, *Whose Child Am I?*, 2, 10.

31. Carlos Holguin, Peter A. Schey, James Morales, and Paul Hoffman, Plaintiff's Appellees' Supplemental Brief on Rehearing en Banc, US District of Court of Appeals for the Ninth Circuit, Jenny Lissette Flores v. Edwin Meese, III, NCLRR, box 402, folder 13, 5.

32. Holgen et al., US District of Court of Appeals, 8, 9.

33. Terrio, *Whose Child Am I?*, 54.

34. Holgen et al., US District of Court of Appeals, 6.

35. *Imperial Valley News*, July 15, 1990, box 403, folder 8, NCLRR, 2.

36. Mary O'Connor, "Undocumented Children in Detention," June 6, 1990, NCLRR, Box 403, Folder 8, 10.

37. "Concerns Regarding Current Detention Conditions and Release Policies for Unaccompanied Minors [in] INS Custody," Working Group on Minors in INS Detention, January 22, 1990, box 403, folder 9, NCLRR, 2.

38. Press Packet, Declaration #2, September 6, 1990, box 47, box 5, AFSCUSMBPR, 10.

39. Press Packet, Declaration #2, 10, 9, 4.

40. Press Packet, Declaration #2, 10.

41. Press Packet, Declaration #3, 11.

42. Press Packet, Declaration #4, 12.

43. Press statement, Lynn Marcus, n.d., 1.

44. Anonymous declaration #4, April 23, 1990, NCLRR, box 403, folder 9, 1.

45. Anonymous declaration #1, April 24, 1990, NCLRR, box 403, folder 9, 1.

46. Anonymous declaration #1, April 24, 1990, 1.

47. Anonymous declaration #3, April 23, 1990, NCLRR, box 403, folder 9, 1.

48. Anonymous declaration #1, April 24, 1990, 1; Anonymous declaration #11, April 23, 1990, NCLRR, box 403, folder 9, 1.

49. Anonymous declaration #5, April 19, 1990, NCLRR, box 403, folder 9, 1.

50. Anonymous declaration #12, April 27, 1990, NCLRR, box 403, folder 9, 1.

51. Anonymous declaration #2, April 20, 1990, NCLRR, box 403, folder 9, 1.

52. Anonymous declaration #2, April 20, 1990, 1; Anonymous declaration #6, April 16, 1990, NCLRR, box 403, folder 9, 1.

53. Anonymous declaration #2, April 20, 1990, 2.

54. Anonymous declaration #8, April 26, 1990, NCLRR, box 403, folder 9, 1.

55. Anonymous declaration #5, April 19, 1990, 1–2.

56. Anonymous declaration #7, April 24, 1990, NCLRR, box 403, folder 9, 1.

57. Anonymous declaration #9, April 23, 1990, NCLRR, box 403, folder 9, 1.

58. Terrio, *Whose Child Am I?*, 14.

59. INS, *Detention Officer Handbook*, 10-4–10-5.

60. Interview with anonymous immigration attorney, El Centro, CA, January 9, 2016.

61. INS, *Detention Officer Handbook*, 13–21.

62. Brett Story, "The Prison Inside: A Genealogy of Solitary Confinement as Counter-Resistance," in *Historical Geographies of Prisons Unlocking the Usable Past* (New York: Routledge, 2015), Karen M. Morin and Dominque Moran, 40.

63. INS, *Detention Officer Handbook*, 12-8–12-9.

64. Carrabine and Longhurst, "Gender and Prison Organization," 249.

65. Letter, Mexican consulate employee Javier Cerritos G. to David Banda, Chief of Deportation," May 28, 1992, CAL-15-31, Secretaría de Relaciones Exteriores, Mexico City.

66. "Written Testimony from Delgadillo," CAL-15-31, Secretaría de Relaciones Exteriores, Mexico City. Translation by author.

67. Additional sources held at the Secretaría de Relaciones Exteriores document INS theft of detainee property, verbal insults, and physical abuse at the El Centro Service Processing Center.

68. Letter, Abelardo Cruz Jimenez, CAL-15-31, n.d., Secretaría de Relaciones Exteriores, Mexico City.

69. Letter, Humberto Villaseñor, CAL-15-31, n.d., Secretaría de Relaciones Exteriores, Mexico City.

70. Newton, "Gender Theory," 240.

71. Hurtado and Sinha, *Beyond Machismo*, 67.

72. Cummings, "Squat Toilets," 261–73; Cavanagh, *Queering Bathrooms*; Maynard, "Through a Hole"; Gershenson and Penner, *Ladies and Gents*, 1; W. Anderson, "Excremental Colonialism."

73. Cavanagh, *Queering Bathrooms*, 5.

74. Cavanagh, *Queering Bathrooms*, 195; Maynard, "Through a Hole," 209.

75. Tyner, *Space, Place, and Violence*, 20.

76. Press Packet, 1.

77. It is important to note that these cases were part of a larger pattern. Reports reveal that specific INS guards were repeatedly accused of committing abusive acts against detainees, and yet investigations led nowhere.

78. White, *Transitional Justice*, 84.

79. Press Packet, 6.

80. Tshumi, "Violence of Architecture," 44.

81. Press Packet, 22.

82. "Border Patrol Tactical Unit (BORTAC)," U.S. Customs and Border Protection, 2014, https://www.cbp.gov/sites/default/files/documents/Border%20Patrol%20Tactical%20Unit.pdf; Dunn, *Militarization*, 52, 59.

83. Press Packet, 2.

84. Press Packet, 3.

85. Wilkinson, *"LA Times*: Refugees Claim Mistreatment."

86. Beverly, *Testimonio*.

87. Wilkinson, *"LA Times*: Refugees Claim Mistreatment."

88. See Press Packet. For example, on September 8, 1989, INS officers at El Centro beat and handcuffed Guatemalan detainee Cesar Agusto Moran-Zuniga. On June 26, 1990, INS guards took Mario Flores Barrientos, a migrant from El Salvador, into the facility's bathroom, where Officer Aguirre insulted him and proceeded to hit him over the head while another agent just stood and watched. This same month, INS guards punished a Nicaraguan detainee for forgetting to close a door. The guards insulted Jorge Alberto Murillo Valladares and then took him to the bathroom at the processing building, where they beat him. Valladares attempted to report the abuse, but nothing was done about the incident, and Valladares was deported after his experience was shared at a press conference.

89. Dunn, *Militarization*, 47.

90. For instance, on August 4, 1990, INS Officer Reyes took Francisco Javier Luna Molina, a Nicaraguan migrant, to solitary to punish him for participating in a hunger strike. Molina was also severely beaten in this process, receiving wounds in his stomach, arms, groin, and shoulders. He was hurt so badly that he had to get treatment for his dislocated shoulder. Although Molina attempted to report the incident, the Justice Department decided not to prosecute Officer Reyes. After Molina spoke with an immigration attorney and attempted to expose his mistreatment, the INS deported him to Nicaragua. This suggests that detention was not just violent, but that if detainees attempted to expose such conditions they could face retaliation or deportation. See press statement, Lynn Marcus, n.d.

91. Patrick McDonnell, "INS Separates 8 Hunger Strikers, Moves Them from El Centro Lockup," *Los Angeles Times*, December 15, 1989.

92. Press Packet, 1, 6.

93. McDonnell, "INS Separates 8 Hunger Strikers."

94. Comision de Derechos Humanos de El Savador (CDHES), "Torture in El Salvador," September 24, 1986, CDHES 1987, ERHA.

Chapter Seven

1. "Deadly Force and Human Rights Violations against Undocumented Workers in CA," AFSCUSMBPR, box 1, folder 3, June–December 1985. I switch back and forth between INS and ICE because after September 11, 2001, the Bush administration abolished the INS and created the Department of Homeland Security, which included Immigration and Customs Enforcement (ICE), United States Citizenship and Immigration Services (USCIS), and Customs and Border Protection (CPB).

2. "Deadly Force and Human Rights Violations against Undocumented Workers in CA."

3. The Service Processing Centers were located at Aguadilla, Puerto Rico; Boston, Massachusetts; El Centro and San Pedro, California; El Paso and Los Fresnos, Texas; Florence, Arizona; Miami, Florida; and Varick Street, New York, New York. Contract facilities were located in Aurora, Colorado; New York, New York; Houston and Laredo,

Texas; Seattle, Washington; and Elizabeth, New Jersey. The PHS Hospital was called St. Elizabeth's Hospital, and the joint facility with the Bureau of Prisons refers to the Oakdale Federal Detention Center in Louisiana. See "INS Detention and Deportation Program," JV6414.DE9B17 1994, USCISHL, 3.

4. "List of Deaths in ICE Custody Report," U.S. Immigration and Customs Enforcement, Freedom of Information Library, www.ice.gov/foia/library; Inda, "Letting Moises Die."

5. Mbembe, "Necropolitics," 27–28; Florida Immigrant Advocacy Center, "Dying for Decent Care: Bad Medicine in Immigration Custody," February 2009, AIJR.

6. Martin, "Trade and Migration," 39.

7. Fernández-Kelly and Massey, "Borders for Whom?," 99; Hing, *Ethical Borders*, 5.

8. Andreas, *Border Games*, x.

9. Nevins, *Dying to Live*, 116.

10. Supplemental Materials to the Intervention before the 55th Session of the United Nations Commission on Human Rights, Submitted on Behalf of Human Rights Advocates by American Civil Liberties Union of San Diego and Imperial Counties and California Rural Legal Assistance Foundation, CSPC, 15.

11. Letter from Claudia E. Smith, Law Offices of California Rural Legal Assistance, to Fernando Trulin, March 5, 1996, CSPC, 1; https://www.law.ox.ac.uk/research-subject-groups/centre-criminology/centreborder-criminologies/blog/2015/04/racism-and.

12. Letter to Doris Meissner, INS Commissioner, from Claudia E. Smith, Regional Counsel for California Rural Legal Assistance, and Roberto L. Martínez, Director of the American Friends Service Committee U.S.-Mexico Border Program, October 24, 1994, CSPC, 3; Letter to John P. Chase, Director, Internal Audit, INS, from Claudia E. Smith, Regional Counsel for California Rural Legal Assistance, March 6, 1995, CSPC, 4.

13. "Letter to Doris Meissner from Claudia Smith, October 24, 1994."

14. Bianca Quilantana, "Remembering the Forgotten," April 10, 2017, *The Southwestern Sun*, Southwestern College, Chula Vista, California.

15. Letter to Marion Standish, California Endowment Public Officer, from Claudia E. Smith, Attorney, California Rural Legal Assistance Foundation, August 8, 1997, CSPC, 1.

16. Nevins, *Dying to Live*, 66.

17. Morgan Baskin, "Field Notes from a Cemetery for the Nameless," *Pacific Standard*, March 31, 2017.

18. Petitioners' Supplemental Memo to the Inter-American Commission on Human Rights of the Organization of American States on Behalf of Petitioners, American Civil Liberties Union of San Diego and Imperial Counties and California Rural Legal Assistance Foundation v. The United States of America, CSPC, 3–4.

19. Tatiana Sanchez, "Remains of Hundreds of Unidentified Immigrants Are Buried in Imperial County Cemetery," *Los Angeles Times*, June 18, 2016.

20. Baskin, "Field Notes from a Cemetery for the Nameless."

21. S. Lee, "Remembering the Lost Dead. Burial costs are approximately $1,200 per person and cremation costs $645 per person.

22. Quilantana, "Remembering the Forgotten."

23. T. Sanchez, "Remains of Hundreds of Unidentified Immigrants"; Baskin, "Field Notes from a Cemetery for the Nameless." Monica Munoz Martínez also writes about remembrance, anti-Mexican violence, and tombstones; see M. Martínez, *Injustice Never Leaves You.*

24. Esther Morales, "Tireless Warrior I;" Escobar, *Captivity beyond Prisons*, 79.

25. Morales, "Tireless Warrior II."

26. Escobar, *Captivity beyond Prisons*, 93.

27. Letter to Doris Meissner from Claudia Smith and Roberto Martínez, October 24, 1994, 4, 5.

28. Letter to John Chase from Claudia Smith, March 6, 1995, 4.

29. Letter to Doris Meissner from Claudia Smith and Roberto Martínez, October 24, 1994, 6. Some of the short-term detention cells inside Border Patrol centers are located in El Centro, Calexico, Indio, Imperial Beach, Campo, San Clemente, El Cajon, and Chula Vista, California, and in Nogales, Ajo, Tucson, Douglas, Blythe, and Yuma, Arizona.

30. U.S. Department of Justice, INS, "Service Processing Center Design Guide," JV6414.DE9F21d, 20, USCISHL; Dow, *American Gulag*, 200.

31. Ordaz, "Protesting Conditions."

32. Dow, *American Gulag*, 200.

33. Dow, *American Gulag*, 201.

34. Florida Immigrant Advocacy Center, "Dying for Decent Care," 11, 21–23.

35. Florida Immigrant Advocacy Center, "Dying for Decent Care," 11, 23.

36. Guadalupe-Gonzales, Department of Homeland Security, *ICE Report of Investigation*, 2013, 1, 3, 4.

37. Guadalupe-Gonzales, *ICE Report of Investigation*, 6, 8.

38. Guadalupe-Gonzales, *ICE Report of Investigation*, 9, 14, 22.

39. Letter to Doris Meissner from Claudia Smith and Roberto Martínez, October 24, 1994, 2; Letter to John P. Chase, Director, Internal Audit, INS, from Claudia E. Smith, Regional Counsel for California Rural Legal Assistance, March 13, 1995, CSPC, 1.

40. Letter to Doris Meissner from Claudia Smith and Roberto Martínez, October 24, 1994, 2; Letter to John P. Chase, Director, Internal Audit, INS, from Claudia E. Smith, Regional Counsel for California Rural Legal Assistance, February 9, 1995, CSPC, 2.

41. Letter to John Chase from Claudia Smith, March 6, 1995, 3.

42. Antonio Gomez is a pseudonym.

43. Letter to John Chase from Claudia Smith, March 6, 1995, 3.

44. Memo to Western District Directors and Chief Patrol Agents from the Office of the Western Regional Director, re: Regional Transportation System Plan, March 28, 1995, CSPC, 2, 6, 13, 8–10.

45. Letter to Doris Meissner, INS Commissioner, from Claudia E. Smith, Regional Counsel for Counsel for California Rural Legal Assistance, September 11, 1995, CSPC, 2.

46. Letter to Doris Meissner, INS Commissioner, from Claudia E. Smith, Attorney, California Rural Legal Assistance Foundation, July 7, 1997, CSPC, 3.

47. Letter to Claudia E. Smith, Regional Counsel for Counsel for California Rural Legal Assistance, from a Concerned Taxpayer and Patrol Agent, October 5, 1995, CSPC, 1, 3.

48. Cacho, *Social Death*, 37.

49. Wong, *Politics of Immigration*, 82; Macias-Rojas, *From Deportation to Prison*, 9.

50. Welch, *Detained*, 3.

51. Wong, *Politics of Immigration*, 83.

52. Jauregui Mariz, "First They Americanize You, Then They Throw You Out."

53. Sanchez de Paulsen, "The Wall Separates Families, but Never Feelings."

54. Nalbach, "Deportation the Effects on the Soul, Part I."

55. Sánchez Pérez, "Cruel Deportations."

Conclusion

1. Krista Daly, "Reasons for US Immigration and Customs Enforcement Facility Closure Uncertain," *Imperial Valley Press*, March 6, 2014.

2. Antoine Abou-Diwan, "Options, Uncertainty for El Centro ICE Employees," *Imperial Valley Press*, May 21, 2014.

3. Krista Daly, "U.S. Immigration and Customs Enforcement Contract Employees Rally Together to Get Message to Imperial County Board of Supervisors," *Imperial Valley Press*, May 14, 2014.

4. Bardis Vakili, phone interview with author, March, 15, 2016.

Bibliography

Archival and Manuscript Collections

American Civil Liberties Union of Northern California Records, California Historical Society, San Francisco, CA.

American Civil Liberties Union of Southern California Records, Special Collections, Charles E. Young Research Library, University of California, Los Angeles.

American Friends Service Committee—United States-Mexico Border Program Records, Mandeville Special Collections, University of California, San Diego.

Americans for Immigrant Justice Records, Rubenstein Library, Duke University, Durham, NC.

Ben Yellen Papers, Mandeville Special Collections, University of California, San Diego.

Centro de Acción Social Autónomo Papers, Department of Special Collections, Stanford University, Stanford, CA.

Claudia E. Smith Private Collection.

El Rescate Historical Archives, Los Angeles, CA.

Ernesto Galarza Papers, Department of Special Collections, Stanford University, Stanford, CA.

Graciela Zavala Private Collection.

Herman Baca Papers, Mandeville Special Collections, University of California, San Diego.

Investigaciones Politicas y Sociales, Instituciones Gubernamentales: Epoca Moderna y Contemporanea, Administracion Publica Federal S. XX, Archivo General de la Nación, Mexico City, Mexico.

Kelly Lytle Hernández Collection of Border Patrol Research Papers, Chicano Studies Research Center, University of California, Los Angeles.

Liberty Hill Collection, Southern California Library, Los Angeles, CA.

Los Angeles Committee for the Protection of the Foreign-Born Collection, Southern California Library, Los Angeles, CA.

National Council of La Raza Records, Department of Special Collections, Stanford University, Stanford, CA.

Protección y Asuntos Consulares, Secretaría de Relaciones Exteriores, Mexico City, Mexico.

Records of the Immigration and Naturalization Service, Record Group 85, U.S. National Archives, Washington, DC.

Roberto Martínez Papers, Mandeville Special Collections, University of California, San Diego.

Ronald Reagan Presidential Library, Simi Valley, CA.

San Diego Union-Tribune Photograph Collection, San Diego Historical Society, San Diego, CA.

U.S. Citizenship and Immigration Services Historical Library, Washington, DC.

U.S. Marshal Collection, Center for Southwest Research, University of New Mexico, Albuquerque, NM.

Government Documents

Bell, Griffin B., and Leonel J. Castillo. "Minorities and Women in the INS." *INS Reporter* 26, no.1 (Summer 1977): 2–3.

Brownell, Herbert Jr. "Address Prepared for Delivery at Naturalization Ceremonies," November 11, 1954, New York City.

Bureau of Immigration and Customs Enforcement. *Detainee Handbook: Service Processing Center, 2003, El Centro, California.*

Carusi, Ugo. Immigration and Naturalization Service. *Annual Report, 1945.* Washington, D.C.: The United States Department of Justice.

———. Immigration and Naturalization Service, *Annual Report, 1946.* Washington, D.C.: The United States Department of Justice.

———.Immigration and Naturalization Service, *Annual Report, 1947.* Washington, D.C.: The United States Department of Justice.

Castillo, Leonel J. Immigration and Naturalization Service, *Annual Report, 1978.* Washington, D.C.: The United States Department of Justice.

Chapman, Leonard F. "Illegal Aliens: A Growing Population." *I & N Reporter* 24, no. 2 (Fall 1975), 15–18.

Farrell, Raymond. Immigration and Naturalization Service, *Annual Report, 1964.* Washington, D.C.: The United States Department of Justice.

———. Immigration and Naturalization Service, *Annual Report, 1966.* Washington, D.C.: The United States Department of Justice.

———. Immigration and Naturalization Service, *Annual Report, 1970.* Washington, D.C.: The United States Department of Justice.

Frankel, Harry D. "INS Research and Development Programs." *I & N Reporter* 26, no. 3 (Winter 1977–78): 33.

Graham, Janet R. *I & N Reporter* 22, no. 2 (Fall 1973).

Guadalupe-Gonzales, Elsa. Department of Homeland Security, *ICE Report of Investigation, Report Number 003,* U.S. Immigration and Customs Enforcement, Freedom of Information Library. www.ice.gov/foia/library, 2013.

Harrison, Earl G. Immigration and Naturalization Service, *Annual Report, 1944.* Washington, D.C.: The United States Department of Justice.

"List of Deaths in ICE Custody Report," U.S. Immigration and Customs Enforcement, Freedom of Information Library. www.ice.gov/foia/library.

Mackey, A. R., Immigration and Naturalization Service, *Annual Report, 1950.* Washington, D.C.: The United States Department of Justice.

———. Immigration and Naturalization Service, *Annual Report, 1951.* Washington, D.C.: The United States Department of Justice.

———. Immigration and Naturalization Service, *Annual Report, 1952*. Washington, D.C.: The United States Department of Justice.

———. Immigration and Naturalization Service, *Annual Report, 1953*. Washington, D.C.: The United States Department of Justice.

Miller, Watson B. Immigration and Naturalization Service, *Annual Report, 1948*. Washington, D.C.: The United States Department of Justice.

———. Immigration and Naturalization Service, *Annual Report, 1949*. Washington, D.C.: The United States Department of Justice.

Nelson, Alan C. *INS Reporter* (Fall/Winter 1984/1985).

Orantes-Hernandez v. Smith, 541 F. Supp. 351 (C.D. Cal. 1982), June 2, 1982. https://law.justia.com/cases/federal/district-courts/FSupp/541/351/2289102/.

Reagan, Ronald. "Statement on United States Immigration and Refugee Policy," July 30, 1981. Online by Gerhard Peters and John T. Woolley, *The American Presidency Project*. http://www.presidency.ucsb.edu/ws/?pid=44128.

Schofield, Lemuel B. Immigration and Naturalization Service, *Annual Report, 1942*. Washington, D.C.: The United States Department of Justice.

Swing, Joseph. Immigration and Naturalization Service, *Annual Report, 1954*. Washington, D.C.: The United States Department of Justice.

———. Immigration and Naturalization Service, *Annual Report, 1957*. Washington, D.C.: The United States Department of Justice.

———. Immigration and Naturalization Service, *Annual Report, 1958*. Washington, D.C.: The United States Department of Justice.

Thompson, William A. "A New Alien Detention Facility at El Centro." *I & N Reporter* 22, no. 2 (Fall 1973).

U.S. Department of Justice, Immigration and Naturalization Service. *Immigration Detention Officer Handbook*. Washington, D.C., 1987.

U.S. Department of Justice, Immigration and Naturalization Service. *Manual of Instructions for Detention Officers*, Washington, D.C., 1955.

Oral Histories and Digital Stories

Anonymous ICE official, guided tour. El Centro Service Processing Center, El Centro, CA, April 2, 2014.

Anonymous immigration attorney. Interview with author, El Centro, CA, January 9, 2016.

Flores, José Rene. Interview with author, Los Angeles, CA, April 30, 2018.

Laue, Gretchen. Interview with author, El Centro, California, January 8, 2016.

Lopez Elizabeth. Phone interview with author, March 22, 2016.

Mariz, Daniel Jauregui. "First They Americanize You, Then They Throw You Out." Humanizando la Deportacion, No. 6, 2017. http://humanizandoladeportacion.ucdavis.edu/.

Martínez, Ramiro Cortez. Interview with author, Oakley, CA, April 25, 2015.

Morales, Esther. "Tireless Warrior I" Humanizando la Deportacion, No.11a, 2017. http://humanizandoladeportacion.ucdavis.edu/.

———. "Tireless Warrior II." Humanizando la Deportacion, No. 11b, 2017. http://humanizandoladeportacion.ucdavis.edu/.

Nalbach, Jessica. "Deportation the Effects on the Soul, Part I: Dwelling in the Past." Humanizando la Deportacion, No. 66a, 2018. http://humanizandoladeportacion .ucdavis.edu/.

Perez, Gerardo Sanchez. "Cruel Deportations." Humanizando la Deportacion, No. 1, 2017. http://humanizandoladeportacion.ucdavis.edu/.

Sanchez de Paulsen, Emma "The Wall Separates Families, but Never Feelings." Humanizando la Deportacion, No. 4, 2017. http://humanizandoladeportacion .ucdavis.edu/.

Trevino, Jesus. "Sudden Death." Humanizando la Deportacion, No. 77, 2018. http://humanizandoladeportacion.ucdavis.edu/.

Vakili, Bardis. Phone interview with author, March 15, 2016.

Velasquez, Lilia S. Interview with author, San Diego, CA, January 4, 2016.

Velásquez, Steve. "Isidoro Ramírez." Bracero History Archive, Item No. 142. http://braceroarchive.org/items/show/142 (accessed June 12, 2019).

Zavala, Graciela. Phone interview with author, April 16, 2014.

Newspapers

Corpus Christi Caller-Times
Desert Sun
Guardian (Los Angeles)
Imperial Valley Press
Los Angeles Times
New York Times
Orange County Register

Pacific Standard
San Diego Evening Tribune
San Diego Union
San Jose Mercury News
The Southwestern Sun (Chula Vista)
Workers World

Secondary and Other Primary Sources

Agamben, Giorgio. Homo Sacer: Sovereign Power and Bare Life. Stanford: Stanford University Press, 1998.

———. State of Exception. Chicago: University of Chicago Press, 2005.

Akashi, Motomu. Betrayed Trust: The Story of a Deported Issei and His American-Born Family during WWII. Bloomington: Author House, 2004.

Anderson, Henry P. The Bracero Program in California. New York: Arno Press, 1961.

Anderson, Warwick. "Excremental Colonialism: Public Health and the Poetics of Pollution." Critical Inquiry 21, no. 3 (Spring 1995), 640–69.

Andreas, Peter. Border Games: Policing the U.S.-Mexico Divide. Ithaca, NY: Cornell University Press, 2000.

Andres, Benny. Power and Control in the Imperial Valley: Nature, Agribusiness, and Workers on the California Borderlands, 1900–1940. College Station: Texas A&M University Press, 2016.

Baldarrama, Francisco E., and Raymond Rodriguez. Decade of Betrayal: Mexican Repatriation in the 1930s. Albuquerque: University of New Mexico Press, 2006.

Barde, Robert E. *Immigration at the Gold Gate: Passenger Ships, Exclusion, and Angel Island*. Westport, CT: Praeger, 2008.

Barde, Robert E., and Gustavo J. Bononis. "Detention at Angel Island: First Empirical Evidence." *Social Science History* 30, no. 1 (Spring 2006): 103–36.

Bender, Steven. *Run for the Border: Vice and Virtue in U.S.-Mexico Border Crossings*. New York: New York University Press, 2012.

Berger, Dan. *Captive Nation: Black Prison Organizing in the Civil Rights Era*. Chapel Hill: University of North Carolina Press, 2014.

———. "Carceral Migrations." In *The Rising Tide of Color: Race, State Violence, and Radical Movements across the Pacific*, edited by Moon-Ho Jung. Seattle: University of Washington Press, 2015.

———. *The Struggle Within: Prisons, Political Prisoners, and Mass Movements in the United States*. Oakland, CA: PM Press, 2014.

Bernstein, Shana. *Bridges of Reform: Interracial Civil Rights Activism in Twentieth-Century Los Angeles*. New York: Oxford University Press, 2011.

Beverly, John. *Testimonio: On the Politics of Truth*. Minneapolis: University of Minnesota Press, 2004.

Brown, Michelle. *The Culture of Punishment: Prisons, Society, and Spectacle*. New York: New York University Press, 2009.

Cacho, Lisa M. *Social Death: Racialized Rightlessness and the Criminalization of the Unprotected*. New York: New York University Press, 2012.

Calavita, Kitty. *Inside the State: The Bracero Program, Immigration, and the I.N.S.* New York: Routledge, 1992.

Camp, Jordan T. *Incarcerating the Crisis: Freedom Struggles and the Rise of the Neoliberal State*. Berkeley: University of California Press, 2016.

Camplin, Erika. *Prison Food in America*. Lanham, MD: Rowman and Littlefield, 2016.

Cannato, Vincent J. *American Passage: The History of Ellis Island*. New York: Harper Perennial, 2010.

Capó, Julio, Jr. "Queering Mariel: Mediating Cold War Foreign Policy and U.S. Citizenship among Cuba's Homosexual Exile Community, 1978–1994." *Journal of American Ethnic History* 29, no. 4 (Summer 2010), 78–106.

Carrabine, Eamonn and Brian Longhurst. "Gender and Prison Organization" in *Gender and Prisons* by Dana Britton (United Kingdom: Taylor and Francis Group, 2011).

Cashin, Edward J., and Glenn T. Eskew. *Paternalism in a Southern City: Race, Religion, and Gender in Augusta, Georgia*. Athens: University of Georgia Press, 2012.

Cavanagh, Sheila L. *Queering Bathrooms: Gender, Sexuality, and the Hygienic Imagination*. Toronto: University of Toronto Press, 2010.

Chacon, Justin A., and Mike Davis. *No One Is Illegal: Fighting Racism and State Violence on the U.S.-Mexico Border*. Chicago: Haymarket Books, 2006.

Chavez, Ernesto. *Mi Raza Primero! Nationalism, Identity, and Insurgency in the Chicano Movement in Los Angeles, 1966–1978*. Berkeley: University of California Press, 2002.

Chavez, Leo R. *The Latino Threat: Constructing Immigrants, Citizens, and the Nation*. Stanford: Stanford University Press, 2008.

———. *Shadowed Lives: Undocumented Immigrants in American Society*. Belmont, CA: Wadsworth Cengage Learning, 2013.

Chavez-Garcia, Miroslava. *States of Delinquency: Race and Science in the Making of California's Juvenile Justice System*. Berkeley: University of California Press, 2012.

Childs, Dennis. *Slaves of the State: Black Incarceration from the Chain Gang to the Penitentiary*. Minneapolis: University of Minnesota Press, 2015.

Cho, Grace. *Haunting the Korean Diaspora: Shame, Secrecy, and the Forgotten War*. Minneapolis: University of Minnesota Press, 2008.

CIVIC. "Immigration Detention Map and Statistics." Community Initiatives for Visiting Immigrants in Confinement (CIVIC): End Isolation. http://www .endisolation.org/resources/immigration-detention/.

Clark, Jane Perry Clark. *Deportation of Aliens from the United States to Europe*. New York: Columbia University Press, 1931.

Cockcroft, James D. *Outlaws in the Promised Land: Mexican Immigrant Workers and America's Future*. New York City: Grove Press, 1986.

Cohen, Deborah. *Braceros: Migrant Citizens and Transnational Subjects in the Postwar United States and Mexico*. Chapel Hill: University of North Carolina, Press, 2011.

Cohen, Deborah. "Masculinity and Social Visibility: Migration, State Spectacle, and the Making of the Mexican Nation." *Estudios Interdisciplinarios de America Latina y el Caribe* (Tel Aviv University) 16, no. 1 (2005), 119–32.

Coolman, Alex, Fateema Johnson, Melissa Roudabush, and Lara Stemple. *No Refuge Here: A First Look at Sexual Abuse in Immigration Detention*. Los Angeles, California. Stop Prisoner Rape, 2004.

Cooper, Betsy, and Kevin O'Neil. "Lessons from the Immigration Reform and Control Act of 1986." Migration Policy Institute, Policy Brief No. 3, August 2005.

Correa, Jennifer G., and James M. Thomas. "The Rebirth of the U.S.-Mexico Border: Latina/o Enforcement Agents and the Changing Politics of Racial Power." *Sociology of Race and Ethnicity* 1, no. 2 (2015): 239–54.

Cortez, David. "Broken Mirrors: Identity, Duty, and Belonging in the Age of the New La(tinx) Migra." PhD diss., Cornell University, 2017.

Coutin, Susan B. *Legalizing Moves: Salvadoran Immigrants' Struggles for U.S. Residency*. Ann Arbor: University of Michigan Press, 2000.

Cravery, Altha J. *Women and Work in Mexico's Maquiladora*. Oxford: Rowman and Littlefield, 1998.

Culley, John J. "The Santa Fe Internment Camp and the Justice Department Program for Enemy Aliens." In *Japanese Americans: From Relocation to Redress*, edited by Roger Daniels, Sandra C. Taylor, and Harry H. L. Kitano. Seattle: University of Washington Press, 1991.

Cummings, William. "Squat Toilets and Cultural Commensurability: Two Texts plus Three Photographs I Forgot to Take." *Journal of Mundane Behavior* 1, no. 3 (2000): 261–73.

Cunningham, Hilary. *God and Caesar at the Rio Grande: Sanctuary and the Politics of Religion*. Minneapolis: University of Minnesota Press, 1995.

Davis, Angela. "Race, Gender, and Prison History: From the Convict Lease System to the Supermax Prison." In *Prison Masculinities*, edited by Don Sabo, Terry A. Kupers, and Willie London. Philadelphia: Temple University Press, 2001.

De Genova, Nicholas. "Migrant 'Illegality' and Deportability in Everyday Life." *Annual Review of Anthropology* 31 (2002): 419–47.

———. *Working the Boundaries: Race, Space, and "Illegality" in Mexican Chicago*. Durham, NC: Duke University Press, 2005.

De Genova, Nicholas, and Nathalie Peutz. *The Deportation Regime: Sovereignty, Space, and the Freedom of Movement*. Durham, NC: Duke University Press, 2010.

Derrida, Jacques. *Specters of Marx: The State of the Debt, the Working of Mourning, and the New International*. London: Routledge, 2006.

Development Management Group, Inc. *Final Report of Findings: Economic Impact Analysis for the El Centro Service Processing Center*. Palm Desert: California, April 16, 2014.

Diaz-Cotto, Juanita. *Gender, Ethnicity, and the State: Latina and Latino Prison Politics*. Albany: State University of New York Press, 1996.

Dicochea, Perlita Raquel. "Environmental Injustices on the Mexico-U.S. Borderlands: The Case of the New River." PhD diss., University of California, Berkeley, 2006.

Dow, Mark. *American Gulag: Inside U.S. Immigration Prisons*. Berkeley: University of California Press, 2005.

Dowling, Julie A., and Jonathan X. Inda. *Governing Immigration through Crime: A Reader*. Palo Alto: Stanford University Press, 2013.

Dubrofsky, Rachel E., and Soshana Amielle Magnet. *Feminist Surveillance Studies*. Durham, NC: Duke University Press, 2015.

DuComb, Christian. *Haunted City: Three Centuries of Racial Impersonation in Philadelphia*. Ann Arbor: University of Michigan Press, 2017.

Dunn, Timothy J. *The Militarization of the U.S.-Mexico Border, 1978–1992: Low-Intensity Conflict Doctrine Comes Home*. Austin: University of Texas Press, 1996.

Escobar, Martha D. *Captivity beyond Prisons: Criminalization Experiences of Latina (Im)migrants*. Austin: University of Texas Press, 2016.

———. "Neoliberal Captivity: Criminalization of Latina Migrants and the Construction of Irrecuperability." PhD diss., University of California, San Diego, 2010.

Epiritu, Yên Lê. *Body Counts: The Vietnam War and Militarized Refuge(es)*. Berkeley: University of California Press, 2014.

Ettinger, Patrick. *Imaginary Lines: Border Enforcement and the Origins of Undocumented Immigrants, 1882–1930*. Austin: University of Texas Press, 2009.

Fernandes, Deepa. *Targeted: Homeland Security and the Business of Immigration*. New York City: Seven Stories Press, 2011.

Fernández-Kelly, Patricia, and Douglas S. Massey. "Borders for Whom? The Role of NAFTA in Mexico-U.S. Migration." *Annals of the American Academy of Political and Social Science* 610 (2007).

Flores, Lori. *Grounds for Dreaming: Mexican Americans, Mexican Immigrants, and the California Farmworker Movement*. New Haven, CT: Yale University Press, 2018.

———. "A Town Full of Dead Mexicans: The Salinas Valley Bracero Tragedy of 1963, the End of the Bracero Program, and the Evolution of California's Chicano Movement." *Western Historical Quarterly* 44, no. 2 (Summer 2013), 124–43.

Flores, William V., and Rina Benmayor. *Latino Cultural Citizenship: Claiming Identity, Space, and Rights*. Boston: Beacon Press, 2004.

Fox, Stephen. *America's Invisible Gulag: A Biography of German American Internment and Exclusion in World War II*. New York: Peter Lang, International Academic Publishers, 2000.

Foucault, Michel. *Discipline and Punish: The Birth of the Prison*. New York: Vintage Books, 1975.

Freed, Joanne Lipson. *Haunting Encounters: The Ethics of Reading across Boundaries of Difference*. Ithaca, NY: Cornell University Press, 2017.

Fritz, Christina G. "A Nineteenth Century 'Habeas Corpus Mill': The Chinese before the Federal Courts in California." *American Journal of Legal History* 32, no. 4 (October 1988): 347–72.

Galarza, Ernesto. *Strangers in the Fields: Rights of Mexican Agricultural Contract Labor*. Washington, D.C.: Joint United States-Mexico Trade Union Committee, 1956.

Gamboa, Erasmo. *Bracero Railroaders: The Forgotten World War II Story of Mexican Workers in the U.S. West*. Seattle: University of Washington Press, 2016.

———. *Mexican Labor and World War II: Braceros in the Pacific Northwest, 1942–1947*. Seattle: University of Washington Press, 2000.

Garcia, Maria Cristina. *Seeking Refuge: Central American Migration to Mexico, the United States, and Canada*. Berkeley: University of California Press, 2006.

Garcia Hernandez, Cesar Cuauhtémoc. "La Migra in the Mirror: Immigration Enforcement, Racial Profiling, and the Psychology of One Mexican Chasing after Another." *Albany Law Review* 72, no. 4 (2009): 891–97.

Gershenson, Olga, and Barbara Penner. *Ladies and Gents: Public Toilets and Gender*. Philadelphia: Temple University Press, 2009.

Gilmore, Ruth Wilson. *Golden Gulag: Prisons, Surplus, Crisis, and Opposition in Globalizing California*. Berkeley: University of California Press, 2007.

Glenn, Evelyn Nakano. "Constructing Citizenship: Exclusion, Subordination, and Resistance." *American Sociological Review* 76, no. 1 (2011).

Golash-Boza, Tanya Maria. *Deported: Immigrant Policing, Disposable Labor, and Global Capitalism*. New York: New York University Press, 2015.

———. *Immigration Nation: Raids, Detentions, and Deportations in Post-9/11 America*. London: Routledge, 2012.

Gonzalez, Gilbert, Vivian Price, and Adrian Salinas. *Harvest of Loneliness*. 2010; New York City: Films Media Group, 2010. Documentary Film.

Gonzalez, Gilbert G. *Guest Workers or Colonized Labor: Mexican Labor Migration to the United States*. Boulder, CO: Paradigm, 2006.

Gordon, Avery F. *Ghostly Matters: Hauntings and the Sociological Imagination*. Minneapolis: University of Minnesota Press, 2008.

Griswold del Castillo, Richard. *World War II and Mexican American Civil Rights*. Austin: University of Texas Press, 2008.

Gupta, Monisha Das Gupta. *Unruly Immigrants: Rights, Activism, and Transnational South Asian Politics in the United States*. Durham, NC: Duke University Press, 2006.

Gutiérrez, David G. *Between Two Worlds: Mexican Immigrants in the United States*. Lanham, MD: Rowman and Littlefield, 1996.

———. "Sin Fronteras? Chicanos, Mexican Americans, and the Emergence of the Contemporary Mexican Immigrant Debate, 1968–1978." In *Between Two Worlds:*

Mexican Immigrants in the United States. Wilmington, DE: Scholarly Resources, 1996.

Haley, Sarah. *No Mercy Here: Gender, Punishment, and the Making of the New Jim Crow*. Chapel Hill: University of North Carolina Press, 2016.

Hallett, Michael. Foreword to *Controlling the Dangerous Classes: A History of Criminal Justice*, edited by Randall G. Shelden. Boston: Pearson, 2007.

Hamilton, Nora, and Norma Stoltz Chinchilla. *Seeking Community in a Global City: Guatemalans and Salvadorans in Los Angeles*. Philadelphia: Temple University Press, 2001.

Hamm, Mark S. *The Abandoned Ones: The Imprisonment and Uprising of the Mariel Boat People*. Boston: Northeastern University Press, 1995.

Hartney, Christopher, and Caroline Glesmann. *Prison Bed Profiteers: How Corporations Are Reshaping Criminal Justice in the U.S.* Oakland: National Council on Crime and Delinquency, 2012.

Harvey, David. *A Brief History of Neoliberalism*. Oxford: Oxford University Press, 2005.

Helton, Arthur C. "The Imprisonment of Refugees in the United States." *In Defense of the Alien* 9 (1986).

Henderson, Timothy J. *Beyond Borders: A History of Mexican Migration to the United States*. Hoboken, NJ: Wiley-Blackwell, 2011.

Herivel, Tara, and Paul Wright. *Prison Nation: The Warehousing of America's Poor*. London: Routledge, 2003.

Hernandez, David. "Detained in Obscurity: The U.S. Immigrant Detention Regime." *NACLA Report on the Americas* 46, no. 3 (Fall 2013), 58–63.

———. "Pursuant to Deportation: Latinos and Immigrant Detention." *Latino Studies* 6 (1-2): 35–63.

———. "The Least of These: Family Detention in America." *Latino Studies* 9, no. 1 (2011): 40, 160–162.

Hernández, Kelly Lytle. "Amnesty or Abolition?" *Boom: A Journal of California* 1, no. 4 (Winter 2011), 54–68.

———. *City of Inmates: Conquest, Rebellion, and the Rise of Human Caging in Los Angeles, 1771-1965*. Chapel Hill: University of North Carolina Press, 2017.

———. "Entangled Bodies and Borders: Racial Profiling and the U.S. Border Patrol, 1925-1955." PhD diss., University of California, San Diego, 2002.

———. "The Crimes and Consequences of Illegal Immigration: A Cross-Border Examination of Operation Wetback, 1943 to 1954." *Western Historical Quarterly* 37, no. 4 (2006), 421–444.

———. *Migra! A History of the U.S. Border Patrol*. Berkeley: University of California Press, 2010.

Hing, Bill Ong. *Ethical Borders: NAFTA, Globalization, and Mexican Migration*. Philadelphia: Temple University Press, 2010.

Hinton, Elizabeth. *From the War on Poverty to the War on Crime*. Cambridge, MA: Harvard University Press, 2017.

Hurtado, Aida, and Mrinal Sinha. *Beyond Machismo: Intersectional Latino Masculinities*. Austin: University of Texas Press, 2016.

Inda, Jonathan X. "Letting Moises Die: Perishing in Immigrant Detention." *Deathscapes: Mapping Race and Violence in Settler States*, 2018. https://www .deathscapes.org/casestudies/punished-to-death-perishing-in-immigration -detention/.

———. "Subject to Deportation: IRCA, 'Criminal Aliens,' and the Policing of Immigration." *Migration Studies* 1, no. 3 (2013), 292–310.

Isin, Engin F., and Greg M. Nielsen, *Acts of Citizenship*. London: Zed Books, 2008.

Johnson, Kevin R. *The "Huddled Masses" Myth: Immigration and Civil Rights*. Philadelphia: Temple University Press, 2003.

Johnson, Kevin R., and Bernard Trujillo. *Immigration Law and the US-Mexico Border*. Tucson: University of Arizona Press, 2011.

Joseph, Gilbert M., and Timothy J. Henderson. *The Mexico Reader: History, Culture, Politics*. Durham, NC: Duke University Press, 2002.

Kahn, Robert. *Other People's Blood: U.S. Immigration Prisons in the Reagan Era*. Boulder, CO: Westview Press, 1996.

Kang, S. Deborah. *The INS on the Line: Making Immigration Law on the US-Mexico Border, 1917–1954*. New York: Oxford University Press, 2017.

———. "The Legal Construction of the Borderlands: The INS, Immigration Law, and Immigration Rights on the U.S.-Mexico Border, 1917–1954." PhD diss., University of California, Berkeley, 2005.

Kanstroom, Daniel. *Aftermath: Deportation Law and the New American Diaspora*. Oxford: Oxford University Press, 2014.

———. *Deportation Nation: Outsiders in American History*. Cambridge, MA: Harvard University Press, 2010.

Kelley, Robin D. G. "What Did Cedric Robinson Mean by Racial Capitalism?" *Boston Review*, January 12, 2017. http://bostonreview.net/race/robin-d-g-kelley-what -did-cedric-robinson-mean-racial-capitalism.

Kinkela, David. *DDT and the American Century: Global Health, Environmental Politics, and the Pesticide That Changed the World*. Chapel Hill: University of North Carolina Press, 2011.

Koulish, Robert. *Immigration and American Democracy: Subverting the Rule of Law*. Oxfordshire, UK: Taylor & Francis, 2010.

Krammer, Arnold. *Undue Process: The Untold Story of America's German Alien Internees*. Lanham, MD: Rowman and Littlefield, 1997.

La Feber, Walter. *Inevitable Revolutions: The United States in Central America*. New York: W. W. Norton, 1993.

Lee, Erika. *Angel Island: Immigration Gateway to America*. Oxford: Oxford University Press, 2010.

———. *At America's Gates: Chinese Immigration during the Exclusion Era, 1882–1943*. Chapel Hill: University of North Carolina Press, 2003.

———. *The Making of Asian American: A History*. New York: Simon and Schuster, 2016.

Lee, Sophia. "Remembering the Lost Dead: Graves without Names on the U.S. Southern Border." *Sophia's World*, March 4, 2019.

LeFlouria, Talitha L. *Chained in Silence: Black Women and Convict Labor in the New South*. Chapel Hill: University of North Carolina Press, 2016.

Lichtenstein, Alex. *Twice the Work of Free Labor: The Political Economy of Convict Labor in the New South*. New York: Verso Books, 1996.

Lindskoog, Carl. *Detain and Punish: Haitian Refugees and the Rise of the World's Largest Immigration Detention System*. Gainesville: University of Florida Press, 2019.

Loyd, Jenna M., and Alison Mountz. *Boats, Borders, and Bases: Race, the Cold War, and the Rise of Migration Detention in the United States*. Berkeley: University of California Press, 2018.

Loza, Mireya. *Defiant Braceros: How Migrant Workers Fought for Racial, Sexual, and Political Freedom*. Chapel Hill: University of North Carolina Press, 2016.

———. "Unionizing the Impossible: Ernesto Galarza and Alianza de Braceros Confront PL78." *Dialogo* 19, no. 2 (Fall 2016), 21–33.

Lugo, Alejandro. *Fragmented Lives, Assembled Parts: Culture, Capitalism, and Conquest at the U.S.-Mexico Border*. Austin: University of Texas Press, 2008.

Macías-Rojas, Patrisia. *From Deportation to Prison: The Politics of Immigration Enforcement in Post-Civil Rights America*. New York: New York University Press, 2016.

Maddux, Thomas R. "Ronald Reagan and the Task Force on Immigration, 1981." *Pacific Historical Review* 74, no. 2 (May 2005), 195–236.

Madrigal, Tomas. "We Are Human! Farmworker Organizing across the Food Chain in Washington." In *Mexican-Origin Foods, Foodways, and Social Movements*, edited by Devon G. Peña, Luz Calvo, Pancho McFarland, and Gabriel R. Valle. Fayetteville: University of Arkansas Press, 2017.

Mancini, Matthew J. *One Dies, Get Another: Convict Leasing in the American South, 1866–1928*. Columbia: University of South Carolina Press, 1996.

Manion, Jen. *Liberty's Prisoners: Carceral Culture in Early America*. Philadelphia: University of Pennsylvania Press, 2019.

Martin, Philip. "Trade and Migration: NAFTA's Migration Hump." In *NAFTA and the Future of the U.S.-Mexico Relationship*, edited by Melissa Floca. San Diego: Center for U.S. Mexican Studies.

Martínez, Douglas R. "Alien Detention Facilities: Overcrowded and Inadequate." *Agenda: A Journal of Hispanic Issues* 8, no. 2 (March/April 1978).

Martínez-Matsuda, Verónica. "Making the Modern Migrant: Work, Community, and Struggle in the Federal Migratory Labor Camp Program, 1935–1947." PhD diss., University of Texas, Austin, 2009.

Martínez, Monica M. *The Injustice Never Leaves You: Anti-Mexican Violence in Texas*. Cambridge, MA: Harvard University Press, 2018.

Massey, Douglas S. "Racial Formation in Theory and Practice: The Case of Mexicans in the United States." *Race and Social Problems* 1, no. 1 (2009).

Massey, Douglas S., and Karen A. Pren. "Unintended Consequences of US Immigration Policy: Explaining the Post-1965 Surge from Latin America." *Population and Development Review* 38, no. 1 (2012): 1–29.

May, Elaine Tyler. *Homeward Bound: American Families in the Cold War Era*. New York: Basic Books, 1999.

Maynard, Steven. "Through a Hole in the Lavatory Wall: Homosexual Subcultures, Police Surveillance, and the Dialectics of Discovery, Toronto, 1890–1930." *Journal of the History of Sexuality* 5, no. 2 (October 1994), 207–42.

Mays, Dorothy A. *Women in Early America: Struggle, Survival, and Freedom in a New World*. Santa Barbara: ABC-CLIO, 2004.

Mbembe, Achille. "Necropolitics." *Public Culture* 15, no. 1 (2003).

McBride, James J. *Fort Stanton Marine Hospital: Public Health Service, 1899–1954*. Santa Fe: Paper Tiger, 2005.

———. *Interned: Internment of the SS Columbus Crew at Fort Stanton, New Mexico, 1941–1945*. Santa Fe: Paper Tiger, 2008.

———. "Internment of SS Columbus Crew during World War II." Master's thesis, University of New Mexico, May 1996.

McCallum, Jack Edward. *Military Medicine: From Ancient Times to the 21st Century*. Santa Barbara: ABC-CLIO, 2008.

McCorkel, Jill A. "Embodied Surveillance and the Gendering of Punishment." In *Gender and Prisons*, edited by Dana M. Britton. New York: Routledge, 2006.

Mckiernan-Gonzalez, John. *Fevered Measures: Public Health and Race at the Texas-Mexico Border, 1848–1942*. Durham, NC: Duke University Press, 2012.

Medina, José Jacques. *De mojado a diputado: Memoria gráfica y documental*. Mexico City: Movimento Migrante Mesoamericano "No nos vamos," 2009.

Mendez, Alina R. "Cheap for Whom? Migration, Farm Labor, and Social Reproduction in the Imperial Valley–Mexicali Borderlands, 1942–1969." PhD diss., University of California, San Diego, 2017.

Menjivar, Cecilia, and Nestor Rodriguez. *When States Kill: Latin America, the U.S., and Technologies of Terror*. Austin: University of Texas Press, 2005.

Minan, Ana Raquel. *Undocumented Lives: The Untold Story of Mexican Migration*. Palo Alto: Stanford University Press, 2018.

Mitchell, Don. *They Saved the Crops: Labor, Landscapes, and the Struggles over Industrial Farming in Bracero-Era California*. Athens: University of Georgia Press, 2012.

Mize, Ronald L., and Alicia C. S. Swords. *Consuming Mexican Labor: From the Bracero Program to NAFTA*. Toronto: University of Toronto Press, 2011.

Molina, Natalia. *Fit to Be Citizens: Public Health and Race in Los Angeles, 1879–1939*. Berkeley: University of California Press, 2006.

———. *How Race Is Made in America: Immigration, Citizenship, and the Historical Power of Racial Scripts*. Berkeley: University of California Press, 2014.

Montejano, David. *Anglos and Mexicans in the Making of Texas, 1836–1986*. Austin: University of Texas Press, 1987.

Morin, Karen M., and Dominique Moran. *Historical Geographies of Prisons: Unlocking the Usable Carceral Past*. London: Routledge Press, 2015.

Mountz, Alison. "Mapping Remote Detention: Dis/location through Isolation." In *Beyond Walls and Cages: Prisons, Borders, and Global Crisis*, edited by Jenna M. Loyd, Matt Mitchelson, and Andrew Burridge. Athens: University of Georgia Press.

Myers, Martha A. *Race, Labor, and Punishment in the New South*. Columbus: Ohio State University Press, 1957.

Navarro, Armando. *Mexicano Political Experience in Occupied Aztlan: Struggles and Change*. Lanham: AltaMira Press, 2005.

Nevins, Joseph. *Dying to Live: A Story of U.S. Immigration in an Age of Global Apartheid*. San Francisco: City Lights Books, 2008.

Newton, Carolyn, "Gender Theory and Prison Sociology" in *Gender and Prisons*, ed. Dana M. Britton. Oxfordshire, UK: Taylor & Francis Group, 2011.

Ng, Wendy. *Japanese American Internment during World War II: A History and Reference Guide*. Westport, CT: Greenwood Press, 2001.

Ngai, Mae M. *Impossible Subjects: Illegal Aliens and the Making of Modern America*. Princeton, NJ: Princeton University Press, 2004.

Ogletree, Charles J., and Austin Sarat. *Punishment in Popular Culture*. New York: New York University Press, 2015.

Okihiro, Gary Y. *Encyclopedia of Japanese American Internment*. Westport, CT: Greenwood Press, 2013.

Ordaz, Jessica. "Protesting Conditions inside El Corralón: Immigration Detention, State Repression, and Transnational Migrant Politics in El Centro, California." *Journal of American Ethnic History* 38, no. 2 (2019): 65–93.

Orozco, Cynthia E. *No Mexicans, Women, or Dogs Allowed: The Rise of the Mexican American Civil Rights Movement*. Austin: University of Texas Press, 2009.

Overmyer-Velazquez, Mark. *Beyond la Frontera: The History of Mexico-U.S. Migration*. Oxford: Oxford University Press, 2011.

Paik, A. Naomi. *Rightlessness: Testimony and Redress in U.S. Prison Camps since World War II*. Chapel Hill: University of North Carolina Press, 2016.

Poniatowska, Elena. *Massacre in Mexico*. New York: Viking Press, 1971.

Pulido, Laura. *Black, Brown, Yellow, and Left: Radical Activism in Los Angeles*. Berkeley: University of California Press, 2006.

Resendez, Andres. *The Other Slavery: The Uncovered Story of Indian Enslavement in America*. Boston: Houghton Mifflin Harcourt, 2016.

Robinson, Cedric J. *Black Marxism: The Making of the Black Radical Tradition*. Chapel Hill: University of North Carolina Press, 1983.

———. Preface to *Futures of Black Radicalism*, edited by Alex Lubin and Gaye Theresa Johnson. New York: Verso, 2017.

Robinson, Greg. *A Tragedy of Democracy: Japanese Confinement in North America*. New York: Columbia University Press, 2009.

Rodriguez, Dylan. *Forced Passages: Imprisoned Radical Intellectuals and the U.S. Prison Regime*. Minneapolis: University of Minnesota Press, 2006.

Rosas, Ana. *Abrazando el Espiritu: Bracero Families Confront the US-Mexico Border*. Berkeley: University of California Press, 2014.

Salinas, Cristina. *Managed Migrations: Growers, Farmworkers, and Border Enforcement in the Twentieth Century*. Austin: University of Texas Press, 2018.

Salyer, Lucy E. *Laws Harsh as Tigers: Chinese Immigration and the Shaping of Modern Immigration Law*. Chapel Hill: University of North Carolina Press, 1995.

Sanchez, George J. *Becoming Mexican American: Ethnicity, Culture, and Identity in Chicano Los Angeles, 1900–1945*. Oxford: Oxford University Press, 1995.

Schoultz, Lars. "Central America and the Politicization of U.S. Immigration Policy." In *Western Hemisphere Immigration and United States Foreign Policy*, edited by Christopher Mitchell. University Park: Pennsylvania State University Press, 1992.

Schwab, Gabriele. *Haunting Legacies: Violent Histories and Transgenerational Trauma*. New York: Columbia University Press, 2010.

Scott, James C. *Domination and the Arts of Resistance: Hidden Transcripts*. New Haven, CT: Yale University Press, 1992.

Sellers, Martin P. *The History and Politics of Private Prisons: A Comparative Analysis*. Madison, NJ: Fairleigh Dickinson University Press, 1993.

Shull, Tina. "Nobody Wants These People": Reagan's Immigration Crisis and America's First Private Prisons." PhD diss., University of Irvine, 2014.

Snodgrass, Michael. "The Bracero Program, 1942–1964." In *Beyond la Frontera: The History of Mexico-U.S. Migration*, edited by Mark Overmyer-Velazquez. New York: Oxford University Press, 2011.

Soss, Joe, Richard C. Fording, and Sanford F. Schram. *Disciplining the Poor: Neoliberal Paternalism and the Persistent Power of Race*. Chicago: University of Chicago Press, 2011.

Stanley, Eric A. *Captive Genders: Trans Embodiment and the Prison Industrial Complex*. Oakland, CA: AK Press, 2011.

Stern, Alexandra M. "Buildings, Boundaries, and Blood: Medicalization and Nation-Building on the U.S.-Mexico Border, 1910–1930." *Hispanic American Historical Review* 79, no. 1. (1999), 41–81.

Stoler, Ann Laura. *Haunted by Empire: Geographies of Intimacy in North American History*. Durham, NC: Duke University Press, 2006.

Sudbury, Julia. *Global Lockdown: Race, Gender, and the Prison-Industrial Complex*. London: Routledge, 2004.

Taylor, Paul. *Mexican Labor in the United States: Imperial Valley*. Vol. 1. Berkeley: University of California Press, 1930.

Tempo, Carl J. Bon. *Americans at the Gate: The United States and Refugees during the Cold War*. Princeton, NJ: Princeton University Press, 2015.

Terrio, Susan J. *Whose Child Am I? Unaccompanied, Undocumented Children in U.S. Immigration Custody*. Berkeley: University of California Press, 2015.

Thompson, Heather Ann. *Blood in the Water: The Attica Prison Uprising of 1971 and Its Legacy*. New York: Pantheon, 2016.

Tibbs, Donald F. *From Black Power to Prison Power: The Making of Jones v. North Carolina Prisoners' Labor Union*. London: Palgrave Macmillan, 2011.

Tshumi, Bernard. "Violence of Architecture." *Art Forum* 20, no. 1 (1981).

Tyner, James A. *Space, Place, and Violence: Violence and the Embodied Geographies of Race, Sex, and Gender*. London: Routledge, 2011.

———. *Violence in Capitalism: Devaluing Life in an Age of Responsibility*. Lincoln: University of Nebraska Press, 2016.

Wang, Jackie. *Carceral Capitalism*. Los Angeles: Semiotext(e), 2018.

Weber, John. *From South Texas to the Nation: The Exploitation of Mexican Labor in the Twentieth Century*. Chapel Hill: University of North Carolina Press, 2015.

Welch, Michael. *Detained: Immigration Laws and the Expanding INS Jail Complex*. Philadelphia: Temple University Press, 2002.

White, Lisa. *Transitional Justice and Legacies of State Violence: Talking about Torture in Northern Ireland*. London: Routledge, 2015.

Williams, Jack. *The Ultimate Guide to America's Weather*. Chicago: University of Chicago Press, 2009.

Wilsher, Daniel. *Immigration Detention: Laws, History, Politics*. Cambridge: Cambridge University Press, 2014.

Wilson, Walter. *Forced Labor in the United States*. New York: International, 1933.

Wong, Tom K. *Rights, Deportation, and Detention in the Age of Immigration Control*. Palo Alto: Stanford University Press, 2015.

———. *The Politics of Immigration: Partnership, Demographic Change, and American National Identity*. Oxford: Oxford University Press, 2017.

Young, Hershini Bhana. *Haunting Capital: Memory, Text, and the Black Diasporic Body*. Lebanon, NH: Dartmouth College Press, 2005.

Index